This Is Our
STORY

HAMPTON BAPTIST CHURCH

This Is Our STORY

THIS IS OUR SONG

THE UNOFFICIAL HISTORY OF HBC
& ITS MEMBERS, CIRCA 1950-2001

BY MIKE HAYWOOD

Hampton Baptist Church: This Is Our Story, This Is Our Song:
The Unofficial History of HBC & Its Members, Circa 1950–2001

ISBN 978-1-304-05978-9

Published at Lulu.com.
Printed in the United States of America.

Contents

Preface

The following manuscript was written simply to tell some stories about growing up at Hampton Baptist Church. But they are not all *my* stories. A lot of people have helped make this book possible—more people than I could hope to name—and they are the reason I wrote this book.

On many occasions, I would be talking with friends who grew up at HBC, and at some point someone would say, "This needs to be written down." After this had happened dozens of times, I decided that I would try to write this narrative. However, before going on, you need to know a couple of things.

This is not an official history of Hampton Baptist Church. Ironically, I am working on that very project with Mary Etta Brown and Alice Erickson. That will be a more formal account of the history of the church, going back to its founding in 1791. *This* book is a rather loose collection of memories and stories about people in the church from the early 1950s to the early 2000s, and they are not usually in any chronological order.

This is also not a list of *everything* that happened at HBC during those years. That would require a series of books (and this one is long enough)! The events in this narrative are mostly memories that I and others have shared. I have talked with and interviewed dozens of people about their "histories," getting their takes on the stories I remember as well those I knew nothing about.

While it is true that my memory is pretty good about interactions with people, I know that I have left out many incidents and, at times, people who were involved. Sometimes I may have added someone who was not actually there. For the most part, I think I have gotten pretty close to what really happened and to whom it happened.

I would like to mention everyone from HBC, but that would not be possible. And I am sure that most of you reading this will remember something and wonder why I didn't include it; this is simply because it didn't make it through the filters in my mental storage. Most of what I tend to remember are stories that are funny (sometimes embarrassing), poignant, or historical.

(Many of my current friends who were around in the old days tell me that the first thing they are going to do after I die is break into my house and wipe my computer clean! I can't blame them. Unfortunately, while that might destroy a few stories and pictures not yet shared, most of what is on my computer is now stored for all time in the books I have written and published.)

I do need to mention several people specifically. Jay Russ, Jay Lawson, Jim Ailor, Mary Etta Brown, Lucille Everhart, and Alice Erickson have spent countless hours reminiscing with me. There are probably a hundred others who have shared a story or an insight about the past.

Before Bill Hurt retired, I asked him if I could get a copy of his annual Church Night scripts. On the evening we celebrated his retirement, Bill called me to the front of the church and gave me a folder with scripts going back to 1963. (There is another copy at the church.) I have drawn upon the information in these scripts quite a bit and, before he passed away, talked with Bill about Church Nights in general.

I have included a lot of photographs. Most are from four sources: John Dawson, Bill Hurt, Jay Russ, and me. I have tried to give credit for each image in this book. But if no photographer is named, there is a good chance I don't know who took the photo. Sometimes I guessed who most likely took the picture. I used a numbering system (additional photographs are individually credited):

1. Mike Haywood
2. Bill Hurt
3. John Dawson
4. Jay Russ
5. Unknown

Going through so many photographs brought back specific memories, which helped in the writing of this book. Sometimes the photo itself tells a story. I have checked with many church members, trying to identify the correct names of the people in the images. Without a doubt, I have made some mistakes. For that I apologize.

MY HOPE

Finally, and this is crucial to understanding this manuscript, I want to point out that Hampton Baptist Church during this time was an almost magical place. I heard this comment time and again when I talked with people about their HBC recollections. They would all say the same thing, using their own experiences and friendships to illustrate what they meant by "magical." I heard dozens of people say that they made special friends and learned how to be a better friend. It was a time of joy and excitement, of learning the Bible, of helping one another and helping others out-side of the church. It was a time of laughing together and crying together, a time of experiencing the wonder of doing life together, and a time of growing into the people we were meant to be. I have even heard the word *Camelot* used to describe these earlier days.

Obviously, the main message of HBC has always been about the power of Jesus Christ to save and the importance of having a personal relationship with Him. We were taught that this was the key to all the other things we discovered. I believe we made one another better Christians.

In pursuing Jesus and sharing the Gospel, the members of Hampton Baptist created a memorable, loving, and one-of-a-kind community. My wish is that every member and former member who reads this book will remember some special times that are not recorded here and that those memories will bring about the same magical feeling—that you would know that attending Hampton Baptist made a difference. I would be happy to hear about any moments not related here that enriched your life. So many people, myself included, oft repeat the sentiment that the people of Hampton Baptist and the spiritual formations developed there impacted and shaped their lives for the better.

Although much younger, Lynne Everhart was a dear friend of mine. She died much too young, but in the course of her life, she touched many people and was always willing to help out. Lynne always had a smile. She, among many youth at the church, helped by serving as a counselor for many of the Peninsula Baptist programs I ran in the early days of my ministry there.

While in junior high, Lynne wrote the following poem. It is currently on display in the Everharts' front parlor. I think this poem catches the essence of what I want to say in this manuscript:

> *This is not primarily the place*
> *where we have to be,*
> *it is the place we are.*
>
> *This is not our prison but our*
> *home. It is the road we must*
> *walk and walking of it is called life.*
>
> *Because we will walk it only once, then*
> *how important it is that we walk it*
> *with some purpose we can call our own.*
>
> *—Lynne Everhart*

This poem typifies the stories you are about to encounter and recall. When we were young, our friends and the adults at HBC helped us grow—spiritually, physically, mentally, and emotionally (Luke 2:52). They helped us discover just who we were and what gifts and talents we had to offer. They helped us learn to live the life God intended.

Lynne, like many others in heaven, are watching us live the life that God intended for us. I miss her, but I am so happy that she was with us during the time she spent walking this life on Earth. To personalize a quote that Chester Brown often used, "I will never be the same—not because she is gone but because Lynne Everhart was once here."

Dedications

John and Ammie Garber, who set an example for all of us

Chester and Mary Etta Brown, who taught us to discover our own gifts and talents and use them in service to God

Phil and Lucille Everhart, Sam and Martha Ailor, John and Myrtle Dennard, and **Milford and Lucille Rollins**, who allowed us to drop by anytime, even unannounced, and made that their witness (They inspired me to do the same later in my life with church teens and Youth for Christ.)

Wayne Erickson and **Dave Carter**, our Royal Ambassador leaders who modeled the Christian life for me and many of my friends

Woody Patrick, who kept us in line (well, most of the time)

Francis and Dottie Lee Jones, who were a steadying influence—a "North Star" to guide us on our paths

Alice Erickson, who allowed the youth at church events to come close to getting out of hand without actually ever getting out of hand

Bill and Jane Hurt, who taught us that you don't always have to make a public "splash" when you mentor others

Gary Lewis, who taught us that good music is a pathway to God (and who had the choir sing Sibelius's "Onward Ye People" a second time because I was out of town the first time they sang it)

Jay and Angie Russ, who performed so many small kindnesses for the people at church, many of which went unrecorded and often forgotten (However, as Chester Brown would say, "It is OK if we forget the deeds of others because God will not forget.")

Sandra and Tom Bundick, who taught us to be willing to help out in any way possible and let that be a guide to others (When the acronym WWJD, or "What Would Jesus Do," became popular, the motto at Hampton Baptist was WWSD—"What Would Sandra Do!")

Of course, **John Dawson**—"Click" to Jimmy George and many of his Tabernacle Baptist friends—who taught us that you could use something as simple as a camera to do ministry and model the love of Christ (John influenced many of us to do the same with our own cameras.)

And finally, the "**Hall People**," who made all of the youth feel worthwhile and important (The Hall People did not operate in any "official" capacity. And yet, whenever I ran across one at church, they talked with me about my life, plans, and visions. They encouraged me and made me feel I had something valuable to add to the conversation or situation. There were hundreds of Hall People, but I will mention one here. After Jack Lawson died, I was inspired to write a sermon about the Hall People. Although indeed special, he was only one of many at Hampton Baptist Church who encouraged me and countless other members and guests.)

Introduction

Dr. Garber at VBS (5)

There is another side to this that needs to be said. We learned at HBC that while it was important to allow our church interaction to enrich our lives, we were not to be oblivious to the world around us. Our closest friends might have been *in* the church, but there was a world out there that was encouraging, instructive, sometimes needful, and always beckoning us to be a part of something bigger.

That is what I learned as a member of Hampton Baptist: I could immerse myself in the church, but I was to enjoy and, when needed, help out in the world. It reminds me of a song by Twila Paris called "The Warrior Is a Child." At HBC, I was taught to be a warrior in the world but to know I could always come home to our friends in the church. I could "go running home," "drop my sword," and be renewed.

Let me begin this narrative with two stories about Chester and Mary Etta Brown's kids. Mary Etta recently told me the first one.

One family who was at the church for a short period of time back in the early 1970s was Jerry and Ellen Sullivan and their three girls: Renee, Lynne, and Lee Ellen. They became friends with many people at the church, including Chester and Mary Etta and their children, Mary Elizabeth and Edward. Ellen Sullivan and Suzanna McKendree also became very close (BFFs, so to speak).

Jerry retired from the Air Force in 1973, and the family moved back to Jerry's hometown, Tylertown, Mississippi. They remodeled an old house that came with a lot of acreage. I and many others from the church started visiting the Sullivans there, starting in the summer of 1973. I can name at least two dozen people from Hampton Baptist who went at least once, but most made several visits. The Sullivans came back this way a few times, but most of the visiting happened in Mississippi.

Jerry passed away in 2001. A group of us went down for the funeral (including Suzanna and Roddy McKendree, Mary Etta, me, and others). Chester was one of the preachers at the funeral. After Jerry's death, friends still traveled to Mississippi to visit Ellen and the three girls and their families.

You will remember, of course, that Hurricane Katrina hit Louisiana and Mississippi in 2005. Although the major destruction was done to New Orleans and Louisiana, there was still considerable devastation in the state of Mississippi, including Tylertown.

Hundreds of trees were blown down and structural damage was done. Ellen Sullivan was not the hardest hit, but hers was one of the homes that suffered major tree loss.

Edward Brown, now out of college and working, found a way that he and some friends could help out. He called a number of his fraternity brothers and got them to come together in the hurricane impact area for a week of hard work. When they met in Mississippi, Edward told them that a large truck would arrive with a load of new chainsaws. The chainsaws were a donation from the author John Grisham (Mary Etta doesn't know how Edward pulled that off), which were to be used for cutting up fallen trees.

Edward's group helped a lot of people with tree damage that week. One of the households that benefited was that of Ellen Sullivan. Mary Etta told me later that when she went to Tylertown for Ellen's funeral in 2022, Lee Ellen Sullivan showed her the stump of one of the trees that Edward cut up.

Alystra Little and Ed Brown (2)

This story is important because it illustrates the main points I have already mentioned. Older Hampton Baptist people repeated these to me when I was young. The first is that growing up in HBC was a lot of fun. Our best friends were there, and the older members modeled the Christian life and encouraged us to mature spiritually. The church was an integral part of our upbringing.

While the church folk made life special and helped us develop into the people we would become, the second lesson we all learned was no less critical. We were taught (and this was modeled to us) to find the areas in which we could use our abilities to help people outside of our church home. We were taught not only to do this in general, throughout our lives, but also when special needs arise.

Edward and his sister, Mary Elizabeth, were not only members of the pastor's household; they were part of the church. They made friends within the church, and they were in Jay Russ's youth group—all of which played a role in their development. Chester and Mary Etta made many friends who became part of the children's lives, including the Sullivans and their three daughters.

In 2005, Edward demonstrated this. Having grown up in the church, he had learned the importance of reaching out to others in need. And so, he called on a group of friends outside his church family, and they traveled to another part of the country to help people who needed it. This they did in abundance. At the same time, Edward had not forgotten his church family. Ellen Sullivan was also in need, and she became one of the people helped by Edward and his friends. Lee Ellen later showing Mary Etta the evidence of this good deed tied it all together.

In 2015, Mary Elizabeth Brown's son Alexander showed up at one of the Peninsula Baptist's sports camps. Chester, now retired, and Mary Etta had brought their grandson to First Baptist Church

Mary Etta, Jessi Barnes (Lynn Sullivan Barnes's daughter), and Alexander Brown (1)

for this week of sports camp. Not only did Alexander take part in the camp, but I was also able to spend time with Chester and Mary Etta.

I was impressed with Alexander from the start. He returned to sports camp the next year, and in 2017, I asked him to be on my Peninsula Baptist summer mission team.

While working with me that summer, he got to meet Jessi Barnes, the daughter of Lynne Sullivan Barnes, who was also on the PBA summer team. She stayed with Matt and Cary Parron, as well as a week with Lucille Everhart. Jessi and Alexander served with a group of teens from Latvia, who had come over for part of the summer.

Mary Elizabeth Brown (2)

In 2018, Jessi and Alexander worked on the summer mission team again and also traveled with other teammates to Latvia. There, we worked with Agenskalns Baptist Church in Riga to put on a children's camp. Jessi stayed with Terize Rozis's parents. Alexander and I stayed together at another home.

Edward, Mary Elizabeth, Alexander, and Jessi typify what has been happening at Hampton Baptist for so many years: people and families gathering for fellowship and spiritual development and then going out into the world together to minister.

I hope that most of what follows will continue to illustrate this two-part commission. First, throughout life, find a special group to be a part of. These friendships and organizations make us the people we become. If that special group is a church, even better; but look for a group who cares for you and gives your life meaning. Second, never stop looking for ways that you can make a positive impact on the world around you. And if possible, do it with the friends you made growing up in church.

Chester with youth (including Tom Bundick and Thomas Goodwin) at a Halloween party (2)

Above: Mary Etta teaching at Vacation Bible School (2)
Below: Dr. and Ammie Garber (3)

Above: Jim Ward (2)

Right: Alice Erickson and Bill
Hurt leading a senior adult
excursion— an appropriate
photo of Bill with camera as he
took about a third of the
photos in this book (5)

Above: Jay Russ with Angie and Caitlyn (4)
Below: Dottie Lee Jones (2)

Gary Lewis and Cindy Garris at a church social (3)

Sandra Bundick and Ann Rosser with Vacation Bible School kids (2)

This would probably be at Centrifuge or a mission trip:
Aaron Whittington (standing), Marcus King, Jay Russ,
Jim Pucket (back to us), Trent Allison, and Corinna Powell,
among others. (4)

John Dawson is shown here in both a familiar and an unusual setting. As you would expect, his well-known camera is in hand, but this is one of a few photographs of John in which he is surrounded by only guys. (5)

Some members of Jay's youth group on a trip, including
Trent Allison, Brooke Puckett, Jon Miller, Jim Puckett, and
Beth Everett (4)

Chapter 1
A Circle of Friends and Caring People

My family first started going to Hampton Baptist in the late 1930s. I don't think any of the three older children—Kimmel, Vernon, or Iris—attended, but the three younger—Carolyn ("Kinky"), Barbara, and me—did, although my journey there was a bit circuitous. During my earliest years, I attended Memorial Baptist Church, and that ties back to Hampton Baptist in events of a later year.

We all know that generally, most guys start going to church because of a girl. That's not a bad thing *if* the guys stay on and are eventually led by the Holy Spirit to the real reason to be involved. It happened that way for me, except that I was only about six years old at the time.

My next-door neighbors on Newport News Avenue were Lil and Leslie Moore. They went to Memorial Baptist. (Lil was Buddy Rosser's sister; Buddy was later the pastor of Memorial Baptist but not when I was there. Reverend Rutledge was the pastor when Lil and Leslie attended Memorial Baptist, while my family went to Hampton Baptist.) The Moores had three daughters: Judy, Pat, and Leslie. Judy, the oldest, was my age.

For whatever reason, I had not been going to church with my mom and sisters. My dad had once been a regular churchgoer but was not at this time. One day in the late 1940s, Judy asked me to go to church with her and, of course, I said yes. Or, it is possible that Lil asked if I would like to go to church with Judy and the rest of their family. Anyway, I went and kept going for a while, even after they moved away from our street a couple of years later. I got my first Bible from Memorial and my first Bible school certificate.

Sometime in the early 1950s, I decided that I should go to Hampton Baptist Church with my family, and so I made the switch. I don't remember there being any great epiphany; it just hit me that I should be going to HBC. I was baptized in Hampton Baptist by John Garber in 1952. All that follows was set up by these events.

So no one can complain about any photo in this book, I am including this one. My sister Barbara is on the far left, and that is me next to her. Then come the three Moore children: Judy, Pat, and Leslie. It does not look like any of us wanted our photo taken! (Photo by Lil Moore)

Many years later, Hampton Baptist would call Ann Rosser, Buddy Rosser's wife, to become its associate minister. During this time, Buddy was the pastor of Memorial Baptist. Buddy was also my friend. He was a good role model and encourager during my early years at the Peninsula Baptist Association (along with George Kissinger and Chester Brown). But in 1951, my job at the PBA was in the distant future.

Ann was still at Hampton Baptist when my mom passed away in 1992. Chester Brown conducted the funeral, and in typical Chester fashion, it was a time when we got to celebrate the life and relationship of someone very special—despite it being a sad occassion. This was an ability Chester demonstrated at all the funerals I attended. He has that knack of eulogizing a loved one in a way that captures their essence. Jerry Sullivan, John Dawson, and George Kissinger are three people I think of when remembering Chester Brown funerals. What he did for those three friends is what he could do at any funeral he led.

One of the sayings he often used is one I love to quote: "We will never be the same—not because they are gone but because they were once here." I feel that way about a lot of my mentors and leaders from the old days at Hampton Baptist.

My mom loved having Chester Brown as her pastor, but she also had a special place in her heart for Ann Rosser. Months before passing away, Madge Haywood, my mom, fell and broke her hip. Chester visited her several times while she was in the hospital. However, on the early morning before she would go into surgery, she wanted to see Ann Rosser. Ann was able to make it to the hospital and pray with her. The surgery was successful, and Mom was all smiles when I got by later that day.

I think that ties a knot in it: my beginnings in church came through the Rosser family, and the Rossers played a big role in my mom's final months on this planet.

But back to the church swap. . . I decided I should go to Hampton Baptist in early 1951, and the rest is history. Or an *unofficial* history rather-er. Again, don't look for any rhyme or reason in how things are laid out in the following pages. There isn't any.

I came across this saying not too long ago: "Friends are God's way of taking care of us."

Chapter 2
Wednesday Night Suppers

Wednesday night suppers have always been special for me for two reasons. The first and most important is that after moving out on my own, they have been my best evening meal of the week. We've had great cooks over the years at HBC. The longest running dinner coordinator was Joanne Corbett, who fed us for many years. Currently, Cheryl and Steve Elder, along with Sandy Tidwell, have kept up the tradition, and for that, I am mighty glad.

The second special thing that Wednesday night suppers have done is give good friends a chance to sit together and talk as we get ready to head to our Wednesday night meetings. They give us a chance to catch up on what is happening in the lives of our friends. Sharing meals, of any sort, has always been a bonding time for friends and families. This seems to have been one of the major ways that Jesus spent time teaching and sharing with His disciples and other friends.

After church suppers, we usually attend meetings, choir practices, or other events. However, on at least two nights in the past, the Wednesday night supper led to a special excursion.

On one of these occasions, David Allison (probably in junior-high school at the time) showed up at supper to tell the youth present that he thought he had come across a body that afternoon in a barn behind a house in the Fox Hill area. He was excitedly telling them that he (I can't remember if he had been alone) had been looking around the area and happened to enter the barn. According to David, he had seen a pile of hay in the back. When he walked toward it, he noticed what looked like an arm and a leg sticking out of the hay. David said it might have empty clothes, but he didn't stick around to find out. He had gotten home just in time to get ready for church supper.

Several of the teens decided that this needed to be investigated, and so they made a plan to go between supper and whatever meetings came after. Nancy Lee Jones, who was in high school at the time, asked me if I would go with them as a "responsible adult." Then she told me that she had already told her parents that I would be going too. After her mom said it was OK, the others had promised their parents that it would be fine because I would be with them. Then they told me that I had to go because they had already cleared it with their parents, who thought I was going. As I remember, it didn't take much effort to convince me, and off we went on our body-searching hunt (kind of like that science-fiction movie *Invasion of the Body Snatchers*).

I remember a lot of excitement in my car as it and several others headed for the barn. David and Nancy Lee were with me, and David told me the exact location of the barn, which made me think there might be something to his tale. (Although, I could not tell you today where the barn was.) We arrived, and everyone parked. If I remember correctly, each driver made a U-turn before parking so that their cars would be pointed in the right direction if we needed to beat a hasty retreat for any reason.

It was twilight, which made the whole scene a little scarier. I was one of only a couple who had a flashlight, and so I was elected to lead the group into the barn. With no nearby houses, we had very little light. To be honest, I was glad there were no houses in sight so that we most likely wouldn't be interrupted by a concerned neighbor (or the owner of the barn) and asked what the heck we thought we were doing!

Nancy Lee Jones, intrepid adventurer and "crafty" person, at VBS (2)

I walked quickly to the barn door, which was open. David said he had left it that way. I hesitated a moment and hoped it looked like I knew what I was doing.

I flashed the light into the barn, and in the glow of the beam, I could see a pile of hay in the back corner. Suddenly, I was not quite as sure as before that I wanted to look into this, but now I was the leader. I had no choice but to appear brave, and so I stepped nervously inside. It occurred to me at this point that if there were a body, it was possible that someone who was responsible for it might still be around. I could only hope that even though our group was young, our sheer number might give us some protection.

There had been a lot of chatter on the walk from the cars to the barn door, but I noticed that we all fell silent as soon as we got into the barn. The structure was probably twenty square feet, with that bundle of hay taking up about a quarter of the space. At this point, there was nothing left to do but walk forward.

Another thought popped into my mind. Perhaps David had left a friend to hide inside the barn to give us all a shock. Too much time had passed during supper for anyone to have remained in waiting, but that didn't occur to me, and I was prepared for anything at this point. My eyes remained riveted as we approached the clump of hay.

There *was* something in the hay pile, which appeared to be a single shoe. Nothing else poked out, but I didn't want to be the one to start feeling around. Somebody picked up a stick—David, I think—and started prodding the hay. Nothing stirred, thank God, and we soon saw that there was nothing at all in the pile of hay except for the shoe.

We looked around the barn, but it was pretty much empty, except for this heap of hay. David said that he was *sure* he had seen a body. But now, there was no body and no clothing of any kind. He continued to insist that he had seen something and wondered if someone had come in the meantime and cleaned up. I think I was happy we did not find anything as we headed back to the cars and then the church. I did check the newspapers over the next several days but saw nothing about a missing person, a found body, or the barn.

It will not surprise anyone to learn that the other time I remember a "story" being told at Wednesday night supper involved none other than Jim Ailor. As all who attended HBC at this time will remember, Jim was nothing if not a great storyteller! During Jim's first year of college, he brought home a fellow student to stay at Martha and Sam's for the weekend. It was a girl, of course.

When I met her at church, she said she had been wanting to meet me. Right away, I was suspicious!

She asked about our ice hockey trophy and thought I was being modest by acting ignorant. It turns out that she thought I was the coach and Jimmy the star player of an amateur, world-champion outdoor ice hockey team. She wanted to see the "pond" Jimmy had been telling her about—the one where we played all our home games.

Later in the weekend, he had convinced her that we used the pond behind the Hampton Coliseum as our practice rink as well as for all of our home games. He had told her that it was "frozen over most of the winter."

By that time, I was so used to Jim Ailor's "stories" that I was able to keep a straight face when talking with her. What was I to do? After all, Jim had made me look good in this story. I was the coach of the world-champion amateur team! So I told her that it was all quite an honor, and we were lucky to win. I told her that Jim would have to show her the trophy because I didn't have it. I don't know if he ever told her the truth or if she figured out she was being had, but I never saw her again.

Anyway, that was *not* the Wednesday night supper story that Jimmy Ailor had earlier told a group of young adults, including Bill Sasser, John Lee Robbins, and me, at church. Jimmy and Phil Everhart Jr. had been in high school at the time. They were sitting across the table from John Robbins, Bill Sasser, and me when Jimmy began telling us what had transpired that afternoon. They had been digging in a field to make a foundation for the fort they wanted to build.

With serious intent and barely contained enthusiasm, Ailor told us how they had been digging all afternoon after school. Just about the time they had to leave to go home and clean up for church, they struck something solid. It was about five feet down, but they could not stick around without getting into trouble with their parents.

Ailor continued, "Mike, I knew we had to leave, but I wanted to know what it was. We scratched away the dirt, thinking it was probably a rock. And you're not going to believe this, but it is true. There is something made of metal in the ground. It looks like some kind of box. We're going back tomorrow after school to dig it up. By this time tomorrow night, we could be rich men!"

Ailor was right about one thing. I didn't believe it. This time I didn't bite. John Lee also saw through the pretense, and we kind of joked during dinner about finding buried treasure and what we would do with it. I didn't notice it at the time, but Bill Sasser was strangely quiet. After dinner, everyone went on their way. I got home and forgot about the tall tale Ailor had spun. But about ten o'clock that night, I got a call from Bill Sasser.

"Haywood! Let's get Robbins, skip work tomorrow, and go get the treasure." I didn't understand at first and asked what he was talking about.

"The treasure," Bill explained. "They have to be in school tomorrow morning. We can get it out of the ground before they get there!"

I wish I had kept my presence of mind and remained serious. It would have been great to have used Bill. Unfortunately, my reflexive laughter gave the opportunity away. I had to tell Bill that there was no treasure to be had. It was just another Jim Ailor Tall Tale.

Later, Jimmy told me that they had really been excited when they did in fact strike something hard at the three-foot level . . . a rock!

Chapter 3
The Petition

This story, one of my favorites, might seem a little unlikely for the beginning of this book. However, because it involved a large group of Hampton Baptist people, it seems like a good one to jump-start us. A lot of you will remember this as you think back on life at HBC.

It all probably began on a Tuesday or Thursday night during the summer of 1968. After a church league softball game (which were usually played on Tuesday and Thursday nights), I went out with Jimmy Ailor and Jay Lawson to get Cokes and coffee. I do not remember the restaurant, but I think it was fast food, and it was close to Eaton Junior High, where we had played the game.

While we were sitting together, enjoying our camaraderie, Jay and Jimmy started talking about some of the things that the church could do better (or in addition to other activities) for the youth. They felt that the youth could be more involved in some more serious mission endeavors. I do not remember everything that came up that night, but I know it included putting youth on committees and providing more ministry activities for them.

At some point, I made an obvious point: "How is the church going to know your feelings if you don't tell them what you think?" We agreed that letting the church know would be the right thing to do. They also said that all youth should have a chance to offer their ideas about what the church could do to help them in the future. We decided that we needed to gather a group of youth together and draft a list of requests.

Left: Jim Ailor helping to run a retreat at Eastover (3)

Below: Jay Lawson speaking at Hampton Baptist (2)

I let Jimmy and Jay decide who should be consulted. The group they named that evening included Jimmy Allison, Jimmy Ailor, Judy Dooley, Phil Everhart Jr., Mike Haywood, Jay Lawson, Tally Mims, Cliff Morris, and Margie Whitcomb. Cliff and I were in college at the time, but they thought it would be nice to include a couple of young adults. (Several other young adults who were active in the church at that time signed the forthcoming petition.)

I can't remember how many times we met before finalizing our suggestions. I also do not remember why we chose to create a petition. I am probably the one who came up with that (bad) idea because it was something that was in the news at the time. It truly was not meant as an "ultimatum" but rather a polite request to involve the youth more. If you read the resolution (which is included in the coming pages), I think you can see this.

Here are youth from the 1960s who were very active at church: (left to right) Bruce Whitcomb, Jimmy Allison, Roddy McKendree, Margie Whitcomb, and Brenda Vick. (2)

A few points of clarification:

- I have no recollection of who wrote the final draft, whether one person put the ideas on paper or whether different people worked on different parts. Diane Roth typed all the handwritten notes for us.
- It is stated in the petition that these "are suggestions and not demands, proposals and not ultimatums."
- The petition went to the youth council, passed, and was then taken to the youth to sign. (I cannot remember who was on the youth council.)
- I wrote a handwritten note on the front page of the resolution that credited Alice Erickson for editing the grammar. I can't remember doing this, but there is no doubt in my mind today that I did so because I thought Alice's name would add legitimacy to our endeavor. I mean, she was a "real adult."
- The mission trips to Dunbar (Eastern State Hospital), led by Phil Everhart Sr., are listed as an example of ministry opportunities. (You will read about Dunbar trips in a later chapter.)

I think all of us on the planning committee knew that the section that requested church-sponsored dances (note that the request was not that dances be held *in* the church) would be the one to potentially spark the most fireworks. That is why a good chunk of the petition was used to spell out the good reasons (in our minds) for this request. You could sign on one of two columns: one that endorsed the whole petition and one that endorsed everything but the request for dances. In fact, one of our committee members signed in the "no-dancing" column, along with five other youth.

Jimmy Allison was that one holdout from our committee. Anyone who ever knew Jimmy knew he was a deep thinker and did not mind being on the short list of opposition if he felt strongly about something. He modeled that mindset for all of us, and it is something we all admired about him.

If my memory serves me, I gave the petition to John Dawson to pass on at the next deacons' meeting. (I'm sure I asked John because he would have given us some measure of respect.) The petition was not a secret, and I think that most people knew that Jimmy Ailor, Jay Lawson, and I were the main instigators. (I never heard that Chester Brown had any problem with the petition. I mean, let's be honest; if this had happened some years later, Mary Elizabeth and Edward would have signed the petition too!) Unfortunately, two words got us into hot water with the deacons. Those two offensive words were, of course, *petition* and *dances*!

I was not at the deacons' meeting, and some of what got back to me may not have been as bad as I'd heard or was said in jest. I was told by some who were there that a few deacons wondered if I were cut out for youth work. (Come to think of it, some people may still wonder this!) At the height of the controversy, it was John Dawson who pointed out that the petition was indeed not an ultimatum but only a series of requests. He went on to say that other than the dancing, it contained some valid appeals and that the youth were actually asking to be more included in the ministry of the church.

So in the end, we didn't get the dances. But some of the other suggestions were indeed carried out. John Dawson told me that some of the deacons were not happy with the whole concept, but that he and a couple of others defended it. I don't remember hearing back from the deacons, except that John Dawson told me that they would consider some of our proposals. I do remember that the next year, several youth were included on some of the church committees.

I'd like to think that we helped pave the way for Jay Russ, who came later as the youth minister. One of his programs taught dancing to the youth at an outside facility. One of Jay's main points (and a good one), which he told the deacons, was this: "If your daughter goes to a dance or the prom with a guy, wouldn't you want to know that the guy had been taught the proper way to dance?"

I have one final point to make. I don't want to throw Jimmy Ailor under the bus, but I must mention this one other thing that the deacons were told that night. Fifty-nine people (mostly in high school, but some college-age and older) signed the petition. I left it up to Jay Lawson and Jimmy Ailor to collect the signatures at Sunday school, so I was not present when it happened. This is what I was later told.

Jay Lawson used normal, polite methods when asking people to sign. But some of the youth told me that Jim Ailor used a stronger, more assertive persuasion: "You need to sign!" (That might have been the reason that Jimmy Allison underlined his signature on the no-dancing portion of the petition.) I even heard the word *coerced* used to describe Jimmy's methods that morning at Sunday school.

It is true that Jimmy could be a little "over the top" in his enthusiasm at times. On the other hand, it is possible that more than one youth who signed the petition had to deal with parents who strongly disagreed with their participation. In that case, it may be that a few hid behind the "I was coerced into signing" defense.

If I'd had the opportunity to do this over, I would have addressed the issue in a different manner. Furthermore, I would have arranged it so that a few of the youth could have presented our ideas in person at the deacons' meeting. I know that Jay, Jimmy, and I really thought it was important to get input from the youth, and that was our intention.

For me, the bottom line is this: If you read the list of signatures, you will note that most of us either ended up in church vocations or strongly supporting the churches we attended. (That even applies to Alice Erickson and John Dawson.) Looking at the list of signees, you can't help but be impressed with what these "revolutionaries" have done with their lives.

And if you read through the list of specific requests, many came into being over the next few decades. Even the request for dancing was partially enacted later by Jay Russ, who set up future dances at the Woman's Club to teach the youth how to dance.

Other than that, youth would be put on church committees in the near future. The church added more youth activities and eventually hired youth ministers to fulfill some of the requests listed in the petition. Other requests were already being made available to members of the church.

We continued to go out to Dunbar, the Eastern State Hospital unit for children, with Phil Everhart to do birthday parties and games. As time passed, our youth began to participate in a variety of ministries, including some for children and special populations, backyard Vacation Bible Schools in other localities, and home repairs for the disadvantaged.

Hopefully, the petition got people thinking about what the church could do for its young people. Perhaps it helped HBC with one of its greatest accomplishments, which would be the number of young members who went into full-time Christian service and ministry. Among those who signed, you can find youth and young adults who became preachers, deacons, "life deacons," Sunday school teachers, public school teachers, social workers, police officers, nurses, and associational workers. Many became Christian husbands, wives, parents, and leaders at Hampton Baptist and other churches. Of those I know, they all have left a positive mark on their church and the world.

To:

Chester L. Brown and the Deacon's of Hampton Baptist Church.

The following resolution was composed by the following committee:

Judy Dooley
Margie Whitcomb
Tally Mims
Jimmy Allison
Phil Everhart, Jr.
Jimmy Ailor
Jay Lawson
Cliff Morris
Mike Haywood

It was taken to the Youth Council and passed as an official resolution by that body. It was then taken back to the young people in the form of a petition. We would now like to present this resolution to you.

I would like to express thanks to alice Erickson for editing this resolution, and to Diane Rath for typing the final copy

mike Haywood

WE THE YOUNG PEOPLE OF

HAMPTON BAPTIST CHURCH

We, the young people of Hampton Baptist Church, would like to present a list of suggestions that we feel will help to further strengthen an already strong and affective church. We feel these suggestions will help by:

1) Making the young people feel more of an integral part of the total church structure, thus instilling a desire to remain as such throughout their lives.

2) Impressing upon the young people what it means, totally, to be an integral part of Christ's Church, this encouraging them to support and participate in the church functions, aims and goals.

3) Involving the young people in the leadership of the church.

4) Making the church more aware of the potential of the young people, both generally and in specific cases.

5) Broadening the Christian fellowship provided by the church.

6) Developing a more mature concept on the part of the young people of the functions and structural organization of the church.

7) Enabling the young people to become more aware of the needs of the church and our immediate community, and to help us in ministering to such needs.

8) Encouraging us to "cultivate the hope" that has been placed upon young people.

Our suggestions are outlined below. We would like to stress that they are suggestions and not demands, proposals and not ultimatums. Still, we hope they will be given serious consideration. The suggestions have been broken down into three parts and are presented in that manner.

AREA I YOUTH LEADERSHIP WITHIN THE CHURCH

1) Two young people should serve on the Church Council, as bonified members. These two persons should be selected by the youth council and approved by the Pastor, with one coming from the High School S.S. and B.T.U., and one coming from the Young People's S.S. and B.T.U.

2) Two young people should serve on the Nominating Committee, one from each of the two groups named above.

3) An official committee should be made to co-ordinate youth activities during the summer, preferably to work with the Minister of Education. (The Youth Council could, perhaps assume this responsibility, though we feel it is too large and does not contain enough college age young people for this particular duty.) Special recreation could include, among others; an interchurch volley ball league, cook-outs, beach parties, dances, picnics, water skiing, a Nags Head outing, a watermelon feast, hayrides, ping pong and tennis tournaments, softball games, etc. Since many of the older people (There are no old people at this church!) might like to participate such a committee should include several adults.

4) An official committee of an equal number of young people and adults should be set up to co-ordinate activities in which the young people could help to serve the needs of the church and the community. (An example of the feasibility of such projects

can be found in the heart warming and successful trips, by the High School and Young People's B.T.U."s, to Dunbar under the leadership of Phil Everhart, Sr.)

AREA II THINGS THE CHURCH SHOULD PROVIDE FOR THE YOUNG PEOPLE

1) Church-sponsored Dances outside the church building. The youth of our church believe that the church should sponsor a dance outside of the church building so that we may have the Christian atmosphere that we would like to see at a dance.

We do not want a dance the the church because we feel that some traditions should be kept. We believe the church is a place for worshiping God and not the place for a loud band. Also, we have been taught since infancy, and we agree, that we should not desecrate our house of worship.

Most of the youth will attend dances held by other groups anyway. Therefore, since we are going to dance we feel that it is the church's responsibility to sponsor a dance in a good place. For this atmosphere we would pick a place in a nice neighborhood, such as the Hampton Women's Club on Columbia Avenue. Control of the dances could be administered by the Board of Deacons or a committee selected by them. They could regulate such things as the hour of closing, mode of dress, chaperons, and the banning of any dances so designated.

The thing that would set the Christian atmosphere would be that one person from every couple would be a member of Hampton Baptist Church (or one of the sponsoring churchs if two or more churches went together.) This in itself, would produce a Christian atmosphere, with good fellowship and lots of fun.

Considering the lack of a real choice in the places that now provide dancing, such a church-sponsored activities would serve a great need for the young people who enjoy dancing as recreation. (Area II, section 1 was passed by an 8 to 1 vote of the committee)

2) Classes in Church Leadership once a year. To serve effectively many of us must be taught. This we feel is a most important duty of the church.

3) Summer activities. (See Area I, #3, a.) This is vitally needed, especially for the younger members of the church (i.e. 9 to 13). We all would like to see this. Life is an interaction of people; fellowship is an interaction of people; (Christian fellowship is essential in developing Christian people who are interested in one another.)

AREA III NOT ONLY TO RECEIVE BUT TO GIVE

We acknowledge that if the young people of the church do not support the functions, goals, aims, and ministry of the church, then they are not, in reality, a part of the church. This does not mean of course, that each person should take part in every activity and program of the church, but it does mean that each should willingly and joyfully take part in many: Those in which they receive, those in which they learn, those in which they interact, those in which they give of themselves, (especially as in AreaI, sec.4)

What we ask is justifiable only if, inthe end, it helps us to find a meaning to life, to find enjoyment in life, and to better give of ourselves: to give of our Christian experience to the world.

Hampton Baptist Church

I am for this petition in its entirety.	I am for all parts of this petition, except for Dancing. I think that section should be omitted.

1- John Ailor	1- Nancy Lee Jones
2- Phil Everhart Jr.	2- _illegible_ Dennis _illegible_
3- Jimmy Ailor	3- Alan W. Townsend
4- Rod M⁺Kendree	4- Bonnie Braswell
5- Judy Dooley	5- Nat Hawley
6- Becky Wood	6- Jim Albertson
7- Beth Robbins	7-
8- Mary L. Upshaw	8-
9- Scott Hawk	9-
10- Scott Miller	10-
11- Marque Whitcomb	11-
12- Nancy Vornom	12-
13- Craig Michael	13-
14- Mike Cleckley	14-
15- MIKE VICK	15-
16- Lynne Everhart	
17- Jean Jones	
18- Jerald Miller	
19- Patricia Wallace	
20- Kay Clayton	
21- Stephanie Northen	
22- Rolanda McKendree	
23- Kathryn McKendree	
24- _illegible_	
25- _illegible_	
26- _illegible_	

16- Lynne Everhart
17- Jean Jones
18- Jerald Miller
19- Patricia Wallace
20- Kay Clayton
21- Stephanie Nother
22- Rolanda McKendree
23- Kathryn McKendree
24- Elen ?
25- Jimmy Snall
26- James ?
27- Jane Jordan
28- Leslie Nevers
29- Peggy Patsons
30- Lynn Murdee
31- Beverly Haynes
32- Pat Gaesser
33- Vernon Rollins [Support Idea)
34-

Hampton Baptist Church

I am for this petition in its entirety.

1- CWMorris
2- Mike Hayward
3- Sally Mims
4- Donald Miller
5- [illegible]
6- Myra [illegible]
7- [illegible]
8- [illegible]
9- [illegible]
10- [illegible]
11- Billy Forbes
12- Jim Dunn
13- Roland Diggs
14- Jane Durand
15- Diane Roth
16- Betty Lou Helling
17- Wm L Sasser
18- Betty P. Sasser
19- Jane Rollins
20-
21-
22-
23-
24-
25-
26-
27-

I am for all parts of this petition, except Dancing. I think that section should be omitted.

1-
2-
3-
3-
4-
5-
6-
7-
8-
9-
10-
11-
12-
13
14-
15-

Note: Some of the signatures did not copy well due to their light pencil inscription and, in some cases, the legibility of the handwriting. Therefore, in order to give equal credit, or equal responsibility, I am listing the names below.

1. John Ailor
2. Phil Everhart Jr.
3. Jimmy Ailor
4. Roddy McKendree
5. Judy Dooley
6. Becky Wood
7. Beth Robbins
8. Mary Oldershaw
9. Scott Hawk
10. Scott Miller
11. Margie Whitcomb
12. Nancy Wornom
13. Craig Michael
14. Mike Cleckley
15. Mike Vick
16. Lynne Everhart
17. Jean Jones
18. Jerald Miller
19. Patricia Wallace
20. Kay Clayton
21. Stephanie Northen
22. Rolanda McKendree
23. Kathryn McKendree
24. Elvin Ahl Jr.
25. Jimmy Small
26. James Caldwell
27. Jane Jordan
28. Leslie Nevers
29. Peggy Parsons
30. Lynn Murden
31. Beverly Haynes
32. Pat Gaesser
33. Vernon Rollins (supports idea)
34. Jay Lawson
35. Cliff Morris
36. Mike Haywood
37. Tally Mims
38. Donald Miller
39. Cathy McBride
40. Myra McBride
41. Ann Ailor
42. Cindy Curtis
43. Timmy Rollins
44. John Lee Robbins
45. Billy Forbes
46. Suzanna Dunn
47. Roland Diggs
48. Jane Dennard
49. Diane Roth
50. Betty Lou Helbig
51. William Sasser
52. Betty Sasser
53. Jane Rollins

Supports the petition, except for dancing:

1. Nancy Lee Jones
2. Jack Dennard
3. Alan Townsend
4. Ronnie Braswell
5. Matt Hawley
6. <u>Jim</u> <u>Alllison</u>

Chapter 4
Church Nights 1964–1968

    Bill Hurt came to the church in 1962 to become our minister of education. He passed away in 2023.

    Bill told me that in addition to his normal duties as education minister, Chester put him in charge of three yearly events. Those were the Wednesday night suppers, Vacation Bible School, and annual Church Nights.

Bill Hurt enjoying a morning at a Vacation Bible School on the church front lawn (5)

Previously, Church Night had been a Wednesday evening meeting in which various organizations presented their yearly reports. It had been a rather cut and dried church business meeting. Bill, however, thought it might be fun to print all the reports in a booklet to be distributed and use drama and musical numbers to highlight the main points. It caught on, and Church Night became a good time of fun and humor as well as of reflection. You will see that it began modestly, but that would soon change. With all the churches in the United States, I would be surprised if there is not another one conducting business meetings in a similar way, but I've yet to hear of it.

It is true that during the first couple of years, we did not see the parodies that pushed the limits, which would eventually come. But in those early days, Bill was feeling his way along as he tried to inject some interest and entertainment into the obligatory reporting.

When Bill retired in 2002, I asked him for a copy of his notes and outlines for the Church Night programs. He gave them to me on the Wednesday night he was honored at church for his years of service. A couple of years were missing, and sometimes the notes were sketchy, but I have tried to highlight each year as best I can.

I will intersperse Church Night presentations here and there throughout this narrative. Keep in mind that Church Night happened on a Wednesday in January and covered the previous year.

As mentioned, the first couple

Disclaimer: A lot of Bill Hurt's notes for various Church Nights give the first names of the people performing in the skits. I have made educated(?) guesses based on the year to identify the correct performer. I'm sure I have made some mistakes, but I think I got most right.

of Church Nights were tame compared to other years, but they were the just the beginning. Bill gave quizzes to the congregation in some of these early Church Nights, and they make for a neat memento, which you will find later in this chapter. The year 1964 consisted of chairmen and women presenting their reports as in years past, but this time, Bill added a slideshow, featuring photos of the reported events, and invited the occasional guest speaker to give their take on things.

The centerpiece of Church Nights 1965 through 1968 were the quizzes. Skits and quiz contestants were used to indicate the correct answers. Then, starting in 1969, the annual Church Nights comprised the off-the-wall skits and one-liners we came to expect and love throughout the years.

1964
"NEWS AND VIEWS"

- On this first Church Night under Bill Hurt, leaders recounted what their organizations accomplished in 1963, while Bill showed slides of each event. These presentations followed the "News and Views" format, which might be applied to a TV news segment.
- Allen Turnbull gave information about the Baptist Training Union. (How many of you remember the Sunday Night BTU meetings, divided by age?)
- Bill told about Youth Week and the youth retreat held at Camp Wakefield. (During Youth Week, the youth "take over," acting as church officers.) Bill pointed out that during the youth retreat, Phil Everhart Sr., who was one of the leaders, took part in the afternoon recreational events.

- Royal Ambassador leaders were Howard Stone, Larry Lawrence, Jim Michael, and John Windham. Pat Patrick, one of the RAs, spoke about their activities.
- Our January Bible study was on the Gospel of Matthew and was taught by Chester Brown.
- Bill Nelson, general superintendent, reported on the Sunday school.
- VBS, for ages 4–16, included Bible study, handicrafts, and refreshments.
- Martha Ailor, the WMU president, gave a report.
- Charlotte Williams was minister of music. She, Tom Inman, and John Crigler gave a musical performance.
- Mrs. George Phoenix was crowned queen of the senior adult Valentine party.
- Baxter Lee emceed a show of the latest Paris fashions, featuring models Jimmy Sinclair, Jules Miller, and Larry Frost.
- Mrs. J. A. Clemmer gave a report on the kindergarten.

Velma Jean Allison was the pianist at Parkview Baptist for many years. (3)

Chester, Jim Michaels, and Bill Hurt at a deacons' retreat (2)

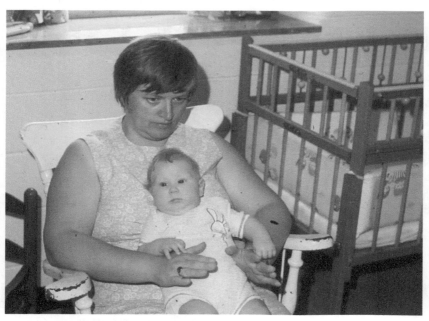

Jane Hurt doing nursery duty (2)

Right: Martha Ailor leading a Bible study at a youth retreat (3)

Below: Francis Jones pointing and leading the way (2)

Right: Gertrude Pearce and Mrs. Downey (1964)—Mrs. Pearce was a chaperone on several Eagle Eyrie weekends for the youth during my early days. (2)

Cynthia Lawson hard at work in the office (2)

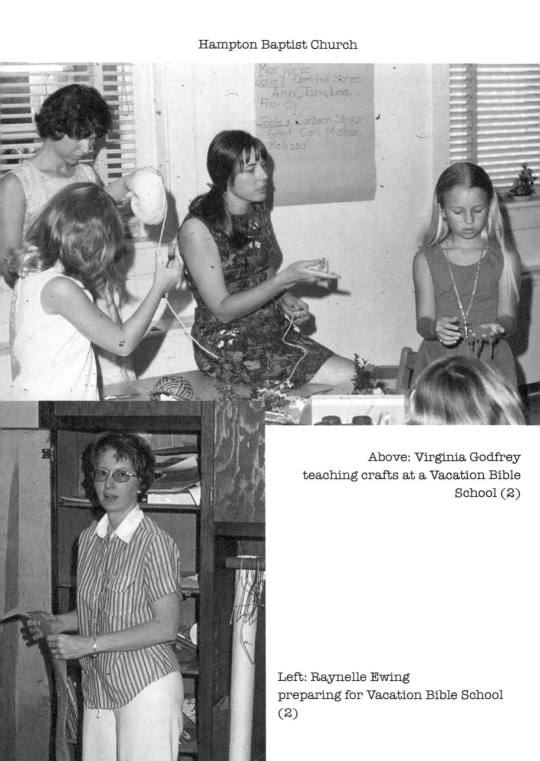

Above: Virginia Godfrey
teaching crafts at a Vacation Bible
School (2)

Left: Raynelle Ewing
preparing for Vacation Bible School
(2)

Jane Hurt, Barbara Gunter, Richard and Virginia Pulley (2)

RA awards banquet: Bryan Lilley, Will Garris, Larry
Brumfield, Chester Brown, Mike Haywood, and Ted Taylor
(I do not remember who the speaker was.) (2)

Everett Whitley reading at a youth choir performance;
John Erickson over his shoulder (3)

Above: Amy Hurt (2)
Below: Becky Riddle (2)

1965
"THAT WAS THE YEAR THAT WAS"

The 1965 Church Night (named after the TV political satire show *That Was the Week that Was*) was one of the few not in the packet that Bill gave me when he retired. In 1991, the program was a history of annual Church Nights; unfortunately, it only mentioned the title of the 1965 event. So until someone comes forward with a record or a memory, this is the "Forgotten" Church Night.

There was a quiz for 1965, which must have been part of the Church Night. Although I'm sure there are copies of Chester's annual letters on file somewhere, this is one of the few included with the Church Night folder that Bill gave me (see opposite page).

Chester at a senior adult gathering (2)

THIS IS OUR STORY, THIS IS OUR SONG

Dear Friends:

Though the past year has not been a dull and uneventful one, it has been mainly a year of "continuation." We have continued to do our Lord's work; we have continued to expand our ministry; we have continued to grow and serve together; and we have continued to mature in Christ. It has not been a year of innovation or new beginnings.

As we consider briefly the statistics for the year, we can be most grateful. Our membership passed beyond the 1300 mark. It is now easier than ever for a person to hide within the membership, as is always true in a large church. Though the Sunday School average attendance dropped seven points below last year, we have continued to offer an effective and profitable Bible Study Period. We would express our gratitude to Mr. W. J. Nelson for his thorough and faithful work as Superintendent of the Sunday School for the past two years. He deserves a vacation, and so we shall let him rest from this job for a while. Mr. Chester L. Robbins is the new Superintendent. He is not a stranger to anyone in the church, and we are confident that he will provide adequate leadership for this the most important organization in our church. The Training Union, under the direction of Mr. Allen A. Turnbull, continues to give us good reports. He is doing a splendid job, and we are grateful to him. Interest in Prayer Meeting (though many of us aren't sure that the mid-week service measures up to the definition of a Prayer Meeting) has grown considerably, and the fellowship at the tables and in our discussions has been a real joy.

Financially the year has been exceptionally good. Every person connected with the Finance Operating and the Finance Planning Committees deserves our sincere gratitude. The total receipts for the year were $126,582.49. The total indebtedness of the church on December 31, 1964, was $216,614.00

It is not fitting that I should relate the busy schedule of a busy year to equally busy people. And even though the singling out of certain people and certain programs presents the danger of overlooking equally isgnificant people and events, I feel it fitting to mention a name or two.

The death of the former Chairman of the Deacons, Mr. C. S. Revell, was both a personal loss to me and to the congregation. I trust that I shall grow old as gracefully and as wisely as he. He never lived in the past, nor did he ever consciously stand in the way of progress. In his judgments he was wise; in his compliments, generous; in his criticisms, kind. Foremost in his mind was his Lord and his church.

We are presently most fortunate to have the leadership of deacons who are personally dedicated to the cause of Christ. It is a pleasure for me to work with each one of them, and I would not exchange any one of them for any one else. Mr. T.J. Northen, Jr., our present Chairman, is a man of exceptional ability, well loved and respected by his church and his pastor.

During the past year the deacons studied the book, What Is The Church? We have given much attention throughout our program to an examination of the nature and purpose of the church. We are now participating with other Southern Baptists in a period of emphasis upon worship. For we believe that when we understand what the church is, then and only then, can we really do what the church is to do.

Mr. John Kersey is to be complimented for leading our church in the Peninsula Baptist Association bond sale. Though the general sale did not go at all well, our church, because of his efforts and your response, went over its goal. This money is being used to purchase new properities intended for the location of new churches here on the Peninsula, one of the fastest growing areas in the country. We have a missionary responsibility, and it begins at home.

The ladies of the Woman's Missionary Union apparently believe this very much. They have been most active in local work, however, they have not relaxed in their vigilance regarding our world-wide obligations. For the first time, the Lottie Moon Christmas Offering for Foreign Missions was church wide. We received the largest amount in the history of our church for this cause, some $2,837.00

Though we have no brotherhood, I cannot interpret this failure as a neglect on the part of our men toward the church. It seems to me that it is merely a lack of concern for additional meetings, and with this attitude, I am much in sympathy. Throughout the program of the church our men are active and dedicated.

The Royal Ambassador Program has enjoyed such success during the year that we must
(continued on back)

publically congratulate both the boys and their leaders. We wish them well during the present year.

The Music Ministry continues to grow in numbers and in quality. We regret the decision of Mr. S. P. Damerel to decline the Chairmanship of the Music Committee, though his long and arduous service on this committee certainly has won for him a rest. Mr. Paul Underhill, the new chairman, is no stranger to the music of the church, and we have confidence in him.

During the past year we were delighted to take note of the graduation of Mr. John L. Blackwell from Midwestern Seminary. He was called to become Pastor of the Waverly Baptist Church, in Waverly, Va. He serves that church today with our prayers and best wishes.

Three gifts during the past year made it possible for the addition of a conference room to the facilities of the church. This room, beautifully decorated, is on the second floor next to the Pastor's Study. We are most grateful to these friends whose generosity has made such a room possible.

The church has voted to accept as memorial gifts, new windows for the sanctuary. Some six windows are now proposed, and we are in the process of negotiating for their installation. Though we plan to build a new sanctuary it does not now seem that it will be in the near future. Even so, these windows will be worthy additions to either a new sanctuary or a chapel.

We are particularly fortunate in having five ordained ministers in our congregation, other than the pastor. The encouragement and devotion of these men to the program of the church is greatly appreciated. Dr. Antonio Martinez continues to serve the Spanish speaking people in the area. His "congregation" now numbers some thirty-five, and during the past year he has baptized five converts.

Dr. and Mrs. Garber continue to minister to us all. They are always willing to serve their church in any way, and we are very happy that they continue to enjoy good health and the pleasure of participating in the work of our Lord.

We welcomed a new staff member during the year, Mrs. Philip Everhart as the new teacher of the Kindergarten. Mr. Hurt, Mrs. Williams, Mrs. Jones, Mrs. Everhart, and Mrs. Wiggs each deserves regular recognition and sincere appreciation from us all. I am most pleased with them, and I am most pleased with you.

In bringing this letter to a close, I would like to reaffirm my confidence in, and my appreciation for each member of the church. You have continued to be generous and kind. We have enjoyed a fellowship of kindred minds and agreement has not been the pre-requisite for fellowship and friendship. We must strive continuously to bring into the inner fellowship all who come to us for a church home.

Patience and understanding are not measured on good days when life goes casually and routinely along. Faith is not measured when we are healthy and wealthy and bubbling over with joy. It is when things do not go our way, when sickness comes, when troubles arrive that the real metal within us shows itself. Let us therefore resolve to seek the will of God in all things, and let us determine to be obedient to that will as we work within the fellowship of God's Spirit.

"Now to Him who by the power at work within us is able to do far more abundantly than all that we ask or think, to Him be glory in the church and in Christ Jesus to all generations, forever, and ever. Amen." (Ephesians 3: 20-21)

Chester L. Brown,
Pastor

February 7, 1965

Mary Etta and Mary Elizabeth with the youth at Eagle
Eyrie (3)

Perry Damerel on a senior adult bus tour (2)

1966
"TO TELL THE TRUTH"

The theme this year was based on the TV game show of the same name, in which four celebrities interview three guests who are all claiming to be the real person of notoriety.

Bill's variation on the game included a printed quiz about the events of the past year. After the congregation was given time to complete the quiz, Bill announced the correct answers. Skits would be performed from time to time to illustrate the subject of some of the questions.

Bill handed out a quiz for three years, 1966 to 1968. **The answers to the quizzes can be found on pages 87–88.**

1966 QUIZ

1. The Training Union held a picnic on July 17th. Where was it held?
   a. Huntington Park
   b. HBC grounds
   c. Gosnold Hope Park

2. The Training Union got a new leader in 1965. Who was he?
   a. Baxter Lee
   b. Phil Everhart
   c. Graydon Elliott

3. How many "seasons of prayer" were held by the WMU in 1966?
   a. 2
   b. 3
   c. 4

4. The GA Coronation service was held on May 16th. How many girls participated?
   a. 23
   b. 25
   c. 30

1967
"HAPPINESS IS BEING ABLE TO REMEMBER 1966"

Skits starring Peanuts cartoon characters highlighted the organizations, people, and functions of the church. These included the classic trope of Lucy pulling the ball away when Charlie Brown tries to kick. Highlights are covered in the quiz that follows.

• The youth presented a Christmas play titled "Gift Wrap, Please."

1967 QUIZ

1. In January 1966, the number of deacons was increased. The number added to the board was:
   a. 8
   b. 10
   c. 12

2. The church librarian in 1966 was:
   a. Jane Hess
   b. Laberta Townsend

3. A youth newsletter was started with the name:
   a. Lucy's Lines
   b. Snoopy's Scoops
   c. Linus's Blanket

4. The name of the coffeehouse started in the
   summer was _____.

5. The annual youth retreat this year was held at:
   a. Eastover
   b. Wakefield
   c. Virginia Beach

6. At the Christmas morning service, the choir used a new
   musical instrument with the anthem. The new
   instrument was:
   a. celesta
   b. violin
   c. handbells

7. The HBC city league basketball team had a tough year
   with a record of:
   a. 1 win/11 losses
   b. 3 wins/9 losses
   c. 2 wins/10 losses

8. The softball team did much better, coming in:
   a. 2nd place
   b. 3rd place
   c. 4th place

9. In RA baseball, which four members of the team made
   the All-Star list:
   a. Phil Everhart Jr.
   b. Lee Feathers

c. John Ailor
d. Michael Vick
e. Doug Thompson
f. Craig Michael
g. Bruce Whitcomb
h. Billy Bosta

10. The church celebrated which anniversary?
    a. 125th
    b. 200th
    c. 175th

11. The Sunday school adopted a new curriculum called
    _____.

12. The book studied during January Bible Study Week was:
    a. Ephesians
    b. Matthew
    c. Deuteronomy

13. The annual WMU banquet was held on March 11th. The guest speaker was a missionary to Colombia, then home on furlough. What was her name?

14. The church was indebted to the WMU for a lovely gift presented to the church in October. This gift was what?

1968
"DO YOU REMEMBER?"

For this year's theme, which was loosely based on *Jeopardy!*, Bill handed out another quiz. Three contestants came forward to sit with Bill, the host, and a scorekeeper. If none of the three contestants could answer a question, the congregation as a whole could try to answer. From time to time, the emcee gave a short break with coverage of special church events.

- Deacons and Wives had a banquet at NASA.
- Bill Hurt and Baxter Lee entertained with musical selections.
- Chester announced his engagement to Mary Etta Mann.

1968 QUIZ

1. What activity did the Sunbeams do to provide gifts to missionaries to give to children for Christmas?
   a. Christmas in March
   b. Christmas in August
   c. Christmas in November

2. Where was the youth retreat held in 1967?

3. HBC had how many church choirs in 1967?
   a. 3
   b. 4
   c. 5

4. Who was the WMU president in 1967?

5. What was the name of the Sunday school class added this year?

6. What was the name of the church softball team?
   a. Snoopy's All Stars
   b. Chester Brown's All Stars
   c. Woody Patrick's All Stars

7. Where was the annual church picnic held?

8. Who won the pie-eating contest at the church picnic?
   a. Phil Everhart Sr.
   b. Baxter Lee
   c. Woody Patrick

9. Who was the kindergarten director in 1967?

10. What was the name of the annual event held on New Year's Eve?

11. Who was the youth pastor in 1967?

12. Who took over the children's choirs?

13. The slogan of the Training Union for the year was "_____ _____—150."

14. What is the name of the coffeehouse started in 1967?

15. (Extra credit) What happened on July 22, 1967?

This must be a WMU circle meeting: back—Sharon Diggs, Carol Harper, Claudia Nock, and Faye Everett; front—Iris Garris, Bobbie Flowers, Vickie Ellis, and Peggy Byrd. (2)

I'm guessing this is a Valentine's Day party. Francis and Dottie Lee Jones sit in the front row, along with Ammie Garber. Bill and Freda Nelson are on the left side of the second row. (2)

Above: Frank Schneider, Dick Whittington, Eddie Hankinson, and Francis Jones (2)

Below: Charlotte Williams leading the children's choir (3)

Hampton Baptist Church

Sonny Ashe, Chet Robbins, and Perry Damerel in the back (2)

Youth choir (3)

Adult choir—too many to name, but you can pick them out. (2)

Jill Godfrey, Susan Lilley, and Sharon Goodwin on a retreat (3)

Becky Parsons, Laura Wood, Linda Hurt, and Cindy Lawson at Eagle Eyrie (3)

This must be an outdoors Sunday morning service that
included communion. (2)

Maynard and Nancy Sandford, Patricia and Craig Michael, and Thelma Killiam get ready to take the youth on a retreat to Eastover. The youth include Theresa Diggs, Dawn Lilley, Alan Hurt, Karen Watts, Mary Elizabeth Brown, John Erickson, Susan Williams, Ben Sandford, Ed Lilley, and Ed Brown. (3)

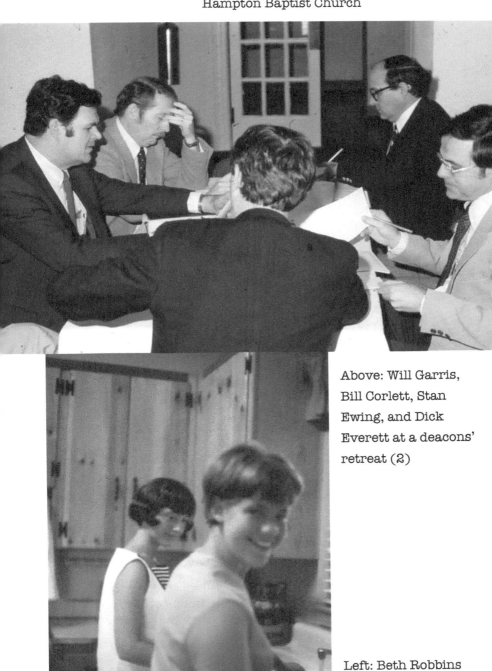

Above: Will Garris,
Bill Corlett, Stan
Ewing, and Dick
Everett at a deacons'
retreat (2)

Left: Beth Robbins
(3)

85

Youth retreat at Eastover: Jim Ailor, Lavonda Simpton,
Martha Owens, Jimmy Michael, Jo Tillery, Sue Ann Tillery,
and Sam Ailor, among others (3)

ANSWERS TO QUIZZES

1966

1. Huntington Park
2. Baxter Lee
3. b. 3
4. c. 30

1967

1. b. 10
2. a. Jane Hess
3. b. Snoopy's Scoops
4. Fisherman's Cove
5. c. Virginia Beach
6. c. handbells
7. a. 1 win / 11 losses
8. a. 2nd place
9. a. Phil Everhart Jr.
   b. Lee Feathers
   e. Doug Thompson
   g. Bruce Whitcomb
10. c. 175th
11. Life and Works
12. c. Deuteronomy
13. Mrs. Zack Deal
14. silver bowl and tray

1968

1. b. Christmas in August
2. Camp Owaissa
3. c. 5
4. Myrtle Dennard
5. Couples Class
6. b. Chester Brown's All Stars
7. Gosnold Hope Park
8. c. Woody Patrick
9. Lucille Everhart
10. Watch Night
11. David Hicks
12. Sidney Swiggard
13. "Think Big—150"
14. Fisherman's Cove
15. Mary Etta Mann married Chester Brown.

Chapter 5
Left Behind, Left Out, and "Leave That Out!"

Phil and Lucille Everhart were two of our youth leaders during the 1960s, when I was in the youth group, along with several others whom we will get to in due time. Phil involved us in several ministries. One of my favorites was Dunbar, the children's unit at Eastern State Hospital, where we threw parties and played games. (You might remember that this was one of the ministries in the petition; see Chapter 3.) As I remember, most of the children at Dunbar were ages ten to sixteen. This was a real learning experience as most of the patients seemed totally normal to us.

The theme was usually "Birthdays of the Month," and we celebrated all the birthdays. We played a lot of games and offered plenty to eat, including cake. However, the best part of the afternoon was the one-on-one interactions with those who lived at the facility. I do not think I could name a single patient today, but I do remember feeling like they were just regular kids and teens enjoying themselves. (I believe this experience had some impact on the vocation I chose later in life.)

For several years, we would go every two to three months on Sunday afternoons. We would usually go home after the morning church service, eat some lunch, and then meet back at the church before heading out to Dunbar. There we would spend a couple of hours in a large recreation room. It was always a lot of fun, and I think that those of us who participated got a lot out of these trips.

We were mostly high-school and college-age youth. As you might expect, we were met at the front door of the building, which was locked, and then escorted to the recreation room. That room also had to be unlocked and relocked once we were inside. We eventually got used to that and had never encountered a problem until one particular Sunday afternoon.

When we finished for the day, we gathered the dozen or of us who had come with Phil Everhart and Freddy Wornam and waited at the door while it was unlocked. We then walked down several hallways to the front door, which the matron, who was also our guide, unlocked and let us pass through. This particular Sunday, someone suggested that we take a group picture on the small front porch. We asked the matron if she would pose with us, and she agreed, as we had gotten to know her over the past visits. I do not remember who took the photo, but it was probably another staff person at Dunbar.

As we lined everyone up on the porch and steps, Phil Everhart said, "Hey, where is Phil Jr.?" Phil Sr. had brought his son on this afternoon. He was about nine or ten at the time. We looked around, and sure enough, Phil was nowhere to be seen! The matron suggested we backtrack to the recreation room. As soon as she unlocked the front door, we saw Phil Jr. and another staff person walking toward us.

He told us that he had been saying goodbye to several of the Dunbar guys. By the time he'd finished his farewells, the rest of us had departed. Phil Jr. tried the door, but it had been locked.

He kept his composure and approached one of the staff people still in the room, trying to explain who he was and what had happened. There were about forty boys and girls in the room, many around Phil's age. He was met with skepticism and the suggestion that he behave himself and stop trying to sneak out.

It took a couple of minutes before the staff figured out that this young person was not one of their patients. Phil took it all in stride with a big smile.

I have the photographic reminder of that day. We retook the group photo after being reunited with Phil Jr.

Freddy Wornom, Jane Rollins, and I are in the front. Eleanor Patrick and Claudette Corbett are on the left, with Jack Sheppard who is wearing the black hat. Phil Jr. is next to Ursula Brown, with Phil Sr. just behind. Barbara Panz and the hospital matron are on the right. (5)

Phil Everhart Jr. was not the only one left behind at a church event. I had not heard about this next story at the time we celebrated the church's 225th anniversary in 2016. There was a lot of reminiscing during the event. At one point, I walked back to the kitchen area and started talking with Sue Coughenour Martinez and Cheryl Bridges Elder. They told me a story about when they were youth at the church in the 1970s. It was during the summer that Jim Ailor and Jay Lawson were co-directors for the HBC youth. (A few more stories will surface about that time.)

Sue Coughenour in a hall at the church Trudy McBride on her left (3)

A multi-church revival was held in the Williamsburg area that summer. Sue and Cheryl attended with a group of about twenty-five from Hampton Baptist. Near the end of the service, the evangelists provided the opportunity for anyone who so desired to come forward and make a profession of faith. A large number of people, including Sue and Cheryl, made their way to the front of the auditorium, where they were divided into smaller groups and directed to other rooms or parts of the venue. Sue and Cheryl went where they were directed and talked with one of the event leaders.

After they finished, the two girls made their way back to where they had previously been sitting with the group. But no

Hampton Baptist people were still there. In the meantime, Jay and Jimmy had gotten their group together . . . or so they thought. Sue and Cheryl had gone forward at the end without telling anyone.

Jimmy and Jay, thinking they had everyone and everything under control, headed back to the hotel where they were staying the night. It was one of those situations that happens in youth groups when everyone assumes everyone is accounted for and with others in the group. (Sue and Cheryl were together, just not with their group.) Keep in mind that this was before the era of cell phones, so there was not a quick way for the girls to contact their leaders. They spent an anxious twenty to thirty minutes before they could contact someone who passed the information on to the intrepid youth directors. Eventually they were reunited, and all ended well.

Now, this next story kind of falls into the "left behind" theme, though it is more of a self-imposed leaving behind. However, it involves Woody Patrick, and that makes it a Hampton Baptist tale and worth remembering.

As most of you may recall, Woody Patrick was our enforcer. If, as a youth, you and your friends were getting a little out of line, your worst nightmare would be running into Woody. It was interesting and uncanny; whenever you were making a little trouble, or thinking about it, Woody would come up behind you unobserved and, with a smile on his face and an even tone in his voice, say, "Mike (or whomever), I don't think you really want to do that, do you?" Sometimes that remark was made with a strong hand (or fingers, actually—Woody had really strong fingers) on your shoulder or the back of your neck.

The following incident shows how certain people leave a lasting impression on your life, sometimes even greater than you realized. Woody Patrick certainly left several impressions on my life (and indentations in my shoulder), including one having to do with how to conduct oneself during a worship service at Hampton Baptist Church.

In the early 2000s, I was at Parkview Baptist for the early (8:30 a.m.) service. Rusty Beck, who later became the pastor there, was the youth minister at the time, and he had started a contemporary worship service. This included a praise band and a more casual atmosphere.

A good number of senior adults attended, but it was mostly teens and young adults. In keeping with the more casual, relaxed setting, you could grab a cup of coffee and a doughnut from the foyer and take them into the chapel (which was the old sanctuary) for the worship service. No one seemed to have a problem with this, including the senior adults.

So this Sunday morning, I decided to do the same. I grabbed a cup of coffee (black, of course) and a doughnut and started to make my way toward the chapel. When I reached the entrance of the chapel, it was as though an invisible hand had reached down from the heavens and grabbed me by the shoulder, stopping me in my tracks. My first thought was that Woody Patrick had reached out to stop me from doing the unthinkable. My mind said, "You can't go in there with food and drink. You just don't do that in a church sanctuary." My feet said, "We know this, and we are *not* moving." That is how I was brought up at Hampton Baptist. Some things were just not done, and that was one of them! I literally could not force myself to take one step into the sanctuary.

I walked back into the foyer knowing exactly what had happened. Back in the days when we were growing up at HBC, we would never take something to eat or drink into the sanctuary during the service. I am certain I never took anything like that into the Hampton Baptist sanctuary at *any* time, day or night.

If I had ever tried, someone (most likely Woody Patrick, but possibly a number of other people) would have grabbed me by the collar, neck, or shoulder and pulled me out, all while delivering a stern lecture about why I should never do that!

Any time after, when I attended the contemporary service at Parkview, two things were consistent. First, it never bothered me to see other people with coffee and doughnuts in the sanctuary (many of these people were seniors). And yet, never once was I able to walk past the threshold of the chapel with those items in my hand. That was a product of my HBC upbringing. I did enjoy my refreshments in the foyer before going into the sanctuary.

One more quick Woody Patrick story: Woody and I had one quality in common: a strong, loud voice! This story was related to me by our then-youth minister, Jay Russ. It was in 1999, after a storm had knocked the steeple down. When the steeple fell on the sanctuary roof, it did enough damage that we could not use that space for a while. Therefore, we held church services in the fellowship hall, where we also served Wednesday night suppers. Jay told me about a meeting in which the staff discussed how the first Sunday morning service in the fellowship hall would go. Jay said that Chester smiled and said he could see it clearly: "I'm going to be saying the opening prayer as Woody Patrick and Mike Haywood come down the hall, talking at the top of their lungs!"

Well, you can't get upset about being compared to Woody Patrick in any regard. But, no, we didn't do that; though I have been asked more than once to please lower my voice!

That was not the only lesson that was taught about how to conduct oneself at Hampton Baptist, especially in the sanctuary. And that is how we come back to the time that Jimmy Ailor and Jay Lawson organized a youth rally one night during the summer they were co-directors. The rally was held in the HBC sanctuary. The dynamic duo were hip on all the latest fads, both inside and outside of churches all over the country.

Well, they wanted to add some pizzazz to the evening. The disco ball was a thing back then. You remember it—a shiny, reflective ball, about the size of a basketball, covered with little mirrors that reflected light at all angles. But one disco ball wasn't enough. Remember, this was Jim and Jay. They hung *two* disco balls from the ceiling of the sanctuary. Ailor later told me that they had used footballs with mirrors attached. Then they spun the footballs in opposite directions. If you had any lights—better yet, colored lights—shining toward the disco ball(s), it would reflect the light back out into the audience.

The guys later told me that the biggest problem was how to hang the disco balls from the cathedral ceiling of the sanctuary. Luckily, they had access to some tall ladders. No one tried to stop them from hanging disco balls in the sanctuary because they didn't actually ask for permission. (OK, I have to admit that one of my guiding principles over the years has been "It is better to ask forgiveness than to ask permission." Much as I hate to admit it, they might have learned that motto from me.)

Long story short, Jay and Jim used the disco balls the night of the rally, which helped make the event a smashing success . . . and caused Jim and Jay to be ordered to report to the personnel committee. After a short but emphatic discussion/lecture, they assured the assembled committee that they would never do it again. And they didn't—at least not at Hampton Baptist.

But wait—that is not the end of the story. In 1985, Hampton Baptist decided to bring in a full-time youth minister. The year before, the church had hired a year-round, part-time youth minister, Terry Laufer. That had gone well, and it was decided that the church would do well to hire a full-time youth pastor. The personnel committee, which included Alice Erickson, Stan Ewing, Bill Nelson, and Jimmy Michael, traveled to Southeastern Seminary, where they met Jay Russ, a senior.

(Now for another Jay and Jimmy: Jay Russ was in seminary with a friend of mine, Jimmy George. Jay and Jimmy had also attended Mars Hill College together. Jimmy had worked for me as a PBA summer missionary in the early 1980s. He had grown up at Tabernacle and First Baptist Churches and knew the Peninsula well. Jimmy was the one who would look after Jay when he came to check out Hampton Baptist.)

Jay was offered the position at HBC, and the rest, as they say, is history. He accepted the youth ministry position and stayed on for twenty-some years before eventually taking the pastorate at Stevens Memorial, where you will find him today.

But we are not through with the disco ball quite yet.

Jay tells the story about one of the many meetings he had with the personnel committee in the early days. During one of these, Jay was told the one thing he must *never* do: hang a disco ball in the sanctuary! There might have been a couple of other things that Jay was told not to do, but that one definitely stood out. Now to be fair, while Jay never used a disco ball in the sanctuary, you might come across a few other things in this narrative that Jay Russ did and was later told never to do again!

Jay Russ, Harald Aadahl, and I, as well as a couple other Peninsula Baptist youth ministers, attended a Baptist conference in Florida during the early 1990s. It was a yearly gathering held in

Lake Yale. It was a great experience because 1) the seminars were excellent and 2) it was during the month of January! At one of the large meetings, the speaker told us to remember the following principle of being a good youth minister: "If the church you are serving at has never made a special 'rule' because of something you did with the youth, then you are not doing your job properly."

If you use that as your guide, then I can safely say that Jim Ailor, Jay Lawson, Jay Russ, Matt Parron, Ed Lilly, Bobby Vann, Ben Sandford, Ann Pulley, Krista Everette, Brooke Pucket, and many other HBC youth ministers all did a first-class job!

Jay Russ did more than his share of transgressions while at Hampton Baptist that landed him in a bit of hot water. I am going to mention a few, but the first incident is one that didn't necessarily get him in trouble, though it might have raised a few adult eyebrows in the church. It is possible that (until now) none of the adults knew about this. It was a graphic example of how we as church members often treat the Bible.

Jay first used this object lesson during a youth meeting one night at church. He later did it again at an evening worship at HBC and at a service during the Peninsula Baptist Work Camp.

Jay would find an old, well-worn Bible that belonged to no one and had probably been sitting in a back room of the church gathering dust. However, it was important that this Bible have its cover intact and be in fairly good condition. He would first talk about how much the Bible taught us and how we should all be spending time reading and learning from it. He would point out that the Bible is a gift from God, and therefore, we should read *all* of it.

He went on to ask the youth if they read from all parts of the Bible, both the Old and New Testaments. They would assure Jay that they did, and he would say that was good.

He continued by saying that most Christians favor certain books or parts of the Bible. Different people have different favorite parts of the Old Testament that may include Genesis, Exodus, Psalms, Proverbs, or Isaiah. The same is true for the New Testament. Most people know a lot from Matthew, Mark, Luke, John, Acts, Corinthians, and a smattering of the other letters.

At this point, Jay would get looks that said, "Oh, no, we've read more than that!" He would flip through the Bible as he mentioned some of the more well-read books that most people are at least somewhat familiar with. He again stated how important it is that we read through all of the Bible, spending time in each book of the Old and New Testaments.

Jay would then say, "Let's find out what the Bible means to us." He asked the youth group how many had read the creation story in Genesis. Most of the youth had indeed read it, and he would say, "Good," and flip past the first few pages of Genesis.

Next, Jay mentioned another story from Genesis, say about Noah or Joseph, and asked if anyone had read it. If even one person raised a hand, Jay would again say, "Good," and leaf through those pages.

He would then pick another, somewhat obscure story in Genesis. When no one raised a hand, Jay would calmly say, "OK, so you've not read that one. That's OK. But since you don't use that part, let's just take it out." Then he ripped those pages out of the Bible. At this point, a couple of the youth would speak up and say he shouldn't do that. Jay replied that if they'd never read it in the past, then it wasn't really in "their" Bible; he wasn't ripping out pages of the Bible but rather superfluous sheets.

This would elicit gasps from many of the youth. Despite that, Jay carried on. He would then ask about another part of Genesis that no one had ever heard about, rip those pages out, and go on to Exodus, Leviticus, Numbers, and Deuteronomy.

All through the Old Testament Jay tore, often removing whole books. He mentioned enough more well-known stories to keep some of the Bible, but they had to have read the account and not just remembered someone telling it to them. By this point, it was quickly becoming a Jefferson Bible!

Most books of the Old Testament had one or two stories the youth had read. Other than Psalms and Proverbs, most of the books were torn out and thrown down. The number of pages littering the floor became quite impressive. A few pages of Isaiah were left but not a lot other than that.

Jay Russ tearing up a Bible at Work Camp: one or more of the teens had to have read a story for it to remain in this Bible. (1)

As Jay worked through the Bible, about 80 percent of the pages were torn out and dropped to the floor. (The only reason more wasn't ripped out is because one or two kids were good Bible students, thus saving some pages in the " Hampton Baptist Youth Bible.") After a short run through the Gospels and Acts, Romans, and Corinthians, which save a lot of pages, Jay was soon ripping pages out left and right. Other than Timothy, not much was left of the rest of Paul's letters.

When Jay got to Revelation, the floor dropped out. There may have been one page left in the last book of the Bible, but that was only because someone had read a specific verse. To say the least, it was a sobering demonstration.

Jay is just getting started. (1)

Jay did stir up a hornet's nest for a couple of other events. I am going to tell one of them now and another later. This first one led to a serious Bible study.

You remember the old Sunday blue laws? These laws determined what kind of stores could be open on Sunday and what merchandise could be sold at those stores. In 1988, the Virginia Supreme Court repelled these laws.

Jay wanted to do a Sunday evening youth Bible study about the Christian perspective on businesses being open on Sundays. He took several of the youth (including Matt Parron and Edward Brown) to a local mall, which was now open on Sundays. They stopped several shoppers and asked permission to film them being interviewed about their views on the mall being open on Sundays to show at their youth group Bible study.

One of the people they ran into was a church member who told them that another church member was working at the mall on that Sunday afternoon. Jay decided that this would make an interesting interview, and so the group went to the store and found the church member, who wasn't helping a customer at that time.

Jay asked her up front if she didn't mind being interviewed on camera. He explained what the questions would be. He also told her that they would be using the video at the church's Sunday night youth meeting. The woman said she had no problem with the video being used for the Bible study and she answered all the questions without any visible qualms.

Jay told me that the youth program that next Sunday, when they played the video of mall shoppers, was a big success.

Unfortunately, the woman who worked at the mall had a change of heart afterwards. She went to Chester Brown and complained about it.

Jay listened to Chester's lecture and tried to explain his purpose for interviewing people at the mall. He said he had asked the interviewees' permission, including the shop employee.

Nevertheless, Jay politely endured the admonitions of "never do that again" and then went on to seek other things he could get in trouble for! By this time, he knew the secret of being a good youth minister. (Don't do that again! Do something else!)

Jay served at HBC for fifteen more years before he moved on to become the pastor of Stevens Memorial Baptist Church. He is still good friends with many of us, including Chester.

Chapter 6
More No-Nos

WEARING SHORTS

During most of my high-school years, we had a rule for youth retreats that said we could wear shorts to any event except worship services and educational seminars. For those, we had to wear long pants and a dress shirt. This was true for many other churches besides Hampton Baptist.

Of course, all of the youth, including me, thought this was an archaic rule, and we let the adult leaders know our feelings. Our feelings, however, were to no avail, and we continued to be told (and yes, we did follow the rules) that we had to wear long pants at these special times. This continued until my junior year in high school when an unplanned coincidence changed all that.

The youth retreat that year included both a main speaker (whose name I've forgotten) and our minister of education (whose name I remember), Bill Hurt, who had a lapse of memory when preparing for the retreat. Both Bill and the speaker forgot to pack any long pants and didn't realize it until they were at the camp and it was too late.

Of course, our leaders had no choice but to concede: for this year only, they said, everyone could wear shorts to all the sessions and events, including worship. I don't remember any of the leaders complaining about it. I think they all discovered how pleasantly comfortable it was. We had been told that this was a "one year only" rule, but you know how that goes. We never went back to wearing long pants after that.

For many years before the previous event, Lucille Everhart and I had a running "discussion" about the short-pants rule. Lucille felt we should dress in a way that showed "reverence," and I felt we should dress in a way that was comfortable. It was always a fun and friendly disagreement, but over the course of it, neither of us budged on our divergent feelings.

A couple of years before the "I forgot my long pants" retreat, Lucille caught up with me one morning at church and gave me a newspaper clipping she had pasted on a piece of construction paper. She said, "I still disagree with you and the writer of this newspaper article, but I did want to show you this." The article said that short pants had become acceptable for events such as church meetings.

I was impressed that Lucille cared enough to give me information that she disagreed with but supported my position. She simply gave me the article, and let me do with it as I desired. Even though I still didn't agree with Lucille's viewpoint, it did raise my respect for her and made me think more about her positions on other matters. She remained on the other side of the debate, which taught me that just because you think you are right, you shouldn't suppress information that supports your opponent's side.

PLAYING CARDS

I remember that playing cards was a big no-no during those days, especially during church-sponsored events. In fact, Eagle Eyrie had a specific rule: no card decks allowed. Of course, that did not mean cards were not played!

I remember one year when HBC was at a weekend retreat at Eagle Eyrie. Larry Brumfield, Cliff Morris, Ted Taylor, and I were playing bridge in the big room at PAL Lodge. I forget who the partners were, but my partner and I had just finished bidding on a "sure grand slam" hand when an adult from another church that was staying at the lodge walked into the room. He came over to the table and said, "It's against the rules to have cards at this retreat." Without another word, he swept the remaining cards off the table, tore them in half, and walked away. We felt that was a bit of an overreaction, but we knew the rules and didn't say anything. He had a change of heart and spent the rest of the weekend apologizing for tearing up the cards.

I read somewhere that "Rook" was developed to give churchgoers a card game they could play that had nothing to do with gambling. Gambling, of course, was the reason that regular decks of cards were frowned upon by the church.

BELLY BUTTONS

I can think of two spinoffs from the above encounter. The youth from Hampton Baptist often attended the annual senior high weekend conference at Eagle Eyrie. It was always a lot of fun and good fellowship, being well attended from churches all over the state. On two occasions, the featured speaker was Grady Nutt, who was very funny.

I think it was the second year he came that Grady got sucked into the "Great Belly Button Conflict." It was when bare midriffs were first in vogue with a lot of teenage girls, and the latest fashions reflected this fad.

Although the weekend began with Friday night supper, lots of youth groups arrived earlier. During the afternoon and supper, a lot of belly buttons were on display. This caused some strong displeasure and discussion among the youth group leaders who were chaperoning. Although, I honestly don't remember there being much of a problem with the Hampton Baptist leaders that weekend.

At the beginning of the first general session, the leadership (from the state Baptist association in Richmond) issued a dress code ruling that there would be no belly buttons in view. (Senior high weekend was always in March, so swimsuits would not be an issue . . . yet.)

After a few more announcements, Grady Nutt was introduced as the main speaker for the weekend. Grady took the microphone and delivered his first declaration:

"Belly buttons are beautiful!"

I saw a few members of the state leadership throw up their hands. Of course, after that pronouncement, there was no going back. Bare midriffs were the order of the day for the rest of the weekend. And that was another rule they never recovered.

SWIMMING POOLS

This is not an HBC story, but it was told to me by John Dawson, which ties it in. When Eagle Eyrie was built in the late fifties, it included the swimming pool that is still there. Eventually, a lot of Baptist conventions built conference centers for their states too. Texas and several other state Baptist conventions voted to install *two* swimming pools, one for girls and one for boys. John told us that there had been a vote on whether or not Virgina would do the same. The argument over whether or not to have separate pools had been loud to downright bellicose. The two-pool amendment was eventually defeated by one vote.

TWO-PIECES

This is probably as good a place as any to tell this story. Truth is, I have never had a problem with girls wearing two-piece bathing suits on any events I have been in charge of. Of course, not everyone agrees with this stance.

For many years, the Peninsula Baptist Association ran a Work Camp, when we repaired houses on the Peninsula. (More on this ministry, which involved Hampton Baptist, later.) Darlene Scheepers, now the office administrator at HBC, always ran the Work Camps, as it was originally her idea. At that time, she was the youth minister at Emmaus Baptist Church.

The first year, they completely built a new home for a woman in Poquoson. After that, Darlene figured out that they could not afford to build a new home each year; however, a lot of homes could be repaired. The number of home repairs ran into the twenties in later years.

Darlene had always been against girls wearing two-piece bathing suits to church events. Whereas it was not a written rule for Work Camp, it was understood. Well, understood by everyone but me and my summer mission team.

My "Smishies" (*summer* + *missionaries*) always helped out at the camp. Most years, the campers would work only half a day on Wednesday and then go to Water Country in the afternoon. I always gave the girls on my team permission to wear what they wanted, as long as it was not scandalous.

For several years in the mid-1990s, Corinna Powell worked as a Smishy. The first summer she worked for me, the team went to Water Country with the other Work Campers, and Corinna wore a two-piece bathing suit. She had a flock of boys following her all afternoon!

That night when we got back to Work Camp, we had a scheduled meeting. The first thing Darlene covered was a new Work Camp rule: "Girls cannot wear two-piece bathing suits. If that is all you have, then you must also wear a T-shirt."

Of course, being someone with a great memory, I love reminding Corinna about this all the time! And I do want to say that once Darlene made it an official rule, I made my teams follow it.

SHORTS—AGAIN!

The other time I ran into a situation like this was when Jay Russ and I took a group to Austria in 2000. It was a Peninsula Baptist—and not a Hampton Baptist—led event, but it did have a lot of Hampton Baptist youth involved.

In 1999, my Smishy team started bugging me to take them on a foreign mission trip. Shirley Gay from Buckroe was the ring leader. Meanwhile, Craig Waddell had contacted me with the same idea; he was the contact person in Austria for mission trips originating with the state Baptist association in Richmond. (The story of that summer is described in another book, *Smishies Through the Years, Volume II.*)

Craig and I organized a trip for the summer of 2000. It would include a number of my summer mission team along with some HBC youth. From Hampton Baptist, we had Jay Russ, David Cox, Ann Pulley, Sarah Martinez, Betsy Trimble, Molly O'Bryan, Laura Williams, Mary Williams, and me. The Smishy team included Shirley Gay, Jeremy Young, and Caroline Lawson, Jay Lawson's daughter. To that mix, I added Jim Ailor's daughter, Dara, and a friend from their church in Afton, Virginia, Debbie Beaver.

We went to Richmond for our orientation in the late spring. When we got back, I received a notification from the mission board that no one could wear shorts on the trip, or at least while the camp was running.

I spoke with Craig, and he agreed that something had probably happened on a previous mission trip involving too-short shorts, and he thought we should be able to change the rule. I contacted the leaders in Richmond and reminded them that we would be helping with a summer camp and that all of the Austrians would be wearing shorts. The powers-that-be agreed, and we were allowed to wear "respectable shorts." Fortunately, we would not be swimming in Austria, so bathing suits were not an issue.

DRACULA AT RAs

OK, this one was totally on me! I was in charge of the older RAs for several years during the time that Jim Ailor, Phil Everhart Jr., Roddy McKendree, Tommy O'Bryan, Ricky Wallace, Bruce Whitcomb, and Bill Sinclair, among others, were members. We studied the Bible and RA materials at the meetings. We also did a lot of fun activities, which included camping and trips to the Haunted Woods in Mathews, Virginia. The trip to the Haunted Woods was always a big event.

Also during that period, I could check out reel-to-reel movies from the library for free, which I did about once a month, to show at the RA meetings. These were mostly old classics, suitable for the guys.

One year, after going to the Haunted Woods, I checked out the old silent film *Dracula*. It is from 1933, and it is a masterpiece. I think my original plan would have worked fine because the older guys enjoyed it. The mistake I made—and it was *my* mistake—was giving the green light to Bill Hurt when he asked if the younger RAs could come in with me that Wednesday night because their leader could not make it. Without thinking, I said, "Sure."

The older boys had no problems with the movie, but two mothers told me the next week that their younger sons had not slept at all Wednesday night. They suggested I not show such films to younger kids. I appreciated Lucille Everhart, who was very kind as she explained how I had messed up. They were right, and I never made that mistake again. (This is not to say that I never made any *other* mistakes!)

GOING TO THE MOVIES ON SUNDAY

Speaking of movies, you might remember that going to the movies on a Sunday was a big no-no for church folks during the sixties. I remember one Sunday afternoon when Eddie Higgins and a friend of his went to the Langley Theater. They missed BTU but did make it to church later in the evening. I can remember how frantic they had been to get back and make sure no one knew Eddie had gone to the movies.

ABE LINCOLN'S FANGS & PEACE SIGNS

Oh, yes. One more story, lest you think it is only I who can get into these kinds of binds. Several years later, my good friend Jerry Sullivan was the leader of the older RAs. They would meet in the Fisherman's Cove coffeehouse at the church. The RAs wanted to paint the walls of the coffeehouse, and Jerry oversaw the painting. The results were far out and psychedelic!

Two parts of the painting caused big concern: Abraham Lincoln with fangs (vampires again!) and the peace sign (not the two-finger "V" but the circle with three lines inside). The fangs on ole Abe speak for themselves, but you might not remember that the peace symbol had been used in antinuclear and antiwar demonstrations throughout the world, beginning in the 1950s. The symbol was first developed in England and became a ubiquitous emblem of youth protest.

Now, irony upon irony. I was a deacon when this mural was painted. I was even present at the meeting when some of the deacons discussed their displeasure with the radical youth painting such abominations in the church. Again to the rescue came John R. Dawson, who pointed out that most of the deacons had not even seen the walls they were critiquing. I pointed out that Col. Jerry Sullivan was their leader. Jerry had been in the Air Force at the time, and it was agreed that he would not have allowed anything disrespectful to be painted on the walls.

So we adjourned for a walking tour to the Fisherman's Cove, and when we returned to the meeting room, they decided to drop the whole issue. Since Jerry was a lieutenant colonel at the time, I took consolation in the fact that anyone could get in trouble with the deacons.

(In case you are wondering, Jimmy Ailor and Jay Lawson were in on that one too. Do we see a pattern here?)

I have no photo of the actual peace symbol painted in the Fisherman's Cove coffeehouse. Rather than copy one off the Internet, I am including one from my days of working with the Hampton welfare department. We called Division I the "Soul Unit" and got one of our members, Linda Walker, who was an artist, to draw the picture above.

Chapter 7

Above: Gary Lewis and the choir entertain the rest of us at a special outdoor event on the grounds. (2)

Left: John Garber (3)

Bill Hurt on the guitar at a youth retreat (3)

Michael Curtis at a church social (3)

Above: A young Jay
Russ (2)

Left: Angie Russ (4)

Above: Courtney and Caitlyn Russ at a sports camp (1)

Below: Dot Little (2)

Above: Libby Sinelnick (2)

Below: Alvin Feathers at Vacation Bible School (2)

Above: Dottie Lee with a young partygoer (2)
Below: Margaret Tillery (3)

Left: John Dawson on a church workday (3)

Right: Wes and Cindy Lawson at Sunday school (3)

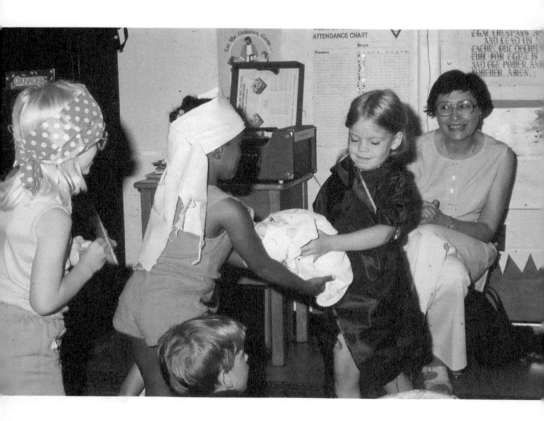

Lucille Everhart at VBS (2)

Chapter 8
Church Nights 1969–1974

1969
"FORWARD TOGETHER"

This Church Night had a political theme. The sanctuary was being painted, so we had to use the Adult 3 Sunday School Department assembly room. Some of the events highlighted by skits included the following:

- Betty Miller gave a speech, running for WMU president.
- Phil Everhart Sr. won the pie-eating contest at the annual church picnic.
- Sharon O'Bryan was crowned queen in May during GA Coronation week.
- Eight GAs went to Eagle Eyrie with Barbara Hixon and Brenda Forlines.
- Nancy Lee Jones led the World Friends (eight-year-old Sunbeams).
- Ida Patrick was the Flower Committee chairwoman.
- Lucky Elliott was the Recreation Committee chairman.
- Trustees were W. T. Sparrow, Felix Hatchett, and Francis Jones.
- Lucille Everhart was the kindergarten teacher.
- Families and individuals who joined the church in 1968:
  - Mr. and Mrs. Garland Goodwin
  - Mr. and Mrs. Cecil Kirby
  - Ms. Tally Mims
  - Mr. and Mrs. Jerry Sullivan, Renee and Lynn

- Mr. Ted Taylor
- Ms. Deborah Ruth Gunter
- Ms. Patricia Ann Riley

Church Night Committee: Tracy Ward, Nannie McKendree, Quimby Collier, Denver Haynes, Herbert Henderson, and Bill Hurt

1970
"HBC IN THE NEWS"

Based on *Laugh-In*, this Church Night had all the silly gags and jokes we loved about the comedy show on television. At one point, Bill Hurt said, "And now, the staff will take a short break," and broke a board on his desk.

In the "News of the Future" segment, it was reported that in 1970, Hampton Baptist would go to a four-day work schedule: March 4, June 13, August 24, and October 19.

A couple of interesting bits of information imparted during the skits were that HBC had twenty-one shut-ins and thirteen births in 1969.

1971
"FORGIVE US OUR CHICKEN COOPS"

This year, Bill planned something different for Church Night, having some of our youth perform a play. "Forgive Us Our Chicken Coops" was a satire on the life of the church. Jean Jones had a starring role.

Chester Brown in the old kitchen with Jim Ward,
the minister of music (2)

1972
"THIS IS YOUR LIFE"

Bill Hurt began the night with the following: "Usually, the highlights of the church year are presented in skit fashion. But tonight's program is in honor of a very special occasion. Ten years ago, on January 1st, 1962, Chester L. Brown became pastor of our church. Now we ask our pastor, Chester Brown, to come to the platform. Chester, have a seat, and we will proceed. Because Chester Brown, *this* is your life."

- 1949: Chester is licensed to preach.
- 1953: Chester comes as a summer youth worker.
- June 12, 1958: Chester is ordained to the ministry by Rev. George Kissinger.
- 1958: Chester is called to be the associate pastor at HBC.
- Wayne Erickson is the first person Chester baptizes while Dr. Garber is away. Chester actually practices at Buckroe Beach because Wayne is so big.
- Summer of 1961: Gertrude Pearce introduces Chester to a girl named Mary Etta Mann.
- January 8, 1962: Chester baptizes his first church member (Scotty Miller) as the pastor at HBC.
- July 22, 1967: Chester and Mary Etta are married.
- December 25, 1969: Mary Elizabeth Brown is born.

Mary Etta and Chester, July 22, 1967 (5)

Church Night Committee: Ann Wood, Pat Corlett, Jerry Sullivan, Mike Haywood, Tom Bundick, and Lou Belle Thorpe, with a special committee appointed by the deacons: Christine Vick, Bill Sparrow, Marge Michael, Phil Curtis, and Lewis Parsons

1973
"1972"

On the last Wednesday of January 1973, Church Night was simply titled "1972." The skit featured Bill presenting various reports on the organizations of the church, during which people from the audience came forward to ask a stupid question or argue about how the report was being presented. Bill answered or gave a retort, a brief argument ensued, and then Bill continued on to the next report. Some of the items spotlighted include the following:

- Trip May was our summer youth worker.
- The church began a Mother's Day Out ministry. Parents could leave their kids at the church for a small fee for a few free hours.
- A senior-high retreat was held at Talbot Hall in Norfolk.
- Two people celebrated their ten-year anniversary: Bill Hurt and Rossie Bernard.
- Delwin Croon Jr. was honored for being awarded the Eagle Scout award. (This possibly happened a year later; the Church Night scripts list it in two different years.)
- Church Night Committee: Max Goode, Alice Erickson, Baxter Lee, Elizabeth Garden, Dorothy Lee Jones, and Bill Hurt

1974
"ON THE AIR"

This Church Night was a news report from station WHBC. Mike Haywood was the studio reporter, and Bryan Hatchett, the star-roving reporter who interviewed key people. Also in the studio was Baxter Lee and Bill Hurt, the singing troubadours.

Bryan interviewed Jane Kirby (WMU), Phil Everhart, Chet Smith (pastor of the Hall Road Mission), Allen Feathers (youth), Gary Lewis, Bill Hurt, Billy Byrd (recreation), and Betty Miller (Stewardship Committee). Bryan also interviewed Margaret Hatchett who was one of the first women deacons added to the board in 1973.

The singing troubadours (Bill and Baxter) sang such songs as "My Sunday School Pin," Sour Notes," and "We've Got a Place for You."

Chapter 9

Jack Miller helping to serve refreshments at VBS (2)

Ben Sandford and Terry Laufer, part-time youth minister, at Eagle Eyrie (3)

Lynn Heard and Alicia Everett (2)

Leigh Taylor Smith, Courtney Russ, and Erika Fields (4)

Greg Schneider, Kim Schneider, and Cindy Garris at Busch Gardens (3)

Talmadge Barbour and Mark Taylor
at Eastover on a youth retreat (4)

Jill Godfrey and Heather Ewing (2)

Brad Whittington, Edward Brown, David Martin, Jay Russ,
and Susan Heard (4)

Above: Courtney Rejzer, Kylee Jordan, and Meghan Forbes
at a youth meeting
Below: Laura Williams and Courtney Russ at church (4)

Left: Sharon Goodwin at a youth trip to either Nags Head or Virginia Beach (3)

Right: There were always a lot of youth help at the yearly VBS. Here, Jon Ewing prepares to give refreshments. (2)

Cynthia Lawson (2)

Virginia Godfrey at VBS (2)

Chapter 10
John Dawson ("Click")

Anyone who knows me well will not be surprised that I did not start my Hampton Baptist Church book at the beginning. I mean, what fun is that? Except for the annual Church Nights, I have been jumping all over the place and probably will for the rest of this manuscript.

I am surprised, though, that I have gotten this far without talking much about John Dawson. I think most everyone has a John Dawson story (and there are many); he was certainly known to most members of HBC. Even my first encounter with John has a story to go with it. And so that is where we will begin this interlude.

Here is John R. Dawson in his normal Sunday morning attire. He could be taking up the offering later! (2)

Most church people—Baptists in particular—in Virginia have memories of Eagle Eyrie, which still operates as a conference center, in the mountains of Lynchburg. A lot of people have attended weeks or weekends at this gorgeous facility. A big event for HBC youth back in the day was the Senior High Weekend, held every spring at Eagle Eyrie. It was on a Senior High Weekend that I first met John in the parking lot of Hampton Baptist Church. I can truly say that life was never the same after.

I was a high school sophomore looking forward to the annual trip to Eagle Eyrie. Several people were driving, but there were no assigned cars. You just kind of jumped into the first open seat you came to or the car your friends were in. When everyone else piled into the other vehicles, four of us were left, and the only empty car belonged to this "old guy." One person was already in his car; I can't remember her name, but she was a high school senior going to Longwood College in the fall.

I do remember that John Lee Robbins, Bill Sasser, Don Miller, and I did not want to ride with him, and most of our friends laughed at us, thinking we were in for a horrible trip. (But they had not yet gotten to know John Dawson.) John did not seem to care who rode with him, but he was ready to head out. We settled into his car, ready for a boring ride to Eagle Eyrie. (Yeah, right!)

I remember three specific incidents on the way to Eagle Eyrie, but I also distinctly remember getting ready to go home two days later. Suddenly everyone wanted to ride home with John Dawson, but the four of us said, "Oh, no! You go home in the car you came in." That whole weekend, John and his camera became the center of attention; but the four of us were believers before we even reached our destination.

We discovered right away that this "old guy" was really interesting. He had a firm grasp on just what fellows our age were all about, and he related to us in those ways. I am not sure if a lot of people realized what a great conversationalist John was. But indeed, he was knowledgeable in a number of subjects.

John further surprised us by breaking away from the caravan so that we could go by Longwood, a women's college in Farmville. He had promised the girl in the car that he would take a detour on the way to Eagle Eyrie so that she could see where she would be going to school in the fall. (We told everyone at the retreat that we were late because John had taken us to see some great architecture!)

The other unusual thing John did was photograph some deer (the four-legged variety) that we encountered along the way. It turned out that John was really into nature and portrait photography. It was not the actual photography that impressed us that day but rather the braking, screeching, 180-degree sliding turn he made on a highway to shoot the deer (with his camera) before they left the side of the road. He swore later that he had checked both directions before making that maneuver! We didn't care. John was our type of guy.

The rest of the weekend just reinforced our initial feelings about John. Another benefit to knowing John was that he seemed to know a lot of girls from other churches. They turned out to be students he had gotten to know while attending Hampton High School athletic events.

John Dawson was indeed a remarkable fellow who had a great love for teenagers and for the Lord. He had been employed at NASA, where he'd held a high-ranking position. A few years prior, he had begun to devote his life to being an encourager and friend to young people.

His specialty was photography. (Actually, his specialty was loving and discipling teens. The camera was merely the hook that kept us around so that he could be a Christian witness and mentor to us.) John and his camera were at every high school function you could imagine. We would go to football games and see John roaming the sidelines, where neither he nor anyone else was supposed to have access. No one ever seemed to mind. He would take thousands of photos each year and give almost all of them to the those he had captured in the images.

It was fun to go on trips with John. If you saw a good-looking girl or guy, you could always ask him to take their picture. Knowingly, he would take two—one for you and one to give to the subject of the photograph.

John seemed to divide his time by priority. Youth from Hampton Baptist got top billing. Next came teens from Hampton High School. The next two ranks in the hierarchy were youth from any other church (mainly Baptist, but not all) and finally any other high school student at an event. From what other teens told me, he spent a lot of time at Tabb High. After I started my ministry at the Peninsula Baptist, John would come to take photos at some of my events.

We would go to youth events and run into teens who, when they found out what church we were from, would ask about John R. Dawson. A couple of years after I met Jimmy George (Tabernacle Baptist), he was talking about an old guy that he and his friends called "Click." Jimmy said that this guy was at Eagle Eyrie and a lot of other youth events. Click would hand out slides of the pictures he took. Even though I had never heard the nickname before, I told Jimmy I knew exactly who he was talking about. It turned out that Jim and his friends knew John well from both Eagle Eyrie and school sporting events. And they were from Menchville High!

When anyone talked about John Dawson, several quirks always came up. Two of these were the gaudy ties and loud socks he perpetually wore. It was a delight to see John taking up the offering in church with his red and green Christmas socks. I think it was John who inspired me to stand up about my hatred of neck-ties. (Although John did wear ties, often ones that matched his socks!) Later, it was me taking up the offering—tie-*less*.

Along with his ties and socks and cameras, John had an obvi-ous love for youth *and* life. He reflected the message that we are all children of God, with special gifts and talents of our own. He let us know that we had the right to smile, laugh, and enjoy life. Being around John made you want to live like that.

He taught us that you could use anything as a prop to do ministry—even a camera—and he was always available when you needed another driver for an activity or trip.

John would do anything in his power to help someone. Many a young person would find their way paid on a church trip that they had no hope of affording. Sometimes young people would receive funds for college or other worthwhile endeavors. Often, they had no idea who had paid their way. John rarely took credit.

Later in life, I was staying at the Eagle Eyrie hotel with John Dawson during an event. At the end of the weekend, I was with John when he approached the front desk. He told the person behind the counter that he wanted to leave a check for one of the occupants. It was a college student who was having a hard time paying their tuition. He explained that the gift was to be anony-mous. He just wanted to help out.

He also loved to give Bibles to his friends. There was one time when I was using a paraphrased Bible called *The Way*. John saw me with it in church and remarked on my poor choice of Bible for church. He had no problem with *The Way* as reading material, but it shouldn't be a main study Bible, he said. The next time I saw John in church, he handed me a present. It was a Bible and one I loved using for years.

John and Mary Etta Brown taught the senior-high Sunday school class, and I guarantee that there was no noticeable generation gap. They worked together for years and were an inspiration to many of the Hampton Baptist youth. Jay Lawson told me that John would use rolls of butcher block paper to make timelines of the Sunday school lesson he was teaching. Jay said that it left an indelible memory in his mind.

Steve Sandford and John Erickson holding a "timeline" (3)

After Jerry and Ellen Sullivan, along with their three girls, retired to Mississippi, I usually spent a week each summer with them. For a couple of years, John Dawson also showed up. One year, he had spent an extra two hours in a rest area along the way so that he could plug his portable television into the cigarette lighter and watch the Redskins game.

Another year, John Dawson and Jim Ailor came down while I was there at Thanksgiving. A group of us took a walk in the woods behind the back pasture. On the way back, several of the Sullivans' horses came up to us. John remarked that he hadn't been on a horse in several years. And then, shocking us all, this seventy-year-old man hoisted himself up on one and went for a ride.

Only once did I ever have a legitimate gripe with John. During my tenure as an RA leader, one of the guys was a future good friend of mine named Bill Sinclair. Bill was a great guy with a sense of adventure. He was also a wealth of strange facts. Sinclair once pointed out that the little seeds you find in the sausage on pizza taste like licorice. (Probably everyone knows that this is the fennel seed in the Italian sausage, but I didn't at the time.) The next time you order a sausage pizza from Pizza Hut, try picking out a seed, washing it off, and biting into it. You will taste licorice.

Or, have you ever tried jumping when riding down in an elevator? This is best done alone; otherwise, you might end up talking to men in white coats! Anyway, Bill told me that if you do the elevator-jumping bit, you will experience an instant of weightlessness. I do not know if that is scientifically true, but I do admit it is a weird feeling, slightly like that first drop on a roller coaster.

Bill Sinclair was also a budding musician who was trying his hand at a few instruments. Two of the many he mastered were the sax and the harmonica. Unfortunately for me, John Dawson started Bill on these two instruments during the time that I was Bill's RA leader. At the time, we were camping a lot.

The morning of the first camping trip after John gave Bill the harmonica, I awoke to the racket. He would later became an accomplished harmonica player, but that morning, it was little more than noise! The next Sunday, I told John Dawson that he should be sentenced to a weekend of having to listen to Bill blowing on that infernal thing. John mentioned that he had put up with me on many a weekend when I was younger. I shut up.

The same thing happened a year later, but this time it was a saxophone. Again, on the camping trip, it was mostly noise, a little louder than the harmonica. However, this time I kept my mouth shut and didn't complain to John R.

Bill and his band would one day release a cassette (tells you how long ago that was) and CD of beautiful Christmas music, titled *Bethlehem Morning*. It is "A collection of instrumental music for acoustic guitar, soprano, harmonica, and keyboard." The band members gave special thanks to the people who inspired them, and one of those is John Dawson. The album includes my favorite Christmas hymn, "O Holy Night."

Another John Dawson story I didn't know until a few years ago when I was talking with Jay Lawson at lunch.

Jay and Jim Ailor grew up at Hampton Baptist, and both (now retired) entered the pastorate. During the time when they were in college and still working out their life plans, Hampton Baptist called them as youth ministers for one summer. This is the story of how that came about.

Jim and Jay have always been friends, but it was that summer that cemented their relationship. For years after that, according to both of them, their dream was to co-pastor a church somewhere in Virginia. That never came about, but it does prove how close they were and still are.

One of Chester Brown's many gifts was that he always encouraged each member of the congregation to use their own gifts to serve Jesus. He certainly influenced me and many others. But Chester would never tell you what God wanted you to do. He would simply let you know that God had a plan for you and that you needed to pray and ask the Holy Spirit to lead you into the ways you should be serving.

Chester didn't mind if you disagreed theologically; he still wanted you to seek God and His plan for your life. I think it is revealing that many pastors, both liberal and conservative, who had been beat up and even let go by their own churches, would end up worshiping for a season at Hampton Baptist. I never heard Chester verbalize this, but I always imagined him saying to the wounded pastor, "We don't have to agree. But if you want, we would love to have you worship at Hampton Baptist for a season to heal and find God's next assignment."

The fact that Jay Lawson and Jim Ailor could grow up in the same church and have the freedom to find their own relationships with the Holy Spirit speaks well of Chester's leadership. He encouraged all of us to find our own way with Christianity. You didn't need a specific theological approach or method to be called. Chester's point was to let the Lord lead you. The path on which the Spirit takes leaders might not say "Hampton Baptist" or "Baptist" or "Church" in the title. If God leads you at some point to be a librarian, school teacher, probation officer, or nurse, then you can be a serve the Lord in that position too.

As people love to point out, I am easily led off topic. Now where was I? Oh yes, Jim's and Jay's theologies were fairly far apart at that time in their young lives. Hampton Baptist still wanted them. The personnel committee wisely put John Dawson in charge of contacting the duo and convincing them to work together that summer.

Jay told me that John contacted him and explained what the church wanted. Jay said that the idea of being the summer youth minister for Hampton Baptist excited him . . . but the idea of working with Jimmy Ailor did not. Jay said that he told John that he didn't think they could work well together. They would argue

143

about theology, he said, and not do the ministry they were called to do.

After Jay told John why the idea would not fly, John simply said, "The church and I think it will work, *and* by the way, Jim Ailor is willing to work with you."

John was a great friend of mine, but I have to say here that John Dawson *lied!* John had not called Jimmy yet; he'd started with Jay!

Jay, who did not detect any ruse, said that in that case, he would be willing to pray about it and get back to John with an answer. John agreed. The future best friends were not so close at that time, so Jay didn't call Jimmy to talk it over.

You can already see where this is going. John then called Jim, and the conversation went almost exactly like it did with Jay. Jimmy said he didn't think it would work but that he would pray about it. John said he had talked with Jay Lawson (true), and Jay was on board to give it a try (false). The rest of the story is that they both eventually said yes and worked together for the summer. The church survived (even the disco-ball incident), and Jay and Jim began a long and beautiful friendship.

A lot of us thought that John R. Dawson would always be with us, but eventually the Master called him home. I have been to many funerals that were, in essence, a celebration, but never have I been to one as joyful as John R.'s. Chester made reference to his gaudy ties and socks, and we couldn't help but remember and laugh. I was going to miss John greatly. Of course, Chester used the phrase I love, and it was so true: "We will never be the same— not because he is gone, but because he was once here."

During the funeral, various episodes kept coming to my mind. I tried not to laugh during the more solemn moments when those episodes hit me: flashing his ever-present camera and smile; taking that 180-degree turn on the highway to photograph the deer; stealing my date, Mary Swift, from me at a church banquet (along with Phil Everhart Sr., Sam Ailor, and Woody Patrick); giving me a new Bible that was not paraphrased; introducing me to a girl (Pam Blewett from Pine Chapel Baptist) who became my summer missionary ("Smishy") at the PBA for four years; watching him walk up to anyone and take a picture. John made you want to enjoy life to the fullest—and to do so while helping others. To those of us at Hampton Baptist, he was John R., but to many of my other friends, like Jimmy George, he was known appropriately as Click.

This may come as a surprise to anyone who knew him, but John really did give away almost all the photos he took. About a year after John passed away, I asked his wife, Celia, if some of us could come and look through John's slides. She told me that she would look around but she didn't think there were any slides; they had all gone to the people in the photos.

Celia complimented John well. John was outgoing and outlandish in both dress and character. Celia was much more reserved; although, like John, she was always willing to pitch in and help at church. She was kind and considerate and made her mark in a less auspicious way than her husband did. Celia, who taught elementary school, was always there to help while John R. was roaming. Many of his photos capture Celia at Eagle Eyrie and other church events.

About a month after I talked with Celia about the photos John had left behind, she saw me at church and kindly gave me a cigar box full of slides.

"These are all that remain," she said. "Do with them as you please."

When I was getting ready to purchase my first serious camera after graduating from college, I'd asked John for his advice about what to buy. I remember telling him that I wanted a camera that would be in the upper tier of quality but at the bottom line of prices. He suggested a Konica, and that camera brought me years of enjoyment.

I once won a small bet with John Dawson. We had stopped to eat on the way home from Eagle Eyrie one afternoon, and I was enjoying my fifth cup of coffee that day. John was giving me a hard time about drinking too much coffee and bet me that I could not go a week without it. I got one more refill on the coffee to start strong and agreed to the bet.

We didn't wager anything. It was just "I bet you can't." I think if we'd had something riding on the bet, I might have cheated. With it being a challenge to my pride, I had to be true to my word and tough it out. I actually made it to the afternoon of the following Sunday before my next fix. John brought me that long-awaited cup of coffee.

John also introduced me to one of my long-running Smishies at the PBA, Pamala Sue Blewett. Pam was a member of Pine Chapel Baptist and a senior at Hampton High School. Jean Jones had made me a judge at the Miss Hampton High contest. The week before the event, John told me that I needed to be sure to meet a certain contestant, who was a great person. He also told me her name, but I promptly forgot it. (Nothing unusual there.) Pam did not win the contest, but her singing did make an impression on me. John briefly introduced me to Pam before the pageant, but in the usual confusion, I did not run into her afterward.

Several weeks later, John and I were chaperones for the Senior High Weekend at Eagle Eyrie. There were young people from several local churches staying at PAL Lodge. The first night, I recognized Pam sitting on a couch on the other side of the lounge but had not spoken with her yet.

Then John Dawson came waltzing into the room. He stopped to snap a half dozen photographs of students in the room and then walked over to where I was sitting. John grabbed me by the wrist and pulled me up. He told me that I needed to meet this young lady on the other side of the room.

"Mike, this is Pam Blewett. You need to get her working with you this summer. Pam, this is Mike Haywood. He is one of the judges who did not vote for you at the pageant. Mike's a little slow sometimes, so you have to make allowances."

Pam was as sharp as John had related. We started talking, and long story short, Pam Blewett worked for me as a Smishy for the next four years.

Now this is the last John Dawson story for now. It is actually more of a Mike Haywood story, but John is the key to it all. For years, I hadn't come across another John Dawson slide and had given up hope of finding any. Then one Sunday afternoon in the early 1990s, I was at church early, with nothing to do for an hour. I was perusing the library for a good book.

I happened to open a cabinet that was below some book-shelves and found a large clear box full of slides. I opened it, grabbed a couple of slides, and held them up to the light. Lo and behold, they were old John Dawson photos. (I never found out why or how they ended up in a cabinet in the church library.) When I went back into the cabinet, I found a second source of slides: a large manila envelope.

Here was a treasure indeed. I took them home and checked them out on a light table. They were mostly from the 1980s, including a deacons' retreat at Eastover. (Some of you have seen these.) I purchased a machine that scans slides and negatives (it was relatively inexpensive) and got to work. I probably scanned all 300 slides to my computer. Fortunately, John tended to take three or four shots of the same scene or person, so that cut back on how many I copied. Then I burned the slides to CDs.

Jay Russ had gotten me working with the senior-high Sunday school, so I got what I thought was great idea. I went through the folder of images on my computer and pulled all those picturing the students' parents when they were young and burned them to a CD. Then one Sunday morning, I showed the slides to the whole youth Sunday school and gave each student a copy of the CD.

What could go wrong, right? I had a lot of Dawson photos that featured the mothers and fathers of the current youth. I didn't get in any trouble with the fathers, but several of the mothers cornered me a couple of weeks later.

"You have really caused us a problem. We are constantly lecturing our daughters about not wearing short skirts. Now you have shown them photos of *us* wearing mini skirts!"

All I could think to say was "Well, your sins will always find you out!"

John Dawson would often join in the hijinks with the youth but never minded cleaning up after. (5)

Chapter 11

Claudia Lawson leading a small group at a youth retreat at Eastover (3)

Mark Talor, Patrick O'Brian, and Phil Everhart visiting Graydon Elliott at a retirement home (1)

Karen Kanoy in Sunday School class (3)

Nancy Lee Trimble, Susie Castle, and Richard Pulley doing
kitchen duty on a mission trip (4)

Elizabeth Patrick, Jo Tillery, and Cindy Garris at Sunday school (3)

Kim Schneider serving punch at an event on the church grounds (2)

Ann and Barry Wood (3)

When I returned to college in 1965, Barry was my English 101 professor at Christopher Newport. He was a fantastic and entertaining teacher. CNU students can tell many stories about him, but here is my personal favorite. I was in his English class one morning when a male student walked in and, without saying a word, kissed a girl on the front row. Barry applauded as the student walked out.

Later, he told us that the student had approached him and asked if he could drop his class. The problem was that it was the day after the drop/add deadline. Barry told him that he would allow it if the student came into his 9:00 a.m. class the next morning and, without any explanation, walk up to any girl on the front row and kiss her.

Ricky Wallace and Wayne Everhart on an RA outing to the Haunted Woods. We found cans of emergency drinking water washed up on the beach. (1)

Sunday School class with John Ailor, Francis Jones, Milton Oakley, and Lib Hutchby (3)

Margie Hill at
Sunday school with
Jimmy Michael in
the row behind (3)

Willard and Iris Garris at a church
dance (3)

Above: Brad Whittington and Edward Brown on a mission
trip (4); below: Nancy Sandford and Jon Ewing prepare
refreshments at VBS. (2)

Chapter 12
The Dating Game

I remember a youth banquet held at Hampton Baptist in the late 1960s. The deacons served as waiters; three of whom were John Dawson, Phil Everhart Sr., and Woody Patrick. I had a date for the banquet: Mary Swift. It is not much of an exaggeration to say that as soon as we walked through the back door next to the social hall, the three of them were immediately at my side, trying to be as helpful as possible. John Lee Robbins and I were double-dating, but at the end of the night, it seemed that John Lee, his date, and I had become a threesome while one or more of the deacons monopolized Mary's time and attention. She was at our table when the food came—that I remember—and I did depart the church with her at the end of the banquet.

Dating among the youth at HBC was a casual and common occurrence, and we intermingled a lot of adventure into our dates. Double-dating was a normal affair. As I think back, a lot of dates involved movies, bowling, miniature golf, tennis (in the summer), and going out to eat. I remember that most of the girls I dated liked to eat. And that was fine with me because eating has always been one of my favorite pastimes!

Going out to eat with a date usually happened on a Friday or Saturday night or on a Sunday afternoon. Even if you were going elsewhere on a date, you inevitably ended up getting a bite to eat.

One comment I remember about eating on dates came from Barbara Panz. Barbara and I both enjoyed eating, and so a great many of our dates involved restaurants. Seriously, I do enjoy a good meal, so I was game. The only small problem was when we went somewhere expensive first and out to eat after. Paying the bill for both activities could cost a few dollars.

That wasn't usually a problem, but one week, I was complaining to John Robbins and Don Miller about paying for a movie—or bowling, miniature golf, or whatever—and then paying for a meal afterward. One of them came up with a super idea.

"Find out what time Barbara has to be home for the evening. Then pick her up later, in time to do whatever activity you had planned, leaving just enough time for coffee and cake before going home."

I'd forgotten to ask her what time she had to be home before picking her up the next Friday night, but I decided I could still utilize the plan John and Donald had suggested. As we were driving away from Barbara's house on the way to our date, I casually asked, "What time do you have to be home?"

Barbara replied, "When I get there!"

Barbara Panz on the front porch of my mom's house on Newport News Avenue (1)

Eating was not reserved for dates only. Often after Sunday night services, the youth and young adults would go out to eat somewhere. We made the rounds to a lot of restaurants. The Chateau, on the left side of Pembroke Avenue when heading toward Newport News, was a popular spot; it was a little past Shoney's (another popular choice) but before the baseball field. The young adults used to go there a lot after church on Sunday night.

I took Brenda Vick out to Nick's Seaford Pavilion for a meal on New Year's Eve. You might remember Nick's, across the street from the river in Yorktown. It was very ornate, and the prices were high, but the food was first-class. I had known that when I suggested the restaurant to Brenda and so didn't mind the cost of the meal. However, I made the mistake of mentioning the price to Sasser, Robbins, and a couple of other friends. The next time we were all together in a group that included Brenda, they started kidding her about how much I had spent on the meal. It didn't faze her, and Brenda had the perfect reply: "Yes, and it was worth every penny!"

During my years as a juvenile probation officer, when I would ride with members of the police youth bureau, they introduced me to their game of "Harassing the Troops." A lot of young adults from the cities would dine out on Friday and Saturday nights. Many of the couples comprised a male of legal drinking age and an underage female. Often, the youth bureau officers, whose faces were familiar, enjoyed strolling around the Chateau restaurant on weekend nights. The "troops" would move drinks from the female's side to join the drink sitting by the male's plate. The officers never said a word—at least when I was with them. They just looked on and smiled before departing.

I know that I will leave out a lot of eating places but some of the one's I remember besides the Chateau and Nick's include Shoney's, Rendezvous, Pappy D's (on Pembroke) and Mama D's in Newport News, Strawberry Banks, Ming Gate, White Oak Lodge, Bill's Barbecue, Bass Brothers Seafood (Sinclair Circle), Providence Ordinary, and B and M Drive-In, among others.

THE NEW YEAR'S EVE THAT ANN AILOR HAD THREE DATES

As I said, the Hampton Baptist youth and young adults often engaged in double-dating. I can remember dozens of times when the same two guys and two gals would go out on double-dates two weekends in a row. The variable was that the couples usually switched the second week.

But Ann Ailor probably holds the record for the number of dates in one night, having extended a double-date into a triple-date. That was the New Year's Eve when Ann had three dates. Because it was unusual, I remember that night well, including my own attempt to cause Ann and her mother, Martha, a bit of grief.

Martha and Ann had clued me in on what was happening because I was the driver for her second round of dating, which was a double-date: I was dating Barbara Panz, and Ann was dating Bill Sasser. Martha and Ann needed me to make sure the exchange went smoothly and quickly when we returned to the Ailors'. They made me promise to drop Ann off by 10:00 p.m. and leave with Bill and Barbara fast. (It was a mistake to make me aware of this ploy and think I would actually try to help!)

I don't remember who her first date was, but if it had been her future husband, Bill Thornton, then all three of her dates were with Bills. I do remember that her first date was an early dinner.

So I picked up Barbara and swung back out to East Hampton to get Bill Sasser. We then headed for the Ailors' to pick up Ann at 7:00 p.m. Before heading to the theater, Martha Ailor pulled me aside and pointed out that the movie should be over by 9:30 and so we should be back before 10:00, which would leave Ann free for her third date of the evening.

"Don't mess this up, Mike" were Martha's final words.

I should point out that I had not revealed to Bill Sasser or Barbara Panz that Ann had another (third) date after we returned to her house. We went to the movies, and I remember Ann made up some excuse for why she couldn't go out to eat after the movie. I think she may have told us that she had gone out to eat earlier with a friend. So we arrived back at the Ailors' around 9:50 or 9:55. As we turned off Mercury Boulevard and onto Charlton Drive, I noticed that Bill Worster (the third "Bill" of the evening) was sitting at a service station, waiting on us to arrive and depart. No one else in our car noticed him except for maybe Ann.

When we parked, I got out of the car as Martha Ailor came out of the house to meet us. "Don't you have to be off?" she said to me.

"I just want to tell Ann goodbye and wish her a happy new year," I replied.

Not knowing what was going on, Barbara and Bill also got out of the car. When we finished saying goodnight, we relieved the anxious mother and daughter by getting back into the car.

"Wait a minute," I said, as though this thought had just occurred to me. "I think I have some fireworks in the trunk. We should stay and set them off to celebrate!"

Ann Ailor (1960) (5)

Martha protested, saying that it was late and we should probably be going, but now Sasser and Panz became unaware co-con-
spirators by insisting that we set off a couple. I got the fireworks
out of the trunk and took my time setting them up for launch. By
this time, Ann knew she could do nothing to speed this up and
graciously played along with the festivities. Martha was a little less
gracious, but there was not a thing she could do.

After about five minutes of fireworks and sparklers, I said we
had to be going. The three of us got back into the car and headed
down the street. The quickest way to leave Riverdale from the
Ailors' had always been to go one block farther down Charlton,
make a U-turn at the corner, and go back, past the Everharts'
on the right, and the Ailors' on the left, all the way to Mercury.

161

I guess I could have turned right instead and took Meadowbrook out to Mercury, but what fun would that have been, and when did we ever cut each other a break? As we passed by the Ailors', I saw that Bill Worster had parked at the neighbor's. Neither Bill Sasser nor Barbara Panz was any the wiser.

Bill Worster called me the next day. My cries of total innocence were not received with complete gullibility, but that would have ruined my fun.

STANDING UP MARY SWIFT

Bill Sasser was not the intended "pigeon" that night, but he did get me back several years later. I had a date with Mary Swift and was supposed to pick her up at her parents' house that night around seven. At the time, several of us, including me and Bill, were dating Mary. (There wasn't a lot of serious dating among the HBC youth.) Several of us that week had been stealing back and forth a picture of Mary that had been in the newspaper. One of us clipped it and others would grab it whenever they found it.

Bill came by my house on Newport News Avenue. I happened to have the picture in my possession and had hidden it pretty well. Bill could not find it in my bedroom, though he'd had free rein because I was in the bathroom getting ready for the date.

I had a wall phone (remember those?) in my bedroom, and I heard it ring a couple of times. Bill picked it up, and I heard him talking. When I walked back into the bedroom, Bill said, "You had better give me the picture of Swift."

I laughed and said, "Not a chance, and by the way, who was that on the phone?"

Then *he* laughed and said, "That was Mary Swift. She was calling to tell you that she's at her aunt's house and you should pick her up there. There's no one at her house now. She gave me her aunt's address, where you should pick her up. I'll give you the address *if* you give me the picture."

"I don't believe you," I said. "Who was that really on the phone?"

Bill had a twinkle in his eye (to which I should have paid attention). "I have to leave now, but I'll give you the address if you give me the photo before I go. If not, then good luck picking up Mary."

As we walked downstairs, I waited for him to tell me who had really called, but Bill said nothing. I decided it had been someone calling for my mom and let him depart without a regret. As soon as he left, though, I started having doubts and thought perhaps I should call Mary's home number, the only one I had for her.

I dialed and grew more pessimistic with every ring, knowing that this was not beyond Bill Sasser and wondering what would I say to Mary next time I saw her. Just as I resigned myself to the fact that I was going to stand Mary up, her mom answered the phone out of breath. When I told her who it was, she told me I was lucky I'd gotten her. She was almost to the car when she'd heard the phone ringing inside and decided to run back in to answer it. She saved the day and gave me the address of Mary's aunt.

And that is how close I came to standing up Mary Swift.

John Lee Robbins actually did stand Mary Swift up one Friday night. John, Don Miller, and I were at Darling Stadium for a football game. We were on the Hampton side near the left end zone. John Lee was a senior at Hampton that year, and he told me he had spoken in the hall with Mary that afternoon. "You know, Mike, I think she said something about picking her up and giving her a ride to the football game. But I'm not exactly sure what she said and if I was supposed to do that." About that time, we saw Mary and a couple of other girls walking into the stadium. When he saw her, John said that he probably should find out if he'd messed up.

He walked down from the bleachers and met Mary and her

friends walking along the sideline. We could not hear what she said, but from the look on her face and the movement of her arms, we could tell that John was getting a proper talking-to at that moment. She then walked past him and proceeded toward the 50-yard line. John came back and told us that Mary did not accept his explanation and let him know in no uncertain terms!

Mary Swift (1)

MY BLIND DATE WITH AN "ARABIAN GIRL"

Don Miller dated Beverly Anderson off and on for several years. She was the daughter of Charlie and Susan Anderson. Beverly had a friend who lived in North Carolina, who was coming to visit her. So Donald lined up a double-date in which I would be matched with the visiting friend. For her and me, it would be a double-date *and* a blind date!

I mentioned this to my mom, and the week before the Friday night date, my mom said something about my upcoming date with the Arabian girl. I hadn't heard what nationality she was, so this was news to me. I didn't think a lot about it but was interested to see what she might be like.

I was driving that night and so picked up Donald at his house, and we drove to Beverly's to meet the two girls. My blind date was attractive and fun to be with . . . but she didn't look *Arabian*. I was too polite to ask and just figured that my mom had gotten her information wrong. I will admit that I was really curious and tried to bring up questions about her background. I only learned that she had been born and raised in North Carolina. Nothing out of the ordinary there. I finally gave up and figured I would never know.

We ended up getting cake, Cokes, and coffee at Shoney's on Pembroke Avenue. While chatting, the topic of religion came up. Of course, Don, Beverly, and I were Baptist. One of us asked the girl what church she attended. She replied that she was Moravian.

All three of my friends sat mystified as I started chuckling. I had to quickly say what was so funny and that it had nothing to do with her religion. We actually got along really well, and whenever she was in town visiting Beverly, we would double-date. She really liked the Shoney's "Big Boy."

I found the following information online:

> The Moravian Church is sometimes confused as its own religion, one that is similar to the Mormon or Amish faiths, but in fact it's not a separate religion. The Moravian Church is a denomination within the Protestant religion and Moravians share the same core beliefs, including that Jesus Christ was born, died, and resurrected.
>
> The Moravian Church has existed for more than 500 years. Moravians originally came from ancient Bohemia and Moravia in what is now called the Czech Republic. Their name comes from the denomination's original birthplace of Moravia.

PLAYING TENNIS

Another popular activity among Hampton Baptist youth was playing tennis. The various courts around town included those at Wythe Recreation, Armstrong Elementary, Fort Monroe, and Langley Field. John Lee Robbins, Don Miller, and I played a lot over the years. I think I played with Jane Dennard at all of these places, but the court we played at the most was the one at Armstrong Elementary School. The interesting thing about Armstrong is that I never paid any attention to the houses across the street from the court. However, in 1993, I purchased the house directly across from the tennis courts on the corner of Cherokee and Fairfax. I bet I never looked at that house twice during all the times I played tennis there, but I have loved living there ever since.

When I became friends with the Sullivans in the early 1970s, Jerry Sullivan and I played a lot of tennis together, usually going to the Sullivans' home at Bethel Manor after the games. Most of the matches I played with Jerry were at the Langley Field courts.

THE CAR BOMB YEARS

You might remember that in the sixties and seventies, most cars did not have a lock on the hood. This meant that it was easy to get to the engine, not only to make repairs but also to give easy access for pranks. A popular gag during this period was the "car bomb." The name was not sinister at the time because the only people putting real bombs in cars were gangsters or secret agents. This was before safety caps on medicines and seals on food containers because no one in the general public was trying to harm random shoppers by putting poisons in our products.

Eagle Eyrie Senior High Weekend with Don Miller and Beverly Anderson; Larry Brumfield and Jack Miller playing chess (1)

Anyway, it's important to know that you could easily gain access under the hood because you had to attach the "bomb" to the electrical system. Then when the "mark" (or victim) tried to start the car, they would hear a loud (and I mean *loud*) whistle, then a pop, followed by smoke that poured out from under the hood.

Once you experienced a car bomb, you never forgot the sensation. As soon as you heard the start of the whistle, you knew you'd been had. At that point, there was nothing to do except let the sound and visual effects run their course. Only then could you raise the hood and detach the device from your car. And you could not drive away and remove it later; the car would not start until the bomb had been extracted.

My most embarrassing moment with a car bomb came when leaving the Center Theater (remember that one?) with a date (Cathy McBride). A line of people were still pouring out of the theater when I started my car and heard the cursed whistle! I had to sit and wait, looking sheepishly at Cathy for the sequence to finish while all the people outside pointed and laughed.

I probably deserved this, as I I loved to plant these devices in my friend's cars. Like many other fads and gags, the car bombs ran their course, and then a time came when you could not get them anymore.

Chapter 13
Church Nights 1975–1980

1975
RECOGNITION OF LONG-TIME MEMBERS
(FIFTY YEARS OR MORE)

- Bill Sparrow and/or Chester Brown gave some interesting facts about the church sanctuary (see below).
- Hall Road Mission building was finished.
- The Concord choir presented a musical about Jonah, called *A Whale of a Tale*. This was also performed at Hall Road and the Veterans Administration.
- The annual Sunday school picnic was held at Gosnold Hope Park on August 14.
- Jay and Claudia Lawson got married.

Twice, during annual Church Night presentations, historical information about the church was given. In the 1975 Church Night folder are several handwritten pages about the history of the sanctuary. Either Chester Brown or Bill Sparrow (or both) presented this information during the Church Night activities. (Due to some comments on the notes, I think it was probably Chester Brown who gave the report.)

- The current sanctuary was constructed in 1883.
- The front of the organ dates back to 1917.
- Most of what you see as you look around today dates to 1941. An extensive renovation project gave the sanctuary its present design.

- In 1940, the entire organ was removed and shipped to the Moeller factory in Maryland to be repaired and updated.
- Now [in 1975], we were looking forward to a completely new instrument.
- In 1941, the present pews were installed. They came from Wisconsin. The original pews were moved to the balcony, which was enlarged to hold more people.
- The communion table also dates to 1941.
- The floor was completely taken out and reconstructed in three places. Specifically, the two outside planes of the pews were designed to compensate for the curvature of the pews. Previously, those seated on the ends tended to slide toward the walls.
- The arch was given its curvature in 1941 also. Previously, it was designed with straight lines and angles.
- The radiators and covers were made in the Shipyard.
- The paneling also came from the Shipyard. It is all white birch, stained walnut.
- There were no side entrances to the sanctuary prior to 1941 (only the two doors at the back of the sanctuary).
- If leaving the education building to go into the sanctuary, you had to "go out" to "get in"!
- The chandeliers were installed in 1941.
- The pulpit and pulpit chairs go back before the 1941 work.
- The Bennie Russell memorial vase dates to 1949. It was made in the Shipyard, being cast of naval bronze.

1976
"DAYS OF OUR LIVES"

Bryan Hatchett and Cindy Garris played a big part in this one, which used a lot of TV commercial skits.

One of the jingles was for Alka-Setzer, when planning for VBS causes headache:

The children, the books, the paper, the glue
The ice cream, the Kool-Aid, the cookies, ooooh
Plop-plop, fizz-fizz
Oh, what a relief it is!

- On May 11, Chester Brown received an honorary Doctor of Divinity degree from the University of Richmond.
- "Lucille Rollins will tell you how, so come and join a circle now."
- Jay Lawson, the summer youth minister, took the youth on a weekend retreat. When he left at the end of the summer to return to seminary, several of our own people took over the task, including Sam Ailor, Eleanor Oakley, Alice Erickson, Mike Haywood, Nancy Sandford, Ida Patrick, Ken and Sandy Matthews. "And then, there is Bob Stockburger, or 'Doc Stock' as he is called. Bob eats, sleeps, and lives young people. This can be hard on the stomach. We recommend Pepto-Bismol for people like Bob."
- Uncertainty reigns within the HBC church office: Will Gary Lewis play the funeral march for Nina Wornom's cat. Dottie Lee calls Francis to see if he has seen her glasses. Chester Brown is calling home to get the details of the latest episode between Mary Elizabeth and Edward. In the middle of all this,

Alice Erickson, pops in with yet another ponderous problem: "Tennis anyone?"

Lucille Rollins and Freda Nelson on a senior adult bus tour (2)

1977
EDDIE HANKINSON ROAST

Eddie was honored for twenty-five years of service as treasurer of our church!

172

1978
"HEROES, BAD GUYS, AND COMEDY"
or
"SAVED BY THE SUPERHEROES"

- Either Linda Riddle or Tracy Ward was "Sensuous Sally Sweet."
- When there were too many empty pews during worship service, Batman and Robin saved the day.
- Dottie Lee wanted to take a vacation, but the bad guy said, "No one can replace you!" Wonder Woman (Cindy Garris) came and began to type, telephone, and file rapidly.
- The WMU needed more women. Charlie's Angels came in to save the day (Martha Feathers, Elizabeth Patrick, and Laurie Wood). One idea was to call it the PMU, or *Persons* Missionary Union, and include men.
- Superman (Bryan Lilly) rescued a girl in Sunday school.
- Dr. Brown took several of our members on a trip to the Holy Land.

1979
"SEVENTY-EIGHT LIVE"

Emceed by Debbie Spencer and Frank Schneider, with reporter Mike Haywood, this Church Night theme was based on *Saturday Night Live* and used interviews and skits to highlight the events of 1978. Several skits involved Cindy Lawson and Mike Haywood.
- HBC is community-minded. Weight Watchers used the building on Tuesday nights and the Peninsula Bloodmobile was here in February.
- The Victory Singers, started by Dean Kershaw, continued. Dean departed this year to Crenshaw United Methodist in

Blackstone when Gary Lewis returned, after a year of study at Northwestern University.

- The senior adults, led by Alice Erickson and Bill Hurt, toured Monticello.
- Cindy Lawson was interviewed regarding a GA recognition service held in May.
- The Concord choir presented *Cool in the Furnace*.
- Terry Babb was our summer youth worker.
- Nancy Sandford directed the summer VBS.
- Bill Nelson was our Premises Committee chairman.
- Gary Lewis and the choir gave us *The Nativity According to St. Luke*.
- Frank Schneider became the new director of Sunday school.
- The RAs had a full year, which included the associational track meet, a day at the University of Richmond, a canoe trip, and a boat trip to Fort Wool.

RAs walking to the boat to head out to Fort Wool (2)

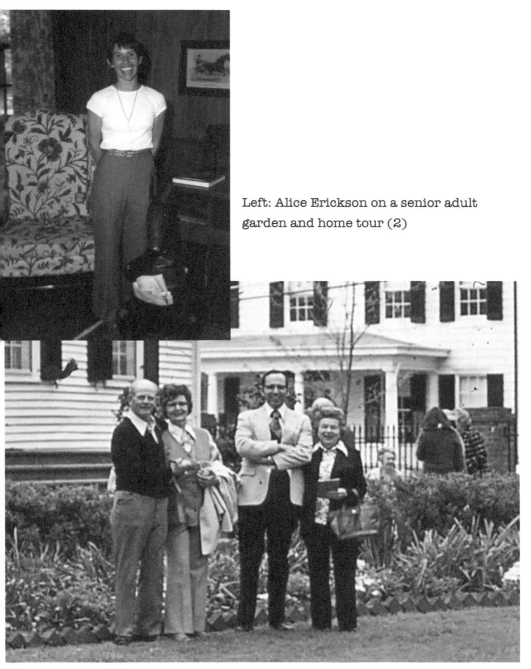

Left: Alice Erickson on a senior adult garden and home tour (2)

Milford Rollins and Bill Hurt (2)

1980
THE WAY WE WERE

A change of pace came during this year's Church Night.
Using the song "The Way We Were," Debbie Spencer and Bill Hurt
presented a slideshow tour of the past decade. After each segment,
someone from each organization gave a projection of the decade to
come (those speakers are in parentheses).

- The WMU supported ministries through the Peninsula Baptist
  Association (Friendship House and Family Services) and
  Hampton Baptist (VBS and High-Rise Apartments) and con-
  ducted the GAs and Mission Friends. (Jane Kirby)
- The WMU also gave Mike Haywood a helping hand with
  blankets.
- The youth group was very active, including retreats. (Steve
  and Mildred Barnes)
- The sanctuary took on a new appearance when it was paint-
  ed and, in 1975, when the new Zimmer organ was installed.
  (Gary Lewis)
- The senior adults enjoyed a good many bus tours. (Alice Er-
  ickson, whose name was synonymous with bus trips)
- Fred King led (and would continue to lead) our Hall Road
  Mission as their pastor.
- Remember the junior-high trip to Nags Head?
- Remember Mike Haywood before his beard?
- Remember when Nancy Lee Jones and Jay Lawson were the
  Valentine King and Queen?
- Remember when Alice Erickson readied some of the guys for
  a Christmas play?

Valentine Banquet King and Queen: Jay Lawson and
Nancy Lee Jones (2)

Here I am being showered with blankets to be used for
PBA ministries. (2)

Above: Faye Everett helping at VBS
Below: Jane Kirby (2)

I don't think
this is the
Christmas play
mentioned
at Church
Night, but for
sure, Alice
would have
helped Larry
Brumfield with
his costume and
makeup. (2)

Mary Etta and Lib Hutchby teaching Sunday school (3)

Above: Victory
Singers (2)

Right: Mildred and Steve
Barnes served as youth directors in the early 1980s.
(3)

There is an interesting side note to this photo of the junior-high students at Nags Head in the early 1970s. That is me in the middle, without a beard or mustache. You will note that Chester Brown, Jimmy Ailor, and Jay Lawson were along to help, but neither Chester, Jimmy, Jay, nor I can remember the trip! My memory is usually pretty good, but this one is wiped clean! It looks like it was a good trip. (5)

Chapter 14
Ghosts and Spirits

I grew up in a family who loved to tell and listen to ghost stories. The house I grew up in at 228 Newport News Avenue was reputed to have a ghost. My parents moved there in 1936, and from the time they moved in, "things" happened: family and visitors would hear talking in rooms that were empty; the doorbell would ring, and no one would be at the door; shadows would be seen moving between rooms; a bookcase fell over in the middle of the night; the record player came on once in the middle of the night and played a funeral march (the record had been on the player earlier in the evening). I would often come home, and my mom would ask if I had come in earlier. I would tell her that I had just gotten home, and she would look perplexed, saying that she'd heard me come in a half hour earlier and shout out to her that I was home.

My father gave the ghost a name: Mrs. Davenport. He actually got the name from a radio drama that featured a ghost of the same name. My dad said that any self-respecting house should have a ghost with a proper name. She—if the ghost were indeed a "she" and *if* she did exist—was already in our home when the radio program aired. She just didn't have a name at first. After the radio program, when anything unusual or weird happened, we said, "That's just Mrs. Davenport."

I will relate some of the events at the house that happened to people from Hampton Baptist. There was one night when Bill Sasser, John Robbins, and Don Miller slept over. My mom was gone for the weekend, and so we had the house to ourselves. We spent the evening telling ghost stories, but I also got to listen to my three friends tell me repeatedly that all this ghost stuff was nonsense. It was fun to tell stories, they said, but nobody believed them and certainly not the three guys sleeping over.

We had four beds in three bedrooms, which we used when we finally called it a night. I am not sure who called out first, but shortly after turning the lights off, the two guys in the middle bedroom decided to share the big bed. I was lying in bed in my own bedroom when I heard the guy in the third room decide to join the two in the big bed in the middle bedroom.

Things were quiet for a few minutes, and then I heard a scream, followed by a loud crash of something hitting the floor. You can believe what you want about what happened, but here are the two sides of the story: Don Miller was in the middle, and according to him, one or both of the other guys, John Lee Robbins and Bill Sasser, grabbed him and threw him out of the bed. John and Bill adamantly denied that either of them had laid a hand on Don and professed that something *else* threw him out of the middle of the bed, or possibly Donald jumped out by himself.

All three of them told me that earlier in the night, when they were in separate beds, someone had whispered to them. None caught exactly what was being said. Then the covers were pulled off of John Lee's smaller bed in the middle bedroom, which was when he decided to join Bill in the large bed. A few minutes later, Don came in from the third bedroom, complaining of weird noises like footsteps his room. He then joined the two in the king-size bed.

Now, all three in the same bed heard footsteps in the middle bedroom, and that was when Don, in between the other two, flew out of the bed and hit the floor. He accused the other two of throwing him out of the bed, but both John and Bill swore they had never touched him! A ghost? Maybe. Of course, knowing the guys involved, you cannot rule out any possible trickery!

Regardless of whose account you believe, there was no more sleeping in separate bedrooms that night. We all got up, including me, although nothing had happened in my bedroom, walked downstairs to the den and living room, where there were several couches, and spent the rest of the night there. Nothing else happened that night.

Jim Ailor, Phil Everhart Jr., Roddy McKendree, and Bill Sinclair came by the house one evening because they heard I had a Ouija board. It was just the five of us. I had just gotten the board but hadn't used it. No one else was at home that night. We turned out all the lights in the downstairs except for one lamp in the living room, and then we gathered in the semi-darkened den. We sat around the Ouija board, everyone with fingers on the planchette, and asked several general questions. The planchette moved to random letters but never spelled out a specific word.

Then I asked if there was a ghost in the house. In a flash, planchette moved and rested on "YES." No one said a word, but we all jumped up and turned on every light in the downstairs. After the guys left, I threw the Ouija board in the trash and never used it or another one again.

I realize that Jim Ailor was there, which makes every part of this event suspect. I will say that to this very day, Jim claims he never moved the planchette. Everyone else also said that they had not consciously moved it.

One afternoon, I was at the house with two friends. We were all upstairs. Bill Sasser and John Robbins were in one room, and I had just gotten back from using the bathroom. John said that my mom had called me while I was in there. I told them that my mom was not at home, and it must have been Mrs. Davenport he'd heard. Bill said I was crazy and went to find my mom and prove me wrong. He looked around downstairs for a couple of minutes, and then the front door opened, and my mom walked in. Bill asked if she had been home five minutes ago, and my mom said that five minutes ago, she had gotten off the bus at the corner and started walking home!

Another time, Bill Sasser and Don Miller spent the night at my house. Again, one of them said they thought my mom had called out for me. I told them that she was visiting her sister and not at home. They looked through the whole house before finally agreeing that we were the only people there.

Milford and Lucille Rollins were a terrific couple who always did anything they could to help the young people at the church.

They, as well as many others at HBC, were a big influence on my life. Their children—Vernon, Iris, Jane, and Tim—were also a big part of my life when growing up at the church.

One night, Bill Sasser, Don Miller, and I went to the railroad track in West Point, where a mysterious light can often be seen. We saw nothing unusual, but here is a picture of Bill there. (1)

A large group of young adults were once gathered at the Rollinses' for a social. This had to have been some time in the late 1960s. At some point, five or six of the guys were in a room talking about ghosts in general when Milford walked in and told us a couple of his own ghost stories. He eventually asked if we had ever heard of the Haunted Woods. We laughed and said no, thinking it was a story he was making up.

Milford, however, quickly let us know that it was a true story and that the location was only about an hour away, across the York River. He held our group of young-adult guys in awe for an hour as he told us about this spooky place located in Mathews, Virginia.

The local people, Milford told us, avidly believe that the woods are haunted and also that several treasures are buried in the area. That night, Milford didn't tell us about all the treasure/ghost stories that were told to us later by the Mathews locals, who we would encounter sitting around a pot-bellied stove in a country store. I do vividly remember him telling us about skeletons in armor that would walk the woods at night. He also told us about the lantern lights that could be seen in the woods at night. I think the vision of skeletons walking in armor through the woods got me more hooked than the tales of treasure, but whichever it was, I was anxious to head out that way to see what it looked like.

After listening to Milford that evening, I conducted a considerable amount of research. I decided to get a group of guys together to check out the Haunted Woods. Ted Taylor, a good friend of mine, and I were working with the teenage guys at church, and I asked them if they were interested. Of course, they were. Ted was from Tennessee and in the Air Force—a super guy with a great southern accent. He was also a top-notch basketball player who had turned our church team into a winner. (Ted eventually moved back to Tennessee and married his childhood sweetheart. He also took a ministry position as director of his church's family life center. He and Don Miller stayed in close contact over the following years.)

Ted Taylor, Jimmy Ailor, Phil Everhart, Roddy McKendree, Bill Sinclair, and I drove over on a Sunday afternoon in the fall to check out the lay of the land. That trip led to many camping trips with the RAs over the years. They were always a lot of fun.

Wayne Everhart, Craig Michael, Bill Sinclair, Gene Kirby, and Jimmy Ailor (in car) (1)

This next story is not strictly a Hampton Baptist story, except that it involved me and Cindy Garris, and it is a great story. Cindy was a camp counselor one summer at the Baptist Lodge, which was a camp for girls (GAs and Acteens) from Baptist churches. It is no longer there, but it was located on the Piankatank River, not too far from the RA Baptist Camp Piankatank. Both were located not too far from the Haunted Woods in Mathews County.

I occasionally served as the camp missionary for one week at each of the camps. One of the years I was the missionary at Baptist Lodge, Cindy Garris was one of the summer counselors there. In the middle of the week, she asked if I would come by her cabin that night and tell some ghost stories about the Haunted Woods. I said I would. The girls were ready and waiting to be scared—but just a little bit scared.

Now, I am usually good at evaluating the groups I tell stories to. By the end, I want them to have about the same degree of fright that comes right before that first dip on a roller coaster. This night, I had done exactly what I'd intended. I was about to bring things to a close. They were a little scared but nothing Cindy and her co-counselor couldn't handle. Most of the girls had made small comments during my stories, but there was one girl in the back who had not said a word the whole time.

I was ready to say goodnight when she suddenly blurted out, "He's not lying! My grandpa is from that area, and he told me the same stories. They're true!"

Things might not have gotten out of hand, except for the fact that this camp was located about five miles from the edge of the Haunted Woods. Unfortunately, I had made that clear at the beginning of the evening. That and this girl's conviction changed the emotional load, which went from mild fright to pure terror in one fell swoop. Ten girls slept on the floor, huddled around their two counselors, who they insisted stay down there with them. They survived and were fine by the next night, when they slept back in their beds. I, on the other hand, was invited by the powers-that-be to feel free not to tell any more ghost stories in the future at that camp. I got invited back a couple more summers but was sure not to talk about the Haunted Woods. (For more stories about the Haunted Woods, see my book *Tales My Father Told Me*.)

Wayne Everhart, Gene Kirby, Bill Sinclair, me, and Jimmy
Ailor (1)

I give Milford Rollins credit for pioneering something
that has become a normal event at most churches. (At
least it was until the pandemic, but that is another story.)
Most church youth ministers utilize the "lock-in." A lock-in
usually runs from midnight to early in the morning, often
ending with breakfast. Sometimes a lock-in is at a church
(although, the building is not actually locked), and other
times it might be at another location, like the YMCA or a
recreation center. The idea is that the group stays in the
facility for the whole night. Lock-ins are a lot of fun, and I
have participated in probably far too many during my time
with the Peninsula Baptist Association.

Back in the 1960s, long before I had ever heard of the
term "lock-in" or the concept, Milford would gather a group
of teens and adults for our own version of a lock-in. We never called it that, but that's what it was.

Milford loved to ice skate, and there was an ice-skating rink in Norfolk. Milford found out that we could get a much cheaper price per person if we skated from midnight until four in the morning. Chester and Mary Etta Brown, our pastor and pastor's wife (well, they were not married at the time but soon would be), often came on these overnight outings. The rink would open the concession stand, and we stayed the whole night. Essentially, it was a lock-in.

I think anyone who can remember going would say that the ice skating was a success. I had always thought that the midnight skating trips were the product of Milford and Lucille Rollins. Recently however, Jane Rollins Garvey told me it was actually Milford's idea. "Lucille merely tolerated it!"

CAMPING WITH THE ROYAL AMBASSADORS

Ghost stories have always been a part of my life. My dad was a master ghost-story teller. So was Milford Rollins. My dad and Milford were probably the two best ghost-story tellers I ever heard spin a tale. Likewise, the three best places for ghost-story telling are related to Hampton Baptist.

One spot was camping in the actual Haunted Woods in Mathews, where the stage was already set. The second best place I can remember telling ghost stories was at the home of Harry and Margaret Hamor. The Hamors were members of Hampton Baptist in the sixties and seventies. They worked with the young adults on Sunday nights, and we used to go to their place a lot. Their apartment was located right next to Oakland Cemetery on Pembroke Avenue. Several members of my family were buried there, and later, my mom would also be buried there.

One monument in the cemetery had the following poem, "Remember Me," engraved on it. It is still there:

Remember me as you pass by
As you are now so once was I
As I am now so will you be
Prepare yourself to follow me

A lot of times at the Hamors', we would walk over to the cemetery and either tell ghost stories there or go back to the apartment for the storytelling.

Jay Russ, however, came up with the very best place to tell ghost stories. For about five years or so, Jay would annually hold a Sunday-night youth meeting at the Wood Funeral Home, which was at the time on the corner of Victoria and Armstead. He would schedule this for the Sunday night closest to Halloween. A couple from the church, Cindy and Mark Andrews, worked at the funeral home and had an apartment on the second floor. (Cindy Garris Andrews was the one who got me to tell ghost stories at the GA camp many years ago.)

First, the youth group would take a tour of the funeral home. After that, they enjoyed refreshments and ghost stories in the Andrewses' apartment. It was an ideal venue. I was honored the first year, as Jay invited both me and Milford Rollins to tell the stories. Since I considered Milford a master, I was a little intimidated but otherwise thoroughly enjoyed myself. Due to health reasons, Milford was not able to come back after that first year, but I was happy to continue.

At that time, one of my PBA summer activities was Camp Opportunity, when we would take at-risk kids from low-income areas to Eastover for a week. These were tough camps, with a lot of kids who could test your patience.

One night, about the fourth year of this particular Halloween tradition, we had finally gotten everyone to bed in the boys' room. (Jamie Lawson, Jay's oldest son, was one of my counselors.) Just as I was about to turn out the lights, I noticed that one of the younger kids seemed to be hiding something under his blanket. When I checked, it turned out to be a glow-in-the-dark "Jason" mask. He was going to sneak over to the girls' window with the mask. If he had been successful, we could have kissed all sleep goodbye that night, and possibly a few nights after that. I took it and truly meant to give it back to him when we went home on Friday. But I got busy and distracted, and when I got home, I discovered I still had it in my suitcase.

By the time Halloween came around, I had not yet caught up with the kid. And so I had the mask when it came time for Jay Russ to gather the youth group at the apartment above the funeral parlor for our annual Halloween ghost-story party. I usually tell local legends, such as the Haunted Woods, but this year, we added another attraction.

The apartment was on the second floor. All the youth were seated on the floor, and I was in a chair in front of them, with the second-story window behind me. Earlier, Jay and Mark had installed a ladder outside that reached up to the window. For this stunt, I made up a story because I knew I wouldn't finish it. When I began, Jay sneaked out the back door and helped Mark, in the Jason mask, cover himself with a coat.

It was great. Sandy Everette and two other girls were sitting cross-legged on the floor, right in front of me. Halfway through the story, everyone in the room let out a scream. The best part for me was seeing the three girls jump three feet in the air from their sitting position. That ended any serious ghost-story telling for that night, but it was well worth it.

Here I am telling ghost stories at the funeral home apartment. The window in the previous story is to my right. (4)

HBC HALLOWEEN PARTIES

Hampton Baptist youth and young adults had a Halloween banquet each year. These were always a lot of fun. I still have a menu from the evening of the 1962 party. Please note that it was a Baptist Training Union event.

HAMPTON BAPTIST
YOUNG PEOPLE AND COLLEGE GROUP
TRAINING UNIONS
October 27, 1962

PROGRAM

6:30 - Arrival
6:45 - Serving
8:00 - Games

MENU

Graveyard Worms with Vampire Sauce
Funeral Flowers
French Stiffs
Creeping Creepers in their super-
        natural juices
Coffin Nails
Corpse-Size Pills
Vampire Venom and Gravemud
Witches' Brew
Ice Screams and Spookies

The above are served with Mummy Spectral's delicious hair-raising biscuits and home-griab vegetabkes-- fresh as the moaning dew - from the Spectral arm's private plot.

The Spectral Arms, located at the coffin coroner of Rip and Dead End Streets, welcomes you to meals that are out of this world. Truly stuperb culinary cremations, fashioned by the finest chef with great skull, and accompanied of corpse, by the best of wines, spirits, and biers. Haunting music by "Spook Jones and his real gone band." We also feature the "Coffin Baggers" with their vacal group "Tie Crypt Kickers Five." Dinners at six-thirty from the groaning board.

Our Skeleton Staff will shadow you with attention. Suppe with us in the Belfry Room, such rattling good food! Drink in our quaint old wrathskeller.

Have a good wail of a time and be sure to float back soon.

WE CATER TO NO BODIES

Above: Virginia Feathers
Below: Melissa Ellis (2)

Claudia Ulsh and Virginia Feathers (2)

Peggy Parsons (2)

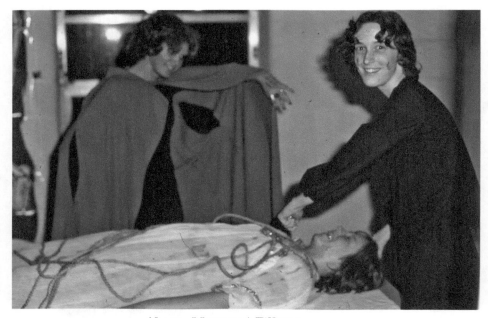

Above: Margaret Tillery
Below: Rhonda Riddle (2)

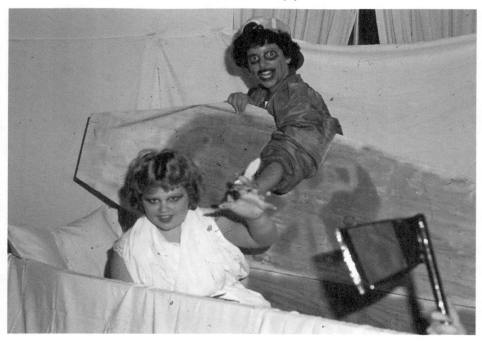

Chapter 15
Lynne Everhart

I first got to know Lynne Everhart because her parents' home was one of my "drop in on a weekend night" houses when I was a teenager. A group of us from Hampton Baptist used to spend a lot of evenings at the Ailors', Dennards', Rollinses', and Everharts'. In fact, during one period, we helped Phil Everhart Sr. build an addition on his house. Well, to be honest, I guess I should say that what we did was stop by on a Friday or Saturday evening and drink a Coke with Phil, thus allowing him to take a break from the construction.

I and a couple of other guys started a tradition back then, which I have carried on for more than fifty years. The tradition was visiting those four homes every Christmas morning. As these good friends eventually went on to be with the Lord, their numbers dwindled, until one year, Lucille Everhart was the only one left. I still visited her each Christmas until COVID hit. I got back on track the next year. Then in 2022, Christmas came on a Sunday, and I was invited to speak at a church that morning and missed again. Last year, 2023, I visited Lucille again for Christmas.

Thus, I got to know Lynne Everhart when she was a kid. Her older brother, Phil Jr., was in my Royal Ambassador group and accompanied us on a lot of camping trips and other activities. Later, Wayne, Bruce, and David joined in on a lot of these trips.

There was always something that impressed me about Lynne, even from an early age. Probably the event that endeared her to me occurred when she was about ten years old. There was a church outing at a cabin on a lake owned by the Rollinses, located in Gloucester. There was a boat available and different groups took turns out on the lake during the day.

When it became my turn, Lynne was also in the boat. We were seated facing each other. We talked and joked. Then, trying to be funny, I pulled the oldest stunt in the book: I tied her shoelaces together and said, "What are you going to do now?"

I watched in amazement as, instead of trying to untie them, Lynne grinned at me and pulled the laces even tighter. Up until then, I had thought Lynne to be a fairly intelligent girl. She didn't try to explain, so I asked, "Why did you do that?"

"So that you can't untie them."

"Why?"

"Because when my mom sees what you have done, you will be in a lot of trouble!"

It took me ten minutes of hard work to get those shoestrings untied, but I knew then that this Lynne Everhart was my type of girl. And we were friends ever since.

Many years later, I attended a meeting with some fellow deacons (it will shock you to know that at one time I was a deacon) and several church youth. The question was whether contemporary Christian music was appropriate for church meetings and worship. Most of the deacons were adamantly against it and felt that contemporary Christian music was one step away from blasphemy. John Dawson and I, as well as a couple of other deacons, felt it was fine for worship.

Lynne Everhart was in the ninth or tenth grade at the time. She and several other youth were in attendance, and Lynne became their spokesperson. She gave the youth's position on this issue and why they felt that Christian music was Christian music, whether it was a hymn or contemporary rock. What I remember most about the discussion is that several of the deacons were not what you

Lynne Everhart, Jean Jones, and Sharon O'Bryan at VBS; Jean and Lynne were good friends, and Jean gave Lucille Everhart a lot of attention after Lynne died. (2)

would call "calm and rational." Lynne, on the other hand, was a model of decorum and politeness. She responded to all the questions and objections in a mild manner and with a smile. At the same time, she was firm and adamant in her position. I do not think that anyone's opinion was changed during the meeting, but I was very proud of Lynne and how she handled herself.

Lynne helped me out with most of the Peninsula Baptist Association ministries that I headed in my early years there. When I left Social Services to go to the PBA, I went with several requests from other agencies. One came from Roy Powell, the director of Big Brothers on the Peninsula. He asked that I, through the PBA, begin a Big Sisters–type organization. I did this with the help of several female social workers. It ran for a good many years. Beginning as a ministry of the PBA, it soon became an independent organization and then an official Big Sisters chapter. I remained on the board of directors, but the PBA was no longer involved. Eventually, it ran its course and was disbanded. Lynne Everhart and Fred Powell's daughter became the first two young ladies I recruited as Big Sisters. Lynne worked with a couple of girls who I had on my caseload at the PBA in the early 1970s.

Another request I received from Wallace Hicks and Jim Thomas (Ivy Memorial Baptist) was for the PBA to run retreats for guys and girls on probation. This was at the time that Wally Hicks retired and Jim Thomas took over as chief probation officer. We included the Newport News and Yorktown juvenile probation offices. My first summer at the PBA (1971), I ran a retreat for boys. Jim Ailor was part of that retreat along with Howard Stone, another member of HBC.

Me and Wallace Hicks at Camp Piankatank on the guy's juvenile probation retreat (1)

Howard Stone is in the center, flanked by me and a Newport News juvenile probation officer. I assisted Howard when I first began working with the RAs. (1)

The next year, we held one for girls from the same three areas. Lynne was one of eight college-age young ladies who helped plan the retreat and serve as counselors. Jim Ailor served as the camp pastor, and Jimmy Allison helped provide transportation. We used Baptist camps: the RA Camp Piankatank for the boys and the WMU Camp Viewmont for the girls.

The third year, I organized a coed retreat for kids on probation. Along with Lynne Everhart and Jim Ailor, I added Laurie Schneider and Bill Sinclair (as well as a dozen other young adults from various PBA churches). Lynne, and her dog Blue, went on to help me with retreats for foster kids and a number of other ministries. Lynne was also a pioneer on the early retreats for the vision and hearing impaired. (Many other HBC youth and adults helped with these retreats over the years, and that is covered in another part of this book.)

Several times, when preparing a retreat for either the vision/hearing impaired or foster kids from York County, I would ask Lynne to come and help out. She would then ask me if it was OK if she brought a teenager she was mentoring. (At that point, she was an unofficial "big sister.") She said it would be a good experience for that person.

(That was a philosophy that Lynne and I both shared. The way to help someone with problems find their way is by giving them the opportunity to work beside you in ministry. I think that Chester Brown and Hampton Baptist encouraged this type of model.)

Lynne Everhart on the girl's juvenile probation retreat at the WMU Camp Viewmont (1)

Easy-going and agreeable, and always with a smile, Lynne was one of those people you just liked being around. She had a great outlook on life and enjoyed being with people. She, along with her brother Phil Jr., Jimmy Ailor, and Bill Sinclair were four of the first younger people whom I considered friends.

Lynne later became an elementary school teacher and a good one. She eventually got married, and a couple of years later, she and her husband were expecting their first child. She was looking forward to showing the same love and compassion for her own child as she had done for so many other children and teens who needed it.

In a world of modern technology and medicine, young people still go blind. They still lose their hearing and the use of their limbs. They still get in trouble and need a little extra help. In a world of up-to-date hospitals and state-of-the-art medicine, Lynne would die of complications during childbirth. In a modern world of all sorts of advancements, some questionable, Lynne would leave an old-fashioned legacy of love and caring for others. I miss her.

Lynne once paid me what I thought was the ultimate compliment, coming from a teenager. Lucille told me that Lynne had wanted me to be one of her pallbearers when she died. That was another unique thing about this cute blonde girl. She'd had a way of looking at life from different angles. For me, it was the sentiment of a teenager, which made that thought so special.

Because the burial was private, I didn't get to do that. However, it was the thought that counted. It was standing room only at her memorial, and Chester recited some of the underlined verses in Lynne's Bible. He also repeated one of my favorite Chester Brown quotes: "We will miss her—not because she is gone, but because she was once here."

It was the only time I have had to wait in a line outside of a home in order to go in and talk with the family of a loved one who was called upward. I think that was one of the neat things about Lynne. She never made a big deal about being popular, but she was. She didn't make a big deal about doing ministry; she just did it. She didn't make a big deal about her walk with Jesus; she just followed Him.

Chapter 16
The Old Guard

Wallace Hicks and Bessie Amory (2)

Two of the "old guard" at Hampton Baptist Church were Wally and Bessie. They were a source of wisdom, encouragement, and humor for us all. I missed being able to work for Wally in his last days at the Hampton probation office. When I went downtown with the intent of putting in my application at both the Social Services and probation offices, I got to Social Services first.

It turned out that I had arrived at the right moment, and I was offered a job at the end of my interview. Wally gave me a hard time in a nice way when I saw him the next Sunday at HBC. He was still encouraging and told me that I would do well at Social Services. I later got to work a year at Juvenile Probation, but by then, Jim Thomas was the chief probation officer. Jim, still a member of Ivy

Memorial, was a super boss, and I enjoyed working for him. It would have been neat to work for Wally, but life takes some interesting twists and turns.

Bessie was one of those "Hall People" I mentioned earlier. Always with a smile and a word of encouragement, she modeled a kind-hearted, caring adult. She was a regular in Bill Hurt's annual Church Nights, which tells you a lot about her fun-loving nature.

Charlotte Williams, who directed the choirs for many years, is here in the kitchen. You know that Charlotte was a "good guy" because she is making coffee. We will forgive her for putting sugar and cream in it! (2)

Left: A father-daughter dance with Jack Lawson and his daughter, Cindy (3)

Below: Linda Miller Riddle getting ready for either VBS or Sunday school (2)

Left: Wayne Erickson on a Saturday church work day (2)

Right: Alice Erickson (You can write your own caption!) (2)

Christmastime with Mary Francis Robbins
and Eddie Hankinson (2)

Nancy Lee Jones with her ever-present smile (2)

Jane Dennard and Alicia Everett hard at work at VBS (2)

Kathryn Thomas, Ammie Garber, and Dr. Garber (1973) (2)

Marion Hankinson (2)

Garland Goodwin, Jules Miller, Tom Bundick, Henry Dixon, and Bob Zigler at a deacons' retreat (2)

Above: Celia Dawson (2)

Below: Lewis and Margaret Parsons with Alice Erickson (2)

Three-legged race at an HBC picnic: Jesse and Toni Wilkins
and Chuck and Angeline Whitcomb (2)

Bill and Freda
Nelson with
Milford Rollins
(2)

Chapter 17
Church Nights 1981–1985

1981
"INSPECTOR CLOUSEAU
AND THE PINK PANTHER"

Roy Powell introduced the opening skit, in which the Church Night Committee discuss this year's Church Night. When they retire for the evening, the Pink Panther steals the church calendar they had been using. Inspector Clouseau is hired to find it.

Roy Powell played the chief inspector, Stan Ewing played Darth Vader, Richard Pulley was a G-man, Bryan Lilly was Superman, Bob Sigler portrayed Jimmy Carter, Linda Riddle was Minnie Pearl, Betty Tillery represented the WMU, and Del Croon played one of the Church Night members.

1982
"HBC NEWSBREAK"

The skits this year were based on television commercials. Debbie and Joe Spencer, along with Richard Pulley, were the HBC seven o'clock news team.

- Camelia Everett, the WMU director, was interviewed.
- On Maundy Thursday, the deacons reenacted the Last Supper and served communion to the congregation afterward.
- Lewis Parsons, chairman of the Hall Road Mission Committee, was interviewed.
- Chester Brown led a Bible study at Gloucester Point Baptist.

- A Work Day was held on June 6.
- Greg Schneider was our youth pastor during Youth Week, August 9–16. Other youth served in various capacities.
- Steve and Mildred Barnes worked with the youth during the summer, leading a Vacation Bible School at the Hall Road Mission.
- Wednesday night suppers continued to be superb. Della Collier, our chief cook, and her associates, Elsie Wright, Thelma Killian, and Anna Marie Hanbeck, were given the credit.
- Ben Riddle, chairman of the Finance Planning Committee, was interviewed.
- On November 15, six more stained glass memorial windows in the sanctuary were dedicated, with Dr. Brown giving a history of each.
- John Kersey, chairman of the Senior Adult Committee, was interviewed.
- During HBC Newsbreak, anchor reporters Debbie Spencer, Joe Spencer, and Richard Pulley reported on the January Bible study, Week of Prayer for Home Missions, Vacation Bible School, and plans for a series of revival services.

1983

The Victory Singers presented the musical *The Kingdom Within*.

1984
"THE CIRCUS PRESENTS: THE GREATEST CHURCH ON EARTH!"

- Craig Michael starred as the ring master.
- In 1983, the sanctuary turned 100 years old and got a well-

deserved painting. The parlor was remodeled, and the senior adults began the Friendship Club. A new Sunday school office was set up.

- Betty Miller was the WMU president. The circle included Jeanette Pierce, Nannie McDaniel, and Lucille Rollins.
- Betty Miller gave a demonstration using a hula hoop!
- We celebrated Dottie Lee Jones's anniversary.
- There was an outdoor church service and picnic on the grounds on July 3. It was the hottest day of the year.
- Terry Laufer (tamer of wild youth) arrived as our part-time youth minister.
- Gary Lewis celebrated his tenth anniversary.
- The grand finale of the show, with circus music playing:
  - Bill worked on the pageant.
  - Terry and youth wrapped presents.
  - Gary directed the choirs.
  - Chester, in robe, raised and lowered a candle.
  - Dottie Lee typed, answered phone, etc.

1985
THE HAMPTON, VIRGINIA, OLYMPICS

- The eternal flame was lit from a torch. The "flame" was in an oven, which represented the "never-ending church suppers!"
- Bob Sigler and John Robbins presented a skit regarding the budget and tithing.
- Linda Riddle was introduced for the Gift Wrap Relay.
- Phil Everhart Sr., Dottie Lee Jones, Leonard Lineberry, Billy Byrd, and Nancy Sandford represented various Sunday school departments. (Nancy Sandford won the event.)
- Commercials included "Raise your pledge if you are sure" and "We do chicken right."

- Bessie Amory reenacted the famous Wendy's commercial for Wednesday night suppers. She ran down one of the aisles yelling, "Where's the beef?"
- We also saw the Sunday School Cross Country, Family Night Pot-Put, and the Budget Tug of War.
- Betty Miller appeared in the WMU Hurdles.
- The Choir Row event featured four choir members rowing and singing "Row, Row, Row Your Boat" and Gary Lewis in back, with a whip and drum, keeping time with the beat.
- Credits:
  - Video director: George Steinmetz
  - Prop director: Alice Erickson
  - Audio director: Leonard Lineberry
  - Producer: Terry Ulsh
  - Hostesses: Judy Watts and Debbie Spencer
  - Director: Bill Hurt

Left: Suzanna McKendree, whose son Will is hearing impaired, teaching "cued speech" to a group at Hampton Baptist (2)

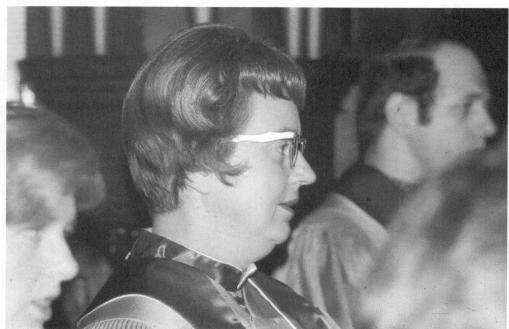

June Ozment (1970) (2)

Mildred Barnes (above):
she and her husband,
Steve (right), led the
youth ministry during
the early 1980s. (3)

Ann Pulley and Julie McKendree on a youth mission trip
with Jay Russ (4)

Tommy Fields, Lloyd Everhart, Ben Hallissy, and Patrick
O'Bryan at a youth meeting during Jay Russ's time as youth
minister (4)

Check out the sunglasses! (Marge Michael on the right) (2)

Matt Parron and David Hurt (2)

Left: Jimmy Michael
and Martha Feathers at
a youth retreat in Nag's
Head (3)

Right: Randy Ware on a youth
retreat (3)

Above: Virginia Trescott, VBS 1967 (2)
Below: Beth McKendree, VBS 1966 (2)

Phil Everhart, Roddy McKendree, Jim Ailor, Tommy
O'Bryan, and Craig Michael, among others, attending RA
weekend at Eagle Eyrie (1)

Chapter 18
Jim Ailor and Jay Lawson

You already know how Jay and Jim got started in ministry by sharing summer youth duties at Hampton Baptist Church. John Dawson got them to work together that summer, and the Holy Spirit took it from there. They have been my friends since their early years, and they continue to bless my life.

Jim Ailor and Jay Lawson were my RAs during their high school years. Later, Jim became my boss as the director of missions for the PBA. That was a lot of fun. Jim always treated me well, and I never harbored any ill will against him. . . Well, except for the afternoon when he made me go outside and clean the PBA van in 105-degree heat.

I had used the van for a big event over the weekend, and now a church wanted to use it. I told Jim it was too hot and I was not dressed for that. Jim smiled and said, "Do it anyway." When I came back inside, soaked to the skin in sweat, Jim was on the phone and said to whomever he was talking to, "Haywood just walked in looking like a drowned rat." To be honest, I'm sure I did many things to Jim over the years that made me deserve it!

Jim Ailor at Eagle Eyrie (3)

Jim did me a big favor in 2020. Because of COVID-19, I had extra time to start writing books about my life and years of PBA ministry. Those of you who know me well, know that my grasp on the English language—written and spoken—is not the best.

Craig Waddell worked for me as a Smishy (summer missionary) for four years and later became my close friend. The summer after he graduated from Washington and Lee University, he entered the Journeyman program through the Foreign Mission Board. He spent two years in Austria doing college student work in the city of Linz. He met his wife, Angelika, there.

Craig returned to the States to attend seminary before going back to Linz to become the pastor at a local Austrian church. Ten years later, his family (including two daughters, Erin and Fiona) moved to the States, and Craig began working for the Baptist General Association of Virginia.

After he returned to work in Richmond, Craig was asked to speak at the Peninsula Baptist Association fall meeting. Craig began his talk with this story:

"When I first went to Austria, I was good at German but was well aware that it was not my first language. I prayed and asked God if I could really do His ministry in a language that I didn't speak all that well. God answered me in a dream, saying, 'Don't worry, Craig, you can do it. Remember, Mike Haywood has been doing it all his life—in ENGLISH!'"

So I kept putting the writing off because of my poor grammar and spelling. Jim told me that his daughter Dara was a professional editor with reasonable fees. I talked to Dara, and she helped me with my first book, *His Love Is Not Blind*. (That book is about the retreats that the PBA sponsored for hearing- and vision-impaired students, which spanned about thirty years. Two dozen or more people from Hampton Baptist helped with those.) She made me sound articulate, and I have loved working with her ever since!

Now, I said that Jim did me a favor by getting my writing career started. Some of you might use a different word to describe it. He kind of created a monster. This is my seventh book, and Dara is still making me look good. I love it. She has not only edited all my books, but she has also designed all the covers and interiors. I have gotten as many compliments on the covers and book layouts as I have on the books themselves.

In addition to the summer he worked with Jay at HBC, Jim remembers the other summers he worked as a youth minister at various churches. He spent a year each at Fox Hill Road Baptist and Buckroe Baptist. It was while at Fox Hill Road that he staged the march on Buckroe Beach (see Chapter 43). Jimmy also worked one summer at a church in

> Jim Ailor once gave me the ultimate compliment (in my mind) by telling someone that "Mike Haywood disciples you without you being aware you are being discipled."

Alabama and for me as a PBA Smishy.

At Buckroe, Jim had the good fortune to work with the Lewis family. Betty Lewis was the PBA children's worker representative. Her oldest daughter, Connie, helped me plan an early retreat for girls on probation. The next oldest, Cathy, helped with several of my early retreats with the PBA. Connie and Cathy were in the Buckroe youth group the summer Jimmy was there, and the youngest, Penny, worked with Jim when he was a PBA Smishy a few years later. Both Penny and Cathy have a high regard for Jimmy to this very day.

After graduating seminary, Jim became the full-time youth minister at Williamsburg Baptist Church. After that, he took the senior pastor position at Pine Street Baptist in Richmond. Several years later, Jim became the pastor of Guilford Fellowship in Northern Virginia. He followed that by becoming the teaching pastor at Leesburg Baptist and the associate of Daybreak in Ashburn. Next, he took the pastorate at Hebron Baptist near Afton Mountain.

In 2004, Jimmy left Hebron to become my boss and the director of missions at the Peninsula Baptist Association. From there, he became a field strategist for the Baptist General Association of Virginia. When Jim retired from that position, he moved to Waynesboro (not far from Hebron in Afton), where he and his wife, Lynne, could be close to their daughter Dara and her family.

Jay Lawson's first summer position, before coming to Hampton Baptist, was as youth minister of North Riverside Baptist. There he got to work with a terrific pastor, Rev. Joe Strother. Joe is another pastor who I considered a friend. When Joe retired, he and his wife, Sue, joined Hampton Baptist. (Everything seems interrelated!)

Jay then accepted the call to come and work as a duo with Jimmy Ailor at Hampton Baptist. The next summer, Jay came back solo for a second year at Hampton Baptist. After graduating from Duke and then seminary, Jay eventually returned to this area as the associate pastor of Temple Baptist Church. The pastor at Temple was Walter Martin. He and his wife, Libby, were good friends of Chester and Mary Etta.

Four days before the Sunday that Jay would start, Dr. Martin suffered a heart attack. He would recover but would be out of action for many months. Because the church hoped that Walter Martin would be able to return as their pastor at some point, they told Jay that he would retain his current position as associate but

Jay Lawson on an HBC youth retreat (3)

that he would also, in effect, become the interim pastor for about eight months. So Jay Lawson went to Temple in kind of a sink-or-swim position as the lead pastor for most of a year. Fortunately for all concerned, Jay was able to "swim" and was an effective pastor there.

Walter was eventually able to return, and Jay assumed the position he had been hired to fill. You couldn't say he *returned* to the associate position because he had not actually served as an associate pastor. Jay stayed on for about a year when Walter Martin decided to retire. Jay agreed to continue as the associate until the new head pastor had settled in.

Jay went from Temple Baptist to North Carolina, where he became the lead pastor of Belhaven Baptist. Jay later returned to the

Peninsula, becoming the pastor of Emmaus Baptist in Poquoson. While there, he teamed up with two people who later influenced Hampton Baptist: Darlene and Scott Scheepers. The Scheepers were members of Emmaus, and, as you know, Darlene much later became the office administrator at HBC, where she is today.

Jay also hired Jimmy George as the church's education minister. If you read Chapter 6, you may remember that Jimmy George and Jay Russ were friends who attended Mars Hill and seminary together. They are all still good friends.

For several years, Jay remained at Emmaus before moving to Hilton Baptist Church, where he stayed for another several years. While at Hilton, Jay hired Harald Aadahl as the youth minister. Harald was a friend and mentor to many of us working within Peninsula Baptist churches (Jay Russ being one of them).

Like Jim Ailor, Jay was always encouraging me and looking out for my best interest. Probably the greatest compliment that Jay and his wife, Claudia, ever bestowed on me was allowing all three of their children—Jamie, Brenden, and Caroline—to work summer missions with me. Caroline even went to Austria with Jay Russ and me in 2000 (as did Jim's daughter, Dara). In 2023, the Lawson grandchildren Conner and Sadie worked as Smishies. Brenden is their dad. Does make me feel old! Jay Lawson is mentioned in several of the books that I have written and published. You can find Jay and Claudia's three children in my book *Smishies, Volume II: 1990–2000*. This book also includes a lot of HBC youth who were Smishies.

During the time that Jay Lawson was at Emmaus and Hilton, I could count on a couple of lunches each year, compliments of Jay. This would occur whenever Jay read a new book about church life that he really liked. He would call and say, "Mike, let me buy you lunch and tell you about this new book I am reading."

I don't know if this was true at Emmaus and the other churches he pastored, but I loved going by Hilton and seeing Jay at his office. His system for writing sermons was to lay everything (Bibles, books, notes) on the floor around his desk as he drafted and put the finishing touches on his work.

For a couple of years, while at Temple, Jay led the Bible study at a Peninsula Baptist youth camp held at Eastover and run by me and Ron Sowers, the pastor of East Hampton Baptist. One year, Jay titled his Bible study "Prayer: A Completely Unique Experience." I was actually hoping it would create a bit of controversy (which, I thought, might help increase participation numbers). Unfortunately, only one adult realized it was the slogan for Colt 45 malt liquor, and they didn't fuss about it too much.

Through the years, Jimmy and Jay have remained close friends and catch up with each other whenever they are able. Both have retired. Several years ago, when Jim's wife, Lynne Ailor, was going to be ordained, Jay Lawson officiated the service.

We get older, but we never seem to get older. The last time Ailor, Lawson, Jimmy George, and I were together, we still managed to find time for an adventure. It was during a big Baptist conference in Salem, Virginia. We got there a day early. George was playing golf, so he missed this little ramble. But the other three of us headed out on a mountain road and found a place to park. We took a trail that led into the woods and just started walking.

Before the afternoon was over, we had become lost several times, explored the base and top of an old dam, worried about getting shot by hunters or bootleggers, and finally found our way back to the overlook parking lot. And it was special because I was with friends.

There really is an adventure waiting out there for you. Just up the trail a bit, past that stand of trees, over the far ridge. Or maybe in that book you have in your hand, with the new kid you've met, or deposited in the memory of the old fellow or lady who lives down the street.

Chapter 19

Linda Brumfield at PAL Lodge, Eagle Eyrie (1)

Barbara (Gunter) Lilly in the blue (Barbara and I graduated from high school together.) (2)

Erin Hallissy and Bill Hurt (5)

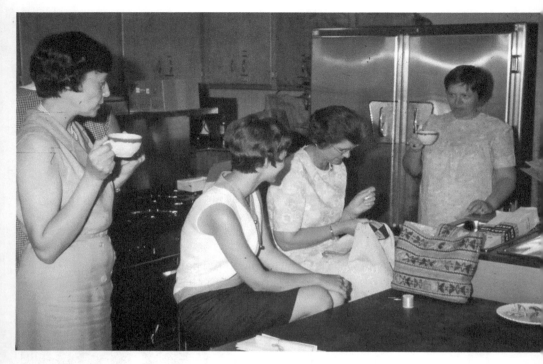

Lucille Everhart, Martha Johnson, and Jane Hurt in the
HBC kitchen (2)

Margaret Allison (2)

Above: Virginia Pulley; below: Eleanor Oakley at VBS (2)

Above: Raye Mathis playing ball at VBS
Below: Trudy McBride making a craft (2)

Raye Mathis (the blonde in the red-trimmed shirt is Susan Forbes (2)

Julie Shepherd (2)

Elizabeth Patrick (2)

Chapter 20
Role Models and Leaders

A lot of different people during my early years at HBC were in charge of different functions of the church, such as Sunday school and youth ministry (before Terry Laufer and Jay Russ). I want to dedicate some pages to them, but first I want to give more details about the aforementioned "Hall People" and a sermon I wrote about them.

I first delivered the sermon at Hampton Baptist on a Sunday night and then many more times at other churches. The point was that a lot of people at HBC, who were never in charge of a Sunday school class or RAs or youth, still made a major contribution to my development as a Christian. I explained that there were many such people, but I used Jack Lawson as an example because he had recently passed away.

I used the term *Hall People* because I mostly interacted with Jack in the halls of Hampton Baptist. For a number of years, it seemed that most Wednesday nights when I was waiting for the church dinner to be served, I would end up next to Jack Lawson. It seemed to happen at least twice each month. During that five to ten minutes, while the line was not yet moving forward, Jack would engage me in conversation.

He would also stop me for a moment as we passed in the church halls and ask a question or make a comment. He would ask how things were going in my life, how I felt about programs in the church, and what my plans for the future entailed. Jack showed a real interest in me as an individual worth talking to. It truly made an impact on my life.

But he was not the only one who did this. Other adults talked with me as we passed in the halls or when waiting for a program to start. As had Jack, they made me feel as though I was someone who had something to offer. There were many of these Hall People, and they were all an inspiration to me. Sometimes we talked about trivial things, but it still made me feel special.

All of us can be Hall People to those we run into at church. You might talk about important matters, or you might just make small talk; whichever it is, it can mean a lot. Just be aware that any person you talk to at church, especially a young adult or teenager, will appreciate your taking an interest in them. It doesn't have to be dramatic, but it can be if appropriate. Regardless, you will make an impression and an impact.

Chester at a church Christmas party (2)

Chester Brown was hired as a summer youth minister in the early 1950s. One Chester quip still sticks in my mind from that time. (It's funny how an odd, off-the-wall comment can stay with you for years.) The youth had been enjoying a bonfire in the open space to the left (when facing the front of the church). There were fewer buildings on that side at the time and a lot of open land. This was before new additions were built onto the church building.

A good number of us circled the bonfire with the coat hangers and plenty of hot dogs and marshmallows. I remember having to get quite close to the fire to get my hot dog to cook. Chester was on my right, doing the same. It was hot, but we had no choice if we wanted to eat a cooked meal.

Grimacing in the heat of the flames, Chester turned to me and said, "Now I know how the hot dog feels."

I was probably twelve or thirteen at the time. It was obviously not a profound remark, but it has stayed with me all these years, and I can tell you why. We were in the midst of a large group, but Chester said to me alone. *We will never know when a remark we make to a young person will make them feel encouraged, worthwhile, important, and accepted.* It's such an easy thing to do, but it can leave a mark.

One other thing that Chester said to me—in writing rather than in speaking—had big impact on me. This was in 1961 or 1962, when I was in college at the Old Dominion Technical Institute. (This was a trade school that taught such things as drafting, surveying, and other skills. I was in the drafting department and after finishing, worked at the Shipyard as a draftsman for a couple of years.) I do not remember if it was before or after Christmas, but whichever it was, I came down with a case of the chicken pox. I didn't have a bad case, but it lasted about ten days.

One day, Chester came by the house, and gave my mother a book for me. He didn't stay long or visit with me personally. The book was *The Meaning of Gifts* by Paul Tournier. I'd recommend it to anyone. I still have a copy, although it's not the same one that Chester gave me. At some point, I lost that copy and got another. But I do remember the inscription Chester had written inside:

Mike, I hope you get well soon. Next time, catch something that I can't catch, and I will come and visit you.

—Chester

Simple gestures and kindnesses can leave lasting impressions! Chester, as well as the Hall People, seem to know this. And speaking of Hall People, I asked several Hampton Baptist members who they would consider Hall People. This is a short list of their answers:

Jay Lawson:	Billy Byrd and John Dawson
Jane Dennard Alston:	Phil and Lucille Everhart
Suzanna McKendree:	Ellen Sullivan
Tommy O'Bryan:	Woody Patrick
Phil Everhart Jr.:	Woody Patrick
Jim Ailor:	Milford Rollins; John and Myrtle Dennard

Jim Ailor has a great story about his time spent with Milford Rollins. Milford had an antique sailing canoe, fondly called the *Kaynoo*. This vessel was fashioned locally from logs that were bolted together and carved into a canoe shape. The hull was five inches at its thickest, and it sat low in the water due to its weight.

Milford would enlist some of the youth and young adults to help him maintain it. The reward for helping was that you got to "crew" during races. A lot of the races were local, and Jim remembers crewing with Timmy and, occasionally, Iris Rollins.

Jimmy was in high school when the *Kaynoo* was ninety-eight years old. He, Milford, and Timmy took the boat to the Lake of the Woods, which is on the border between the United States and Canada, for a five-day race. Each crew sailed from island to island, keeping a record of their time. They would spend the night on an island before heading out on the next leg. It was cold enough that they would wear wetsuits during the day. Jimmy remembers that on one leg of the race, Timmy had only worn his wetsuit top and that by the time they got to the next island, his legs were purple.

On another leg, Jimmy remembers sailing at night through rain and a fog thick enough to cut with a knife. Jim was the navigator, and though they knew they were close to the finish, he had no idea where to direct them. Then, through the gloom, he heard music and thought, "That's as good a direction as any," and sent them toward the music. The fog thinned out as they reached the island on the Canadian side of the lake. On the pier was a brass band, drenched and decked out in red, playing a jolly tune.

The crew arrived to cheers from a crowd that stood in the rain with the band. They were treated to a buffet dinner and for the first and only night of the race did not have to sleep in a tent. After the buffet, they were escorted to a second-story bedroom with three beds. It was a real treat. However, they noticed a big iron ring bolted to the floor under the window with a knotted rope attached. When they asked their host about the rope, they were told, "That's the fire escape!"

The next morning, they were back out on the cold lake and heading for another island, where they would spend the night in a tent. They finished ninth out of fifty boats.

Milford's Chesapeake Bay log canoe is in a museum in Poquoson today; in this photo, it is about 100 years old.

Let me make one other quick comment about Chester and good books. Joe Strother was the pastor of North Riverside Baptist in Newport News during his last pastorate. During that time, my PBA office was in North Riverside. I occasionally attended on Sunday evening, but Joe was around the PBA a lot. He was a pastor who, like Chester, was a mentor to me. In the late 1980s, Joe developed cancer in his back and had to retire. When he did, he and his wife, Sue, joined Hampton Baptist. Joe and Chester were a lot alike, and so this made sense.

Chester doing "show and tell" at Vacation Bible School (2)

When Joe retired, I asked him to give me one of the books from his study at North Riverside. He gave me a Bible I still cherish and use a lot. A couple of years ago, I mentioned this to Joe's daughter Donna. She told me that it had been one of his favorite study Bibles. That did make me feel special. Donna had been one of the teens who helped a lot with my ministries.

When Chester retired in 2001, I also asked him for a book. He did me a double honor; he gave me two: one of his and one he had kept from Dr. John Garber. I am blessed to have both. I have made this request four times, receiving books from Joe, Chester, Dr. Garber, and Larry Biermann of Parkview Baptist.

For many years, HBC didn't have a paid youth minister. In the early 1980s, Terry Laufer was hired part-time. Terry was a member of First Baptist in Newport News. Terry's sister Lynn worked for me as a PBA summer missionary for one year in the 1970s. Terry was followed by Jay Russ, who came on as a full-time youth minister in 1985, and as they say (as far as youth ministry goes), "the rest is history!"

During the time I was growing up at Hampton Baptist, all of the youth work was done by volunteers. I want to mention some of them, and yes, I know will inevitably leave out a few. Obviously, Sunday school classes, the Baptist Training Union, RAs, GAs, and Girls Auxiliary were always run by volunteers.

Whoever was serving as a youth director was usually in charge of a Sunday night and a Wednesday night program at the church. These folks rotated from year to year, and in my memory, they were always around. After being hired as the director of education, Bill Hurt would serve as the staff person who oversaw the youth group at Hampton Baptist. Bill did a splendid job at that until Terry Laufer and later, Jay Russ were hired.

Thelma Killian, Nancy Sandford, Sam Ailor, and Phil Everhart during a youth retreat at Wakefield (3)

Lucille Everhart with VBS kids (2)

Kenny Matthews, Martha and Sam Ailor, Nancy and Billy Trimble at a deacons' retreat at Eastover (3)

I think of six people who seemed to be leading the youth group in the sixties and seventies: Lucille and Phil Everhart, Martha and Sam Ailor, and Alice and Wayne Erickson. A while later, Margaret and Harry Hamor also worked with the youth. Alan Turnbull was usually associated with the Baptist Training Union. Dave Carter and Wayne Erickson served as our RA leaders.

A very special group of people opened their doors to the youth group—to the group as a whole or to any members who might just show up. Some were called youth leaders and some were Hall People. These included Martha and Sam Ailor, Lucille and Phil Everhart, Alice and Wayne Erickson, Milford and Lucille Rollins, John and Mrytle Dennard, and Harry and Margaret Hamor. Jane Dennard Alson remembers going to the home of Francis and Dottie Lee Jones many a time.

This is a deacons' retreat at the PBA retreat center at Eastover. Several photos of the retreat, taken by John Dawson, exist. In this one, we have Gary Lewis playing the guitar while Milford Rollins, Terry Ulsh, and Wayne Erickson hover near the door. (3)

Above: Dottie Lee Jones (2)

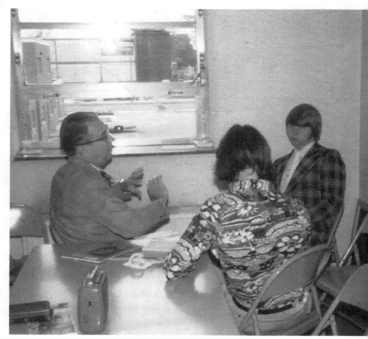

Right: Francis Jones teaching Sunday school (3)

There were a lot of Friday nights when my friends and I would go by one of those homes. On Christmas morning, John Robbins, Bill Sasser, Don Miller, and I would visit several: the Ailors', Dennards', Everharts', and Rollinses'. (I especially liked going by the Everharts' because with five kids, their living room always looked like Christmas!)

We even had an unofficial "sergeant at arms" at church. With a loving smile, firm voice, and hand on your shoulder, Woody would always steer you back to the middle of the road when things got a little out of hand. Woody seemed to show up whenever we started to act up.

My Sunday school teachers from 7th grade on:
- 7th—Wayne Erickson
- 8th—Phil Everhart Sr.
- 9th—Sam Ailor
- 10th—Bill Nelson
- 11th—Chet Robbins
- 12th—Francis Jones

Alice Erickson remembers her preschool and elementary Sunday school workers:
- Bessie Sparrow
- Bennie Russell
- Ammie Garber
- Bessie Amory
- Kathryn Bully

Nothing unusual here: Alice Erickson taking a ride on a vine while leading a senior adult bus trip (2)

Others remember the following teachers/leaders (lots of people left out):

Sunday school—Katie Bully, Henry Dixon, Mr. White, Debbie Spencer, Mary Etta Brown, John Dawson, Pat Corlett, Alice Erickson, Billy Byrd

Sunbeams, GAs, Acteens—Martha Ailor, Belinda Adams, Nancy Sandford, Lucille Everhart, Ellen Sullivan, Alice Erickson, Nancy Lee Jones

Lots of guys were in Sunday school and regular school together. This included Billy Forbes, Dick and Billy Everett, Jack Shepherd, Cliff Morris, Tom Matthews, Don Miller, Bill Nelson, Vernon Rollins, Allen Turnbull, John Robbins, Billy Hughes, and Roddy Diggs.

Barry Wood, Francis Jones, and Ann Wood (3)

Marion Hankinson: VBS 1963 (2)

Sam Ailor and Cecil Kirby (2)

I remember Sam Ailor, on the first day of Sunday school class, telling us his last name was Ailor. He said it is like "Jailor" without the "J."

And I still remember a puzzle that Chet Robbins had for us on the blackboard one Sunday morning. He said it was a puzzle for us to figure out. The letters were written on a wooden sign outside a saloon in the old West.

TOTI
EMUL
ETO
=
"To Tie Mule To"

And that, of course, reminds me of a riddle that Faye Estes, one of the secretaries at the Peninsula Baptist Association, once recited to me:

M R DUCKS
M R NOT
O S M R
C M WANGS
L I B
M R DUCKS

Chapter 21

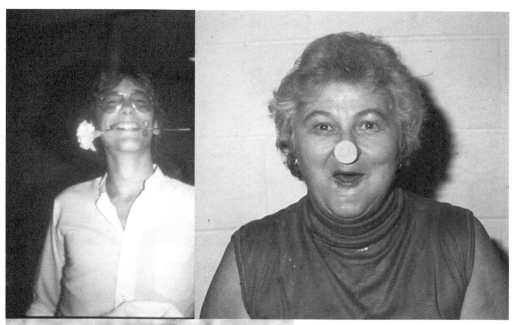

Above left: Bret Godfrey (3)

Above right: Iris Dunn (2)

Left: Dawn Lilley (2)

Betty Corbett (above) (2)

Hampton Baptist Church

Raynelle Ewing (2)

Martha Feathers (2)

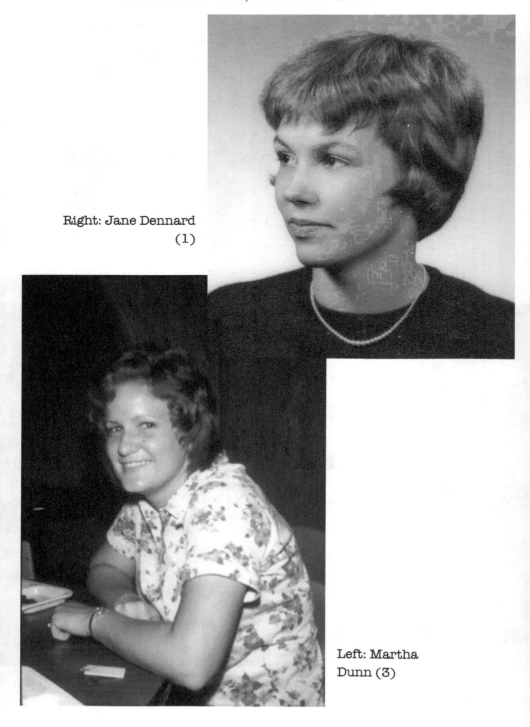

Right: Jane Dennard (1)

Left: Martha Dunn (3)

Left: Sandy Aust (5)

Below: Amy Hurt (1966) (2)

Chapter 22
Youth Retreats

Phil Everhart, Marianne Gaesser, Jimmy Allison, and
Martha Dunn on the bus heading for a youth retreat at
Wakefield (1966) (1)

Events at Eagle Eyrie, especially Senior High Weekend and other retreats were the big activities that the youth and young adults enjoyed the most back in the 1960s. I think we had more chaperones than we needed at Senior High Weekend, but that was because we had a bunch of first- and second-year college students who wanted an excuse to tag along.

Until Bill Hurt came, the supply of youth workers from Chapter 20 was in charge of the retreats. After Bill arrived on the scene, he became the leader and the planner. Early on, we would meet at someone's home to plan a youth retreat. About the same time that Bill came on, the small conference room (next to Chester's office on the second floor, above the main church office) was where the youth retreats were planned. When Jay Russ became our youth minister, all of that changed. (We will get to that in a bit.)

One of the most enjoyable parts of youth retreats was the planning. I can remember many others saying the same thing. I can't recall everyone who helped plan, but I do have memories of planning meetings being times of laughter and fun. In the midst of all that, the actual event was scheduled and planned. I will admit, at least during the meetings I attended, that it probably took a little longer than one would expect because of all the interruptions and "rabbit-chasing."

For this chapter, I will be laying out the things that stick in my mind about HBC youth retreats over the years. I have already mentioned that in the 1960s, everyone was expected to wear long pants to the serious parts of the retreat (Bible study, worship, etc.), but we got wear shorts the rest of the time. That policy, as you know, met its doom when Bill Hurt and the invited preacher for the weekend forgot to bring any long pants. We were given permission to wear shorts for all sessions that weekend with the understanding that afterward, the rule would return. As you also know, it is hard to go back to a rule once it's been broken. And so it happened with the "long pants rule."

During the early years, we went to Camp Wakefield (in Wakefield, Virginia) and used a camp in Virginia Beach (Camp Owaissa). By the time Jay Lawson and Jimmy Ailor came on the scene, the Peninsula Baptist Association had established a camp (Eastover) in Surry County, and most of the Peninsula Baptist churches held their retreats there. Eastover was purchased in 1972, and the buildings were constructed soon after. However, even Lawson and Ailor used Camp Wakefield and Camp Owaissa.

MIDNIGHT FISHING

One event I remember well because I got caught in the middle of new challenge. I was in my first year of college and deemed a worthy chaperone for the youth retreat, which was in Virginia Beach. This was my first chance to act like an adult! I felt really good about being a chaperone, but I would soon regret this milestone of maturity!

The camp was located not far from the coastline. Roddy McKendree and Scotty Miller (both still in high school at the time) brought their fishing rods. A fishing pier was not too far from the camp, and they were told it was OK to fish during free periods, as long as an adult was with them. I can't remember if they fished during the first afternoon free time. When evening came, we enjoyed the usual activities, including a campfire. Then it was off to bed in order to be fresh for the next morning.

I was awakened about 1:00 a.m. by someone who told me to go outside. When I did, I saw Alice Erickson and several other adults talking. I was informed that Roddy and Scotty were missing from their room.

Someone suggested that we wake Bill Hurt, who was in another room, but to do so discretely so as not to wake up the others.

Alice said that she could find him with just a flashlight because she knew "what his pajamas look like!" The humor in that comment was lost in the gravity of the situation, but it has been remembered, to Alice's chagrin, and we still like to give her grief about it. She embarked on her quest and returned about five minutes later with Bill in tow.

Scotty Miller and Phil Everhart at what looks to be a paper drive collection at HBC (2)

It didn't take too much thought to figure out what had probably happened. Someone suggested that Scotty and Roddy had probably sneaked off to the pier to go fishing. We couldn't see them anywhere around the camp, and so nothing else made much sense. Several of us headed toward the pier, about 100 yards away, while a couple remained in the camp to keep an eye on things and in case the two guys returned from elsewhere.

Indeed, they had gone to the pier to do a little night fishing. I can't remember if they had caught anything. We read them the "riot act," they packed up their gear, and we all returned to the camp. All the adults agreed that we could best discuss this in the morning after getting a little sleep.

No one was the worse for wear in the morning, but the transgression still had to be dealt with after breakfast. The guys were sheepish and apologetic. Several of the adults gath-

Roddy McKendree at an RA camping trip in Gloucester (1)

ered to decide what the appropriate consequence would be. I remember being told that I was one of the "adults" and needed to be in on the conversation. We talked with Roddy and Scotty and then among ourselves. I truly cannot remember who spoke in favor of what outcome, but I do remember the results of our meeting:

1) We realized that the guys had not wanted to cause problems or give us grief. They had just wanted to go fishing (although they obviously had enjoyed the sneaking out too).

2) The main thing we tried to impress upon them and the rest of the youth was our worry about what could have happened. Accidents do happen around water, especially in the dark.

3) They had broken camp rules, which specified that campers not go to the water without an adult. It was also a rule that leaving the campground without permission would lead to being sent home.

Therefore, our ruling was that they be sent home. The main reason for this decision was that they had acted in a way that was dangerous. Obviously, we didn't want anyone else to think they could do the same thing or something similar. Roddy and Scotty accepted their punishment and did not seem terribly upset. Their parents came to pick them up that morning.

Not all the youth took this as calmly as the two culprits. When I got back to the guy's dorm later in the morning, I found all my clothes packed and sitting out on the front porch. This was courtesy of Jim Ailor! Jim refused to speak to me for the rest of the day. I could not be upset by this. I realized that this was the first event in which I was not just "one of the guys" anymore. I felt really bad for Roddy and Scotty. I also learned that once you become an "adult," you cannot "go home again"! Fortunately, Jim Ailor got over it and is currently one of my best friends.

I was recently talking with Lucille Everhart who was also on the retreat. We both agreed that if we had it to do over, we would suggest a punishment short of being sent home.

GIVE ME A "J"!

You might remember that during 1970s, a lot of the teenagers got into the Jesus Movement. Ailor was one of them. You might also remember Jimmy sporting an afro during that time.

Being in the Jesus Movement meant, among other things, that you were very vocal about your commitment to Jesus Christ. One of the fads at the time was a Jesus cheer. This was similar to when high-school cheerleaders lead a cheer with the name of the school. Someone would shout out, "Give me a J! Give me an E! Give me an S! Give me a U! Give me another S! What have you got? JE-SUS!" This was done with a lot of emotion and volume as the rest of the group shouted "Jesus!" several times.

Ailor did this a lot, and one of the places one would hear the cheer was on youth retreats. One year, I got in the spirit and started the cheer, momentarily forgetting that my poor spelling could get me in trouble.

A large group were playing volleyball, and the ball got bumped onto a low roof at the camp. I climbed up to the roof and rescued the volleyball. But before throwing it down, I yelled, "Give me a J!" I got an animated response and so continued with the cheer. Without realizing it, I proceed to shout out the letters: J, U, S, E, S. I realized at the end that I had mixed up the letters, but at that point, there was nothing to do but yell as loud as I could: "What have you got? JESUS!"

SWAN LAKE

One of my most enjoyable memories at Wakefield was when Bill Hurt asked a group of young adults to do a parody of a classic ballet. We danced Swan Lake to music played on a tape recorder. This recital was performed around the campfire on Friday in the late evening. The highlight of our performance was the tutus that Bill had gotten one of the ladies of the church to sew for us. We only performed for about ten minutes, but it was beautiful. The other ballerinas included Bill Sasser, John Robbins, Don Miller, and Cliff Morris.

SUZANNA'S MIDNIGHT CONCERT

I was on this retreat and can remember the incident, but most of the details came from Ellen Sullivan and Suzanna (Dunn) McKendree. Suzanna Dunn was still a youth when the Sullivans first joined the church. She and Ellen eventually became best friends and remained so even after the Sullivans moved back to Jerry's home. Both Jerry and Ellen have passed away, but Suzanna remains very close to all three of the daughters, especially the youngest, Lee Ellen.

Something happened on a retreat during those early years that could have sidetracked their relationship. But as such things often do, the tension helped to cement the friendship instead.

A sidenote to all this is that my own friendship with the Sullivans dated back to the time Bill Hurt asked Jerry and Ellen to lead this particular youth retreat. I was also on the planning committee, and on a Saturday morning in the spring, Bill Hurt got the Hampton Baptist van and took a group of us over to Wakefield, where the retreat would be held.

The thing I remember most about that Saturday trip is that Bill suggested we eat lunch at the Virginia Diner on the way over, which was fine with me because I loved the food there and so did the rest of the group. The trip itself got us all excited about what the retreat would hold for Hampton Baptist youth. Anyway, after much planning, both at the Sullivans' home and the church, the retreat was planned and ready to go.

It was on this retreat that Suzanna Dunn got it in her head that the curfew was way too early. By "way too early," Suzanna thought that 1:00 or 2:00 a.m. was a more appropriate time for lights-out. Not surprisingly, Ellen (who had been appointed director of the retreat) and the other leaders disagreed. The curfew had been set for 11:30 p.m., which they felt was more than fair. But after several discussions between the youth and the adults, the curfew may have been moved back to midnight.

The youth still felt short-changed, and Suzanna was hell-bent on making it later. All the discussions finally dwindled down to the "last men standing": Ellen Sullivan and Suzanna Dunn. Neither was going to budge on their preferred curfew time.

A lot of the youth and adults were in the dining hall as the clock ticked toward midnight. Suzanna and Ellen might have continued to talk until around 11:45. Then Ellen acted as director and told everyone to head for the dorms. They had fifteen minutes to get ready for lights-out at midnight.

Everyone started to move. Ellen and the rest of us headed for the exit. Suzanna, however, moved to her drums, which had been set up in the dining hall, and started playing. Ellen waited at the door and asked Suzanna if she were coming. Suzanna kept on playing the drums, now a little louder.

Ellen thought that if she left and gave Suzanna time to cool off, the issue would work itself out and everyone, including Suzanna, would go to bed. But Suzanna played even louder. It didn't seem like she was going to stop, and so Ellen thought, "Fine, if she wants to stay up and play the drums all night, she can."

Ellen returned to the dining hall and told Suzanna that she could stay up as long as she wanted, playing the drums to her heart's content. "But know this," Ellen said, "I will make sure you are up at 7:00 a.m. with the rest of us, and you will stay awake all day!"

In fairness to Suzanne, she did not play a long time after curfew, just long enough to make her point. In fairness to Ellen, she thought it was a little longer than Suzanna remembers!

This was one of those situations that could have gone in several directions. Thankfully, after that confrontation, the two of them were drawn together, and a beautiful friendship developed in the years after.

Lynne Everhart, Suzanna Dunn, and Phil Everhart waiting in line at church (2)

LEFTOVER COMMUNION GRAPE JUICE

I remember one retreat—I think it was at Virginia Beach—where we had communion on the beach at sunrise. It was an uplifting experience.

After the service was over, Lucille Everhart and I, as well as a couple of others, stayed behind to clean up. We picked up everything but realized we had several communion cups still filled with grape juice. We had a serious, five-minute discussion about what to do with the juice. Nothing theological was brought up; we simply didn't know the proper way to dispose of leftover communion juice. We thought of pouring it out, but we were just not comfortable doing that. In the end, we drank all the leftover juice. Fortunately, I don't think it affected our future in any way.

IN THE DARK AT CAMP WAKEFIELD

I pulled one of the oldest tricks in the book to get Jim Ailor and a girl back to camp for an evening meeting. I didn't often succeed in getting one over on Jim Ailor, but this time, I succeeded.

Several of the youth were missing as we got ready for an after-dark conference in the dining hall. Everyone was fairly quickly found (they were not hiding but just not nearby) and sent to the meeting place. Soon, only two were unaccounted for: Jim Ailor and a girl whose name I've forgotten.

The leaders spread out and began to look. I was told to check out an unused building at the edge of the camp. I ran off without a flashlight, and when I got to the building and tried the light switch, there was apparently no electricity connected to this old building.

I was sure they were in there, but I knew I would never find them in the pitch blackness. So I simply yelled, "Hey, Jim! I know you are in there, so come on out, and let's go to the meeting." If he were in the building, I did not expect Jim to bite. But he did. Ten seconds later the two of them walked out, and the three of us headed for the cafeteria.

AILOR AND THE BARKING DOG

This is the one that made me think that perhaps Jim Ailor did have a special connection to God. I can't remember if this was during the summer that Jimmy and Jay were co-directors of the youth ministry or another year, when Jimmy was in college or seminary and helping out with the retreat. Anyway, I do remember the events of this episode vividly. Jimmy was in charge of leading a devotional at the campfire, which was around 10:00 p.m. This was at Camp Wakefield.

About a half hour before we gathered, a dog started barking, loud and clear. The dog was not at the camp, but neither was it too far from us, and it was making a racket. I remember thinking, "I hope the dog shuts up or someone brings it inside before we begin the serious part of the campfire."

We did the usual—s'mores, drinks, and songs—around the roaring fire. It was a great bonfire! The dog was a distraction but not overly so for the raucous events so far. I kept hoping and praying that the dog would quiet down before Jimmy started, but the dog was not listening to my prayers.

Finally, it was time for Jimmy to begin his part of the program. He grabbed his Bible and stood to speak to us. The dog kept barking. Jimmy paused for a second and then spoke to the group. "Folks," he said, "that dog is going to cause a problem for me when I'm trying to talk to you this evening. So here is what I want us to do. I am going to lead us in prayer and ask God to quiet the dog. I want each of you to say a silent—no pun intended—prayer for the same thing."

This is what the "super-spiritual" Mike Haywood thought at that moment. (Fortunately, I did not verbalize this.) "Jim, I wish you had not said that out loud because that dog is not going to shut up. It's been barking all night, and that is going to make you look bad when what you ask God for in front of all these kids does not happen."

But Jim started praying, and about thirty seconds later, the dog stopped barking! "OK," I thought, "let's see how long this will last."

Jim finished his prayer and told us that now we could proceed with the devotional. Jimmy began, and the dog kept quiet. He spent about thirty minutes speaking. No one said a word, and we didn't hear the the dog again that night.

THE WATERMELON CAPER

Since I am telling on everyone else, I guess it is only fair to tell a story on myself.

After work one Friday, I was driving over to Wakefield for a retreat with John Robbins, Bill Sasser, and Cliff Morris. On the way, we passed a watermelon patch. (More than a patch actually, it was a rather large parcel of land.) As we passed by, someone in the car said, "It would be nice to have some watermelon at the camp."

I thought, "Why not?" And so I pulled to the side of the road.

The road was deserted, and there didn't seem to be anyone in the field. There was not even a house in sight. We ran to the edge of the field, and two of us grabbed one.

And that is how, on the way to a church youth retreat, I stole a watermelon. I would like to point out that I never did anything like it again.

MUDDY EASTOVER

It's a funny thing, slipping a vehicle into a ditch at Eastover.

One year, I went to Eastover for a youth retreat with Jay Russ and the teens from Hampton Baptist. I could only stay the evening, but I was there long enough to see Jay Russ, our fearless leader, drive the church van into a muddy lane. It took a tractor and eight guys to get it out. Jay made me a part of the excitement by telling the Eastover camp staff that *I* had been the one to get it stuck.

Oh, and it gets better. A year later, Jay had two counselors—Mark Taylor and Talmadge Barbour—who had four-wheel vehicles. On the last morning of the retreat, several of the guys, including Jay, went out four-wheeling.

Later in the morning, they had to ask one of the Eastover staff to find a farmer to pull one of them out.

And the beat goes on.

Jay Lawson, Alice Erickson, and John Erickson preparing to head to Eastover (3)

Chapter 23
The Tallest Climbing Wall on the East Coast

Aaron Whittington, Chris Ellis, Jim Puckett, and Trent Allison on the tall wall at Eastover (4)

In the late 1980s or early 1990s, Harald Aadahl, Jay Russ, and I decided to build a confidence course in the wooded area behind the swimming pool and cabins at Eastover. It consisted of several initiatives for individual or group participation. The only thing out of the ordinary was proposed by Harald.

Usually, a confidence course consists of two scaling walls, one shorter and another taller. The shorter wall is usually eight feet high and the taller is twelve feet. Harald decided that we would make the taller wall a *bit* taller than usual—fourteen feet. In the end, we had probably built the tallest climbing wall on the East Coast. But it could be scaled if the teens worked together. The confidence course and walls are no longer in existence, but they were a lot of fun for the decades they lasted.

Kneeling: Angela Peele, Mary Williams, and Paul Pavlik; Front row: Molly O'Bryan, Corinna Powell, Emily Shuart, Leith Taylor Smith, Kaitlyn Rejzer, Sarah Martinez, Jenny Field, Amy Shuart, Katie O'Bryan, Laura Williams, Meagan Tucker, Mark Taylor, and Sandy Everett. Back row: Gary Powell, Will McKendree, Talmadge Barbour, Katie Hanson, Will Rawls, Juli McKendree, and Betsy Trimble among others at the high wall at Eastover (4)

Cindy Garris getting ready to
wash Jo Tillery's feet (3)

A classic game you might remember playing on a retreat or other youth gathering involves a plank. The person in the middle of the plank is blindfolded and told to put their hands on the shoulders of the two people kneeling in front of them. It is explained to the blindfolded that they are going to be raised about three feet off the ground.

Foot-washing was a popular activity in the 1970s. After you got your feet washed, you picked another person and took them up to the stage and washed their feet.

Then, while keeping their hands on the shoulders of the two people in front, they will jump off and try to land without losing balance.

Here is the trick: the two people holding the plank at each end will only raise it about six inches off the ground. They will jiggle it as though having a tough time lifting the plank and the person up to the proper height. Meanwhile, the two people facing the blindfolded person will slowly rise, giving the blindfolded a feeling of being raised up high.

The time I was blindfolded, I would have bet money that I had been lifted up several feet. By shaking the plank, the person on it loses their sense of perception. You must do this one time to understand the full impact of the trick. When you jump, you expect a three-foot descent, and so you are totally unprepared when you hit solid ground after a short fall.

Craig Michael on the right end of the board (3)

Cindy Garris, Jo Tillery, Cindy Lawson, Margaret Tillery, and Elizabeth Patrick watching a game in the recreation area at Eastover (3)

Terry Laufer at Eastover (3)

Lunchtime at Eastover (3)

Patricia and Craig Michael getting ready to lead a
devotional (3)

Branch and Jay Lawson at Eastover (3)

Jimmy Ailor at Camp Owaissa; probably Renee and Lynn
Sullivan opposite Jimmy (3)

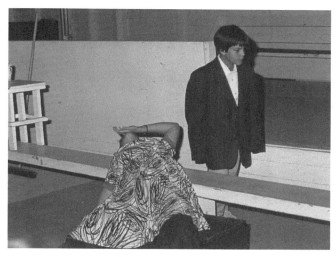

Performing a skit at the youth retreat (3)

Ellen Sullivan at Camp Wakefield (3)

JERRY SULLIVAN DEMOLISHES
AT CAMP WAKEFIELD

Jerry Sullivan, the ping-pong king of Camp Wakefield (3)

One year in the early 1970s, Bill Hurt asked Ellen Sullivan
to direct the youth retreat at Camp Wakefield. That was the year
that Suzanna Dunn played her drums well into the night to protest
the early(?) curfew. (See the previous chapter.) That was the same
retreat when everyone (youth and adults) found out just how good
Jerry Sullivan was at ping-pong.

Jerry did not lose a game that weekend. I can't remember exactly, but I do believe that no one got more than ten points on any game to twenty-one that they played against Jerry. Jerry was definitely the king of ping-pong!

This reminds me of the time I went to visit the Sullivans at base housing for Langley Field. They always had table tennis set up under the side porch roof. Lynn Sullivan asked me if I wanted to play a game, and I said yes. So I grabbed a paddle and began to warm up with Lynn . . . or so I thought! After I hit one that missed the table, Lynn informed me that she was winning five to zero! I could not convince her that we hadn't started playing yet. It did not make a lot of difference because she beat me pretty bad even after I started playing for real!

JAY RUSS AND THE WHOLE-FLOOR WRESTLING MATCHES

Laying out the mattresses for the wrestling matches at Eastover: Aaron Whittington, Jim Puckett, Brooke Puckett, Debbie Puckett, and Sarah Trimble (4)

I think that many of the youth would tell you that one of the main attractions of youth retreats during the Jay Russ era were the massive wrestling matches held in the middle of the X-Building at Eastover. They would lay mattresses on the floor, on which they would compete in one-on-one and group events. Jay said it took most of the mattresses from the four dorm rooms. That did make it a lot safer. I think Jay used the "it is better to ask forgiveness than permission" method for informing the Eastover staff.

I didn't get to go on many of the youth retreats then (my summers being filled up with PBA events), but one of my fondest memories involves Jay, Mark Taylor, and a skit titled "You Can Go to Hell!" The skit was comprised of young people being asked how they would handle different life situations. They would be presented with three possible reactions. One was the world's way, one the Christian way, and the third, an off-the-wall way. Those who took the world's way were immediately told, "Well, you can go to hell!"

The other great line from the skit was spoken by Mark Taylor. When asked how he would handle a specific problem, Mark's reply was "Oh, in that case, I always call the psychic hotline!" That was met by the "Go to hell" response!

MESSY GAMES

Messy games have probably been around forever, but they became really popular at youth events beginning in the 1970s. One of the biggies was one we usually played on youth retreats. We would pass out shaving cream, fruit pies, flour, and anything else messy and harmless. In a place like Eastover, we would give boundaries, outside of which no one could go. While the game is in progress, participants can run down anyone they choose and plaster them with whatever substance they had. Supposedly, you were not allowed to go after anyone who is out of bounds. (Some youth have been known to violate that rule!) The next couple of photos were taken during a HBC youth retreat at Eastover.

Sometimes, if a youth or leader lost at another competitive game, they would have to sit and wait to be splattered. I was also the target of this activity at many a Campus Life—Youth for Christ—club. Lots of adults do not approve of this. I usually refer such adults to the website for Youth Specialties, which is considered the premier source for youth group games. Several of us used to go to seminars they conducted. They usually had a photo on the front page of their website similar to the one below.

The Pucketts at Eastover: Jim, Brooke,
Debbie, and Jim (4)

Above: I'm not sure, but I think that is Chris Ellis, second from the right in the back.

Left: If I am correct, the above situation led to this photo of Chris cleaning up after a messy game. (4)

Right: Mike
Haywood after
a messy game
(1978) on a
Peninsula Bap-
tist youth camp
(1)

Jimmy Michael, Bill Sinclair, and Harry Hubbard at
Eastover (3)

Above: Gary Lewis and Susan Lilley (far right) at Camp Wakefield (3)

Below: Susan Williams at lunch at Eastover (3)

Chapter 24
Church Nights 1986–1990

1986
"THE PRIZE IS SLIGHT"
(OR "YOUR GUESS IS AS GOOD AS MINE")

Bill Hurt was the host of the show. Richard Everett introduced new contestants.

Contestants, including Chester Brown, competed to win the prizes. Most questions involved the contestants guessing numbers and the winner being the one who got closest to the correct number. One of the questions was how many pictures were in the church directory (answer: 261).

One question that did not involve numbers had to do with roles in the church. The contestant had to match four jobs with women: Claudia Ulsh, Raynelle Ewing, Patti Robbins, and Betty Miller.

1987
"CLB XXV"
"THE WILDCARD GAME"
"THE BROWN BOWL"

This was a celebration of Chester Brown's twenty-fifth anniversary. Since Church Night is held in January, Bill used another popular January event as the inspiration: the Super Bowl.

Our bowl game was modeled after a church service, with Jay Russ playing the part of John Madden. Jay illustrated the service on an overhead projector.

The cheerleaders were not named in the script, but here is one of their cheers:

Chester, Chester, that's our man
If he can't do it nobody can
He's got the books
He's got the looks
And you can see we're his biggest fans!

1988
"IRAN? YOU RAN? WHO RAN HBC?"

Richard Pulley conducted interviews, trying to identify the author of the plot to sell WMU cookbooks to the Methodists and give the money to the Lottie Moonies!

Jay Russ played the part of J. (Jollie) South. One of the skits was an interrogation of Jay:

Senator:	You were in charge of the gift wrap?
J:	Yes, I was in charge of the whole operation.
Senator:	And what did you do with the money?
J:	I gave it to Ayatollah Khomeini.
Senator:	For what purpose?
J:	He had taken my youth group hostage.
Senator:	You used other people's money to pay a ransom for hostages?
J:	Heck, no. I was paying him to keep the kids. I didn't want them back!

Senator:	Did Pastor Brown have knowledge of this?
J:	You bet he did. In fact, he approved the whole thing. Two of the kids were his. I was only doing what my superior ordered!

Later, Richard interviewed J. South's secretary, Fawn Bundick (Sandra Bundick), who came to the stage carrying a paper shredder.

Dollie Lee Jones, "The Manager," is named the organizer of the HBC cookbook scheme.

1989
"UNCONVENTIONAL CONVENTION"

This Church Night was based on a political convention.

Church Night Committee: Jimmy Michael, Linda Riddle, Gary Powell, Beth McKendree, Ida Barnes

Bill Hurt and Neil Cox were the anchor reporters.

Other participants included Martha Ailor, Terry Ulch, George Gratto, Claude Corbett, Lit Little, Dottie Lee Jones, Betty Miller, Gary Lewis, Jay Russ, Wallace Hicks, Buck Chandler, Matt Parron, Stan Ewing, Chester Brown, Mary Etta Brown, and Roy Powell.

All of the above gave a speech or presentation. Jay Russ and Gary Lewis engaged in a debate. Matt Parron represented the youth group party.

1990
"THE SHADOW KNOWS"

(*Who* knows what goes on within the walls of HBC? The Shadow knows.)

Church Night Committee: Tom Bundick, Joanne Barbour, Bryan Lilley, Elizabeth Buchen, Steve Barnes, Beverly Doyer

Renovation of the vestibules and the completion of the stained-glass window installation was a major item. At times, it seemed this project would never get finished, but on November 5, we held the dedication service. Hats off to Cynthia Lawson who chaired this committee.

Carlton Yates was the Finance Planning Committee chairman. Dottie Lee Jones was the WMU director. In order to reach the Lottie Moon offering goal, Dottie Lee set up a lottery called the "Dottie Lee Lottery for Lottie Plan," or the "Dottie Lottie" for short. George Gratto was the Sunday school director.

Jay Russ was ordained to the gospel ministry. He was now entitled to be called Reverend Russ, but to most of us, he was still just Jay.

Jack and Ruby Shepherd made appearances. And Anne Rosser joined us this year as associate minister.

Chapter 25

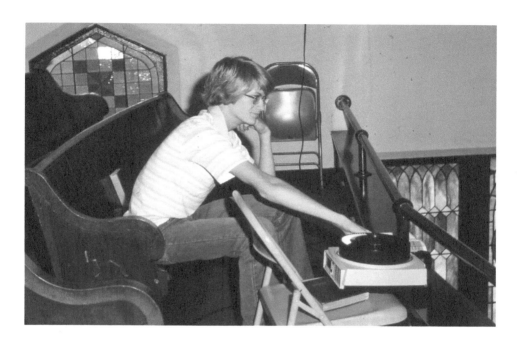

Above: Thomas Bundick running the slide projector in the church balcony (2)

Left: Margaret Allison, probably at Bible school (2)

Mary Etta, Ann Kilgore, Ida Patrick, and Woody Patrick (2)

Martha Ailor
(2)

This was taken at a PBA RA baseball league game. Jimmy Allison is wearing a sling, and thus not playing; the rest are Howard Stone, Mike Haywood, Margie Whitcomb, Christine Vick, and Alan Vick. (Do you remember where the Dresden Arms apartments used to be?) (3)

Harry Hubbard on a senior adult garden tour (2)

Mary Cibinic, Eunice Rountree, and Everett Whitley playing
a board game at a senior adult social (2)

Velma Jean Allison and Mary Cibinic waiting on lunch (2)

Deacons' retreat: Henry Dixon, Milford Rollins, and Bob
Zigler (facing) (2)

Left: John Kersey leading a hymn sing. (2)

Below: Jerry Sullivan attends to Lynn Sullivan's foot. (I'm guessing she was running around without shoes.) (3)

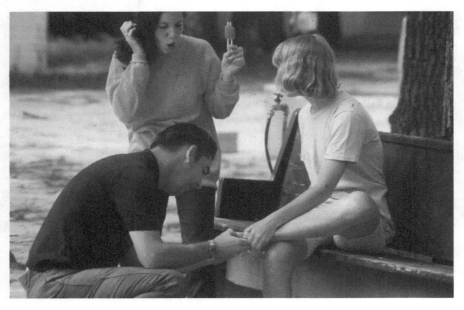

Chapter 26
Weekends at Eagle Eyrie

Cindy Parsons (3)

You've already heard some about the Senior High Weekend at Eagle Eyrie. This annual event, at the beginning of March, meant a lot to all of us. After graduating from high school, many of us served as chaperones, which extended the experience for a couple of years. As a consequence, Eagle Eyrie will always be a special place for me and countless others who attended events there. I also spent several Royal Ambassador weekend retreats at the conference center on the outskirts of Lynchburg.

The lodges at Eagle Eyrie are for the most part owned by Southern Baptist associations throughout the state. PAL Lodge stands for Peninsula Association Lodge. PBA churches pay the association a fee for each student who stays at the lodge. The association covers the cost of repairs and upkeep. First choice is given to churches from the PBA.

If a church from an association that doesn't own a lodge wants to rent space, they can check with Eagle Eyrie to find out if any lodge space is available. I can remember so many people from Hampton Baptist going to Senior High Weekend that there was not enough room in PAL, and we had to put a number of them in another lodge.

Dawn Lilly and Becky Riddle at Eagle Eyrie (3)

JIM AILOR RINGS THE BELL

This was a long time ago, but some of you might remember the well-enforced curfew at Eagle Eyrie. Paid staff would patrol the campus, making sure that everyone was in their lodge by midnight. As I recall, this was not a big deal with HBC youth because you could hang out in the big front room of the lodge for as long as you wanted to stay up. We often did.

From time to time, a group would try to sneak out of their lodge for whatever reason. But I don't remember any destructive pranks being pulled during these times. Usually, the group sneaking out would be found by one of the night watchmen and ushered back to their lodge.

In the midst of the lodges was a bell on a tall wooden stand. I really don't know what they used the bell for, but I think I may have heard it rung early in the evening to mark the time of an event or gathering.

One year (I think 1966 or 1967), when I was going as a chaperone, Jimmy, who was a student, came to me with a request. He didn't need me to OK the idea, but he just wanted one of the "adults" to know what was going to happen and so be prepared. It was not a big deal, he said. He and a couple of others—Phil Everhart Jr. and Roddy McKendree were two in on this escapade— wanted to sneak out after midnight and ring the bell.

It was pretty obvious that the reason to do this was to prove to themselves and the adults (the ones who did not know this was coming) that they could pull it off without getting caught. I said, "OK, whatever," and I was happy to keep the secret and see what they could accomplish.

Prior to the Senior High Weekend, Ailor and his band of merry men schemed. I even ran into them at church as they were planning the caper. They put a lot of work into the planning and were confident of their success. They figured they would not have much of a problem sneaking around the grounds once they were loose, but they needed a good strategy for getting in and out of PAL Lodge. That made sense, but I actually had no doubts that they would pull it off.

On that Friday afternoon, I arrived at the Hampton Baptist parking lot, and everyone started piling into the cars. Hampton Baptist always had a good number of high-school students going on this particular trip. Ailor came to me to make sure I would not rat them out, and I assured him that their secret was safe with me. The event included two nights at Eagle Eyrie, but Jim wanted to pull this off the first night before anything could go wrong.

We arrived at Eagle Eyrie in time for supper and then trekked up to PAL Lodge to move in and claim our bunks. After this, we headed down to the auditorium for the first evening's program. Ailor and his group added a detour, going by the pole with the bell on top. It was still there, as it had been for several years. When they got to the gathering (later than the rest), they found where I was sitting. Ailor, Everhart, McKendree, and the rest of the gang, who were up for some nightime extracurricular activities, all sat in the same row. They were refining their plans even at this late hour. I reminded Jimmy that I was not going to help them in any way except not to blow the whistle on their conspiracy.

I think that Cecil Marsh was in charge of Senior High Weekend during that time. He got up to go over the general schedule for the weekend before introducing the speakers. Having finished his announcements, Cecil told the assembled group that there would be one major change this weekend.

"This year," Cecil said, "we are instituting a new policy. As far as Eagle Eyrie is concerned, there will be *no curfew*! Each individual lodge can set a curfew for their students, but as far as we are concerned, you can stay out all night!"

I wish I had a photo of the faces of the three guys to my right. They were devastated. Three months of planning down the drain. I leaned over to Ailor and whispered, "Perhaps we can get our leaders at PAL to set a curfew for you to break, but you might have a problem *sneaking* to the bell with half of Eagle Eyrie walking all over the mountain!" Jimmy hit me, but not too hard. I think the guys did walk down to the bell and ring it after midnight!

THE OLD HOUSE AND THE BLOCKHOUSE ON THE MOUNTAIN

I remember two side trips while at Eagle Eyrie. Both destinations were on the mountain, on the opposite side of the highway from the conference center. You could cross over the highway by traversing a walking bridge. After crossing the bridge and following a dirt path past some tennis courts, you would be on your way up the mountain. After a distance, you would come across a short cinder-block building on the right side of the path. It looked dangerous and forbidden . . . but not as spooky as the old abandoned house farther up the trail. The house was located in a wooded area on the right, a ways off the path.

We visited that house during several Senior High Weekends. It was a great site for photos. The one story I remember about the house was one of the years that Phil Everhart Sr. was a youth group leader. We had plans to go to the house in the evening, and Phil said he would go with us.

To get an early start, we wanted to skip a fellowship time in the auditorium. Phil said that we had to go to the assembly for at least a short time before heading out to the house. We agreed.

About a dozen of us were planning to go, and so we filed into the conference room and took seats near the back. About ten minutes into the meeting, Phil looked at our group and said,

"OK, we can go now." We lost no time in escaping, which was not too noticeable in such a large-group setting, and there were still people coming in late.

It was a fun trip that night, and we took a lot of photos at the house. The group was mostly from HBC, but we had made a few new friends who accompanied us on the hike.

The ruins of the old house on the mountain at Eagle Eyrie: Sydney Garris, Margaret Northern, Ann Ailor, Kenny Higgins, Jeannie Hankinson, Eleanor Patrick, John Mann (Mary Etta's brother), and me standing; Betty Northern and a girl we met at Eagle Eyrie kneeling (1)

Left: Phil Everhart and Ann Ailor posing in the ruins. (1)

Previous: At the cinder-block house is Ann Ailor, the girl we met while at Eagle Eyrie, Sydney Garris (hidden), Kenny Higgins, John Mann, and Eleanor Patrick. (I am not sure who is being carried, but they had a hole in their shoe.) (1)

During the day, we had to make the blockhouse look scary. That is a "headless" Jim Ailor carrying Phil Everhart's head. The others are Lee Feathers, Roddy McKendree, Tommy O'Bryan, and Craig Michaels. (1)

"GET ME TO LYNCHBURG, AND I WILL GET YOU TO EAGLE EYRIE"

My favorite memory about Eagle Eyrie is not about something that happened there but rather about *getting* there. This was a Senior High Weekend, and several of us in college were going as "leaders." The group in my car included Mary Etta Mann, Cliff Morris, David Levy, and probably a couple of others.

I didn't mind driving, but I was not sure how to get to the conference center. (This was not unusual, as directions and navigation were never my strong suits.) Most of the groups had gone up right after lunch, but my group could not get away until later. I was not sure how to find Eagle Eyrie, but Mary Etta kept saying, "If you can get me to Lynchburg, I will get us to Eagle Eyrie!" So I drove us into Lynchburg, without getting lost even once, although we stopped for dinner because we knew we would be too late to eat at Eagle Eyrie.

We were all sitting at one table, which was close to another table with a young couple and their son, who was about four years old. Mary Etta was teaching school at the time. The four-year-old kept staring at her. The boy's mother told him to be polite and not stare at the lady. The admonishment didn't faze the young boy; he kept looking at Mary Etta, and they exchanged smiles.

We were close enough to hear the conversation at the other table. The boy told his parents that "the lady" was very pretty and nice. The parents agreed with him. Then the boy asked, "Can we take her home with us?" Everybody at both tables laughed, except for the four-year-old who continued to give Mary Etta the eye. Fortunately, it was time for us to depart, and so we exchanged pleasantries with the parents while the kid kept staring at Mary Etta.

We left and thought we were heading for Eagle Eyrie. About ten minutes later, we came to the Lynchburg city limits. I asked Mary Etta, "Where do we go from here?"

"I don't have the slightest idea," she said.

"But you said—"

"Oh, I know what I said. I just figured if we got this far, we would find our way there."

It gets better. We pulled into a service station, where I got gas and asked the attendant if he knew how to get to Eagle Eyrie. Even after I explained what Eagle Eyrie was, he was still mystified and had no idea where it was located. We drove a little farther into Lynchburg and stopped at another gas station. Same results. The people had never heard of it. A couple of guys got out of the car with me at the third gas station. I think they assumed I must be asking the wrong questions. But we were met with the same puzzled looks at the third station as the first two.

After the third stop for directions, as the three of us walked back toward the car, I noticed a bar located next to the service station. Not a restaurant that served alcohol but an actual "stand-up" bar! Joking, I said to the other two, "Let's go in there. They'll probably know the way to Eagle Eyrie."

We walked into the bar, and I asked the bar-tender for directions to Eagle Eyrie. He smiled and replied, "Oh, the Baptist conference center!" Then he told us exactly how to get there, and we had no problems following his directions!

> This reminds me of an old joke: Catholics do not recognize Methodists as true Christians. Methodists do not recognize the pope as God's emissary on Earth. And Southern Baptists do not recognize each other in a liquor store!

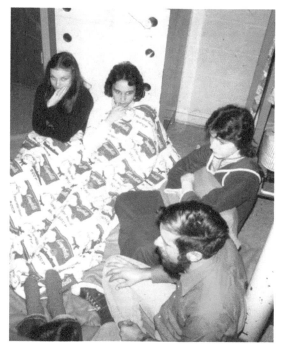

Right: Telling ghost stories at Eagle Eyrie: Mildred Barnes, Martha Feathers, Laura Woods, and me (3)

Bill Sinclair jamming with a couple of the musicians at Eagle Eyrie (3)

Mary Etta and Edward Brown at PAL Lodge (3)

Kim Sok and Cindy Parsons in the parking lot at Eagle Eyrie (3)

Above: Ben Sandford and Alan Hurt
Below: Laurie Schneider, second from left (3)

Left: Chef Everhart preparing popcorn in PAL Lodge (1)

Right: Brenda Vick and Roberta Corbett outside PAL Lodge in the early sixties (1)

Above: Tracy McBride, Becky Riddle, and Susan Williams (3)

Left: Alan Hurt at lunch (3)

Susan Williams, Melissa Ellis, and Kathy Haynes eating ice cream (3)

Mary Etta at dinner. (3)

Above: David Hurt (3)

Below: Ed Lilly (as per the usual), Ben Sandford, and Jay Russ (4)

How many of you remember the "white house" at Eagle
Eyrie? (3)

Chapter 27
The Sullivans (The Cat in the Lap)

Jerry Sullivan died in 2001. Chester and Mary Etta went to the funeral in Tylertown, Mississippi. Chester, along with the pastor of Tylertown Baptist, spoke at the funeral, and I was a pall-bearer. Of course, Suzanna and Roddy McKendree attended. John Dawson had passed away several years before or he too would have made that trip.

Lynn, Ellen, and Jerry Sullivan at the Haunted Woods, where we spent the night; Lee Ellen with her back to us (1)

Ellen had told me earlier that Chester and Mary Etta came by the week before Jerry died. She said that when she opened the door and saw the two of them, it was like the weight of the world fell off her shoulders. (My sister, Carolyn, made the same comment about Chester in 1964, when he saw her at the hospital soon after my father passed away.) Chester and Mary Etta were able to spend some quality time with Jerry during his final days.

The local pastor told Ellen that God must have needed a special person like Jerry to help out in heaven. Chester told Ellen that he could not think of a single good reason for God to have taken him. "The fact is that Jerry is now in heaven and no longer with us here on Earth. You and your girls will have to live with the memories of a wonderful husband and father." That may have been the first time I heard Chester's saying: "We will never be the same—not because he is gone but because he was once here."

Chester made an interesting observation during the funeral. He said it was hard to believe that the Sullivans had only been at HBC for five years. They seemed to have been a fixture for much longer. They were dear friends who left a legacy of friendship at Hampton Baptist.

After they moved to Mississippi in 1973, I visited almost every year. Chester and Mary Etta, Roddy and Suzanna, and others in Suzanna's family—sisters Martha and Fubs, children Will and Juli, and Eric Burge—made the trip many times. It was never a surprise to see John Dawson show up while I was there. And many others made that trip at least once. Those would be Jimmy Ailor, Bill Sinclair, Larry and Linda Brumfield, Alice Erickson, Edward Brown, Martha Dunn, Jimmy George, Rusty Beck, Melanie Beck, Anna Jones, and Harald Aadahl.

Some went to Mississippi because they been friends with the Sullivans; others went for different reasons but returned because they had became friends.

len prepares hamburgers at the Haunted Woods. (I ate better on this trip than any other RA trip to the Haunted Woods.) (1)

During the time that the Sullivans were at Hampton Baptist, they made many close friends, but they had a special friendship with Chester and Mary Etta Brown. I was not able to make it to Ellen's funeral in 2022, but Mary Etta and Suzanna did.

I became friends with the family because of a cat. Shortly after they were stationed on the Peninsula, the Sullivans started going to Hampton Baptist. They were renting a house on the Sinclair property off of King Street. The girls and I think that it was probably Jimmy Sinclair who first invited them to HBC. They soon moved to base housing in Bethel Manor.

When it was time for the HBC youth retreat, Ellen was put in charge, and the planning committee met at the Sullivans' one night. I took a seat in their living room, where there were two Siamese cats, Tina and TC. Almost as soon as I sat down, Tina jumped into my lap and made herself at home. I started petting her and noticed that all five of the Sullivans were staring intently at me. I wondered what I had done wrong. Perhaps the cats weren't allowed on the furniture. But before I could say anything, Ellen blurted out, "Tina doesn't sit on anyone's lap!"

"Oops," I thought. "They don't want anyone holding her." But that wasn't it. Jerry explained, "I can't believe this. As long as we

319

have had Tina, she has not warmed up to anybody except family, and usually only Ellen. This is remarkable!"

It seemed to be a sign that I was to become a good friend of the family. Sadly, Tina didn't live much longer, and she never sat in my lap again. It was as though she had given me her approval and could now go on to other things. It was up to us to take it from there.

Now TC and I did become good friends for many years. For a while, I thought that TC was spelled something like "Tse Cse" or some other Far Eastern name. Jerry had been in Vietnam, and I assumed he brought the name back from there. One evening, I finally asked Jerry what "Tse Cse" meant in English. He replied, "It stands for Tom Cat." TC never had the same mystique for me after that, but he did remain my friend.

I started hanging around their house and playing tennis with Jerry. (After about twenty sets, I finally won one.) They even got interested in scuba diving and, along with Tom Rish, became certified divers. Ellen had been convinced she couldn't swim the length of a pool much less pass a course, but she did fine.

Renee, her friend Anita Bradshaw, and Lee Ellen on the camping trip at the Haunted Woods (1)

I had known the family for more than a year, and the three girls and Ellen had always been quite talkative around me. We had lots of great conversations about growing up and life in general. Then one afternoon, I was at the house when neither Renee, Lynn, or Ellen would say a word to me. At first, they refused to say why, but then Lynn blurted out, "We know why you like to talk with us. You just want to analyze us, but we aren't going to tell you anything else about us. So there!"

"Yeah," Renee echoed. "We just found out that you majored in psychology and that's the reason you like to get us talking!"

I didn't do any talking at that moment; I was too busy laughing! You have to keep in mind that this was the family who decided I must be an OK friend thanks to the approval of their stand-offish cat. (Lee Ellen never had a problem with my major and so was thankfully still talking to me at this time.)

The other time I got a lot of grief from Ellen and Renee was when they went to Florida on a week-long vacation, which included trips to various springs I had recommended where they could do some snorkeling. They loved the springs and the nearby Holiday House, where they served great meals. The mistake I made was in suggesting a place to stay near Blue Springs in DeLand, Florida. My diving buddies and I had stayed at Chimney Corners Motel many a time, and we had always liked the motel. Then again, all we desired was a comfortable bed and a good night's sleep.

When I went by the house in Bethel Manor after they returned, Ellen and Renee told me that the Chimney Corners Motel was terrible. Both had a particular gripe with the facility. Horrified, Ellen told me that the motel room had no carpet—just bare floors—and Renee complained about the color and shabbiness of the curtains! I just shook my head and said that I had honestly never noticed these defects. They did agree that my other recommendations were worth the trip.

Probably the best Sullivan story involves Lee Ellen, who was in second grade at the time. Her schoolteacher's name was Virginia Dare (like the first English settler born in the New World). Lee Ellen decided that her teacher and I should go out on a date. She spent the first semester convincing Miss Dare to go on a blind date with this friend of the family. After she convinced her teacher, she began working on me during the second semester. Her efforts eventually paid off.

Miss Dare and I went out on a Friday night in May while school was still in session. I took her out for a steamed shrimp dinner in Norfolk. (Actually, Lido's was little more than a bar, but I loved the steamed shrimp.) After the meal, Virginia and I went to the Sullivans' for dessert and coffee. Lee Ellen was thrilled!

My scuba club friends and I used to eat at Lido's fairly often. But after a while, it had run its course. Many years later, Gene and Sidney Jordan invited me to go with their Sunday school class out to a place that had great shrimp. That's right—they were going to Lido's! I had not been in years but enjoyed that meal too.

The Sullivans moved to Jerry's hometown of Tylertown in the spring of 1973. They purchased a large tract of land that came with an old house, which they planned to remodel. For the meantime, Jerry acquired a twenty-one-foot trailer (or was it seventeen?) in which the five of them lived for more than a year. (I'm not sure if the girls would refer to it as part of the adventure!)

I followed them a few months after they moved. I was in between jobs and so was able to visit three times that summer. When I arrived for the first visit, the three Sullivan girls—Renee, Lynn, and Lee Ellen—were waiting on the front porch steps. That evening, Jim Ailor showed up for the weekend. It was like I had never left Hampton. Jimmy was in college at Samford University in Birmingham, Alabama, which is not too far from Tylertown.

We actually began helping with the house repairs that weekend. Ailor, the Sullivans, and I worked hard for two days, taking off long enough at noon on Sunday to eat a great home-cooked meal. Jim Ailor headed back for college early Sunday evening, but I remained for three weeks. Ailor later returned several times.

Renee and Ellen watching the iron, circular staircase being installed (1)

I do recall one specific work project a year later. Jerry, Ailor, and I were working on something under the house while professional brick masons installed a new wall under the side porch. The three of us under the house had to crawl near the new wall. Jimmy, who was six feet, six inches, was on his hands and knees. He turned to tell us something and lost his balance.

You guessed it. Trying to regain his balance, Jimmy reached out for any solid object. He happened to find the brick wall, except at this point, it was not so solid. In slow-motion sequence, the bricks looked like a stack of dominoes as the wall collapsed outward. I must admit, it made crawling out from under the porch a lot easier!

It was not all work at the Sullivans. I also got to swim in the river and eat Fourth of July breakfasts at the riverbank. We also did a little snorkeling in the river. In fact, on a few occasions when we got extremely dirty, Jerry would grab a couple of bars of soap and load us all up in the pickup to bathe in the river.

It was at the Sullivans' that the girls taught me to ride a horse bareback. They always kept a good herd of horses.

One of the most enjoyable parts of visiting the Sullivans was eating Ellen's cooking. She was a masterful cook. Unfortunately for the family, she spent most of that first year working on the house instead of cooking. Living by myself in an apartment, I didn't get to eat as much of my mom's excellent cooking and sorely missed it.

When I returned to Mississippi the next year, I arrived on a Sunday, and Ellen had prepared a big afternoon lunch. When I finished dessert, I remarked that it had been the best meal I'd had since I was there last summer. Without missing a beat, Lynn replied, "Yeah! And it's the best one we have had since you were last here!"

Lynn, bless her heart, is also a good cook. I used to get excited when she was making banana pudding, although I never did get to eat one of the best-looking ones she ever made. She was carrying it out of the trailer with a smile and a song, when she tripped and splattered it all over the ground. I was tempted to drop down on my knees and clean it up with my tongue!

The other dessert I never got a chance to eat was made by Ellen, back in Virginia. I had gone to Florida and brought back a recipe for key lime pie, which is wonderful. About a week later, I went by the house in the evening. Ellen proceeded to tell me she had made the pie and just how fantastically delicious it was. My mouth watered as she took her time describing it. Then she finished by saying, "I would offer you a slice, but we ate it all for dinner!"

For several years, I was able to enjoy a few rounds of golf on Jerry's personal "Thunderhead Golf Course" in the two back pastures of the farm. It was actually a beautiful par-three, nine-hole course, where you could pet one of the many horses that roamed the fairways and the greens while waiting your turn. The presence of these animals prompted the first rule, which was printed on the scorecards: "Watch your ball and your step!"

Jimmy George went down with me one year and got to play a lot of golf, including Thunderhead and another local golf course. Jimmy gave Jerry much better competition than I ever could.

Ellen told me this story long after they had moved to Tylertown, even though it happened while they were in Virginia and attending HBC. She had thought that perhaps God was calling her to teach Sunday school, but she was questioning her decision. She approached Chester Brown and asked him what he thought of the idea. Ellen told me quite frankly that she wanted Chester to tell her if God was really speaking to her.

But Chester told her, "Ellen, you have the same access to the Holy Spirit that I or anyone else has. My advice would be to go home, get in a room alone, and ask God yourself if He is calling you to become a Sunday school teacher." She did what Chester suggested. She prayed, asking for guidance, and the Holy Spirit answered her prayers.

I like to tell this story because it shows the trust she had in Chester's guidance. And yet, it also shows Chester's trust in his congregation to go to the Holy Spirt, to be led by the Holy Spirit, and to discern answers to their questions. This was something that he taught. Each of us has access to the Holy Spirit, and there will be times that the Holy Spirit will speak to us. It's up to us to arrange a quiet time when God can speak to our hearts. Chester encouraged us to look for times when we could follow God's leading in our lives. He would not, however, tell us what it was God wanted for us, only that God would indeed speak to us if we gave Him a chance.

When in Hampton, Jerry and Ellen would often invite the Browns to lunch at the Officer's Club at Fort Monroe. (I am happy to say, I got to go there a couple of times too.) We got talking about those lunches one time when I was visiting the Sullivans long after they'd moved to Tylertown. We agreed that the beef and burgundy was one of the best meals. Most diners would order a glass of burgundy wine with the meal.

One time, the two couples went to lunch and enjoyed the the beef burgundy. Ellen said that their only disappointment with the meal was that they were not able to enjoy a glass of wine. They said that Chester and Mary Etta kept their glasses turned upside down when the waiter came around with the wine. Jerry said that they didn't think it would be polite to ask for wine in that situation.

Shortly after returning home, I was talking with Chester and Mary Etta about my trip. The lunches at Fort Monroe came up, and they said how much they enjoyed eating there with the Sullivans. Then Mary Etta said, "The only drawback was that Jerry and

Ellen did not ask for wine when the waiter came around. To be polite, we also chose not to order wine."

After breaking out in laughter, I told the Browns that they had misunderstood one another and missed out for no reason. Next time I talked with the Sullivans, they also laughed about it.

Ellen Sullivan had been raised in a conservative church, and while at Hampton, she sometimes disagreed with Chester's scriptural views. After moving to Tylertown, she found more time (especially after she retired from the library) to read the Bible and biblical commentaries.

During one of my visits, Ellen told me to give Chester the message that the more she read her Bible, the more she found herself agreeing with him. I relayed this to Chester, who told me to tell Ellen that "contrary to popular belief, I get most of my theology from the Bible." I did so during my next visit, which brought forth a smile and this comment from Ellen: "Well, I am learning!"

I think the largest group to ever come from Hampton at the same time (other than for Jerry's funeral) was a couple of weeks before the Thanksgiving holiday in the late 1970s. I arrived on a Friday to find that Jimmy Ailor was already there. I had not known he was coming. Jim was only there for the weekend. The next day, Suzanna and Roddy McKendree came in for a week. This I had known about. Jerry let me know about another guest who would arrive on Sunday in time for dinner. That was John Dawson, who visited a couple of times when I was there.

On Sunday, John called and said he would not arrive until dinner. He had stopped at a rest area and was watching the Redskins game on a small portable TV that he had brought. It was halftime, and he said he would depart when the game ended. He was a couple of hours away and would arrive at 6:00 p.m. Jerry said we would hold supper for him. We did, and we enjoyed a wonderful meal after John arrived.

The next day, we went for a walk in the woods and pasture. The girls were getting ready to ride their horses when John said that he had not done so in many years. Without missing a beat, he hopped on one of the horses and rode off. The day after that, Ailor, the McKendrees, Renee, Lynn, and I spent the day on Bourbon Street in New Orleans. That turned out to be an interesting trip!

This must be between 1973 and 1976 because I have a mustache but no beard. Here I am with Jim Ailor, Jerry, Renee, Lynn, and Ellen Sullivan, walking in the first pasture. This was the time that John Dawson rode the horse. (3)

The Sullivans came back to Hampton a couple of times, but for the most part, it was folks from Hampton Baptist and a few other churches making the trip down to Tylertown. Bill Sinclair went with me twice and on one trip, spent a good amount of time working on their sound system.

In 2005, Katrina hit that area of the country. Harald Aadahl and I spent a weekend with Ellen, surveying the damage in Gulfport. We returned with more than a hundred volunteers over the next two years, repairing houses and doing a sports camp for the kids in the Gulfport area. Ellen took Harald and me to a church that was housing volunteers, and we used it for lodging in 2006, when we returned for a work week during the summer.

We only worked half a day on Wednesday. While the rest of our group went swimming in the Gulf, Jim Ailor and I had dinner at Ellen's. Our group from the PBA returned again in 2007. On that trip, Alice Erickson and Melanie Beck joined me for dinner at Ellen's on Wednesday.

Jessi Barnes, Lynn's granddaughter, came to our area in 2017 and 2018 to work with my summer mission team, which included a trip to Latvia in 2018. Jessi stayed with Matt Parron and Lucille Everhart while working for the PBA.

One year after Ellen had passed away, I made it back to Tylertown to spend time with each of the daughters and their husbands. While there, I talked to them about their memories of Hampton Baptist. Here are a few of the comments they made. All of them were in grade school at the time, and all three shared the memory of feeling safe and loved at church.

LEE ELLEN

- Miss (Mrs.) Godwin, nursery worker (Lee Ellen loved her so much, she would run to the nursery.)
- Ellen being the matron of honor at Suzanna's wedding
- Bible drills at GAs (This encouraged her to learn the books of the Bible.)
- Eating dinner on the church grounds
- An older man who gave kids Dubble Bubble gum
- Jerry beating everyone in table tennis at the youth retreat

LYNN

- John Dawson walking around with two cameras around his neck and spare film in his pocket
- Being mad at Jimmy Ailor, for some reason, and grabbing hold of his leg and not letting go
- Bill Sinclair playing instruments at youth retreats and at home when the Sullivans lived near Bill's parents
- Being babysat by Suzanna McKendree
- Wes Lawson
- Going to the Fisherman's Cove
- When Jim and other youth painted Abe Lincoln with fangs and the peace symbol on the walls of the coffeehouse
- Discussing the sermon after coming back home for dinner
- Youth song book (Lynn really liked the songs in it.)
- A special speaker who came and did Chalk Talks

RENEE

- Bill Sinclair, Phil Everhart Jr., and Jim Ailor
- Hating John Dawson taking her photo
- Going to the coffeehouse, which made her feel grown up
- Jim Ailor with an afro
- Going on her first-ever date with Jim Ailor and seeing the movie "Patton"
- Loving going to Sunday school and GAs
- Thinking the sanctuary and organ were beautiful
- Having a copy of the Bible paraphrase "The Way"

Chapter 28

Angela Peele and Ashley Everhart (4)

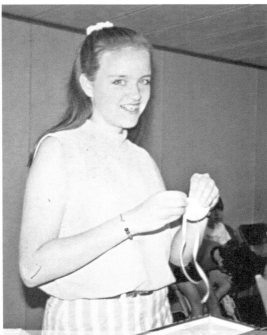

Left: Beth Everett (4)

Below: John Ailor showing a lot of "Joy" (2)

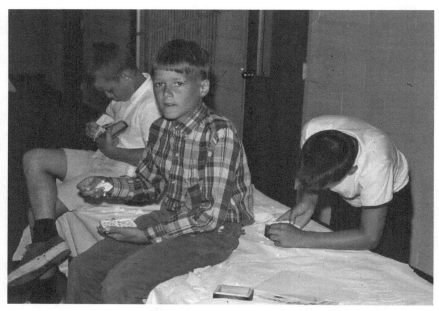

Wayne Everhart (2)

Tracy McBride working with VBS kids (2)

Sue Ann Tillery and Mary Oldershaw at Sunday achool (2)

Linda Riddle at a church Halloween party with Rhonda
Riddle, Tom Bundick, Becky Parsons, Mildred Barnes, and
Tom Goodwin (4)

David Hurt (2)

Rhonda Riddle, Laura Williams, Brooke Puckett, and Sarah
Trimble ("driving") for a dramitization of a youth trip (4)

Virginia Feathers at VBS (2)

Looks like a party. Jim Michael is in the center. (2)

Chapter 29
Bits & Pieces

JIM AILOR SELLS ZIF TO THE EVERHARTS
(OR SO HE THOUGHT)

Usually it was Jim Ailor who "got" other people. It could be a tall tale like the buried treasure in a field or the march on Buckroe Beach, when he was the youth minister at Fox Hill Road Baptist Church. These are some of what you could expect from the Big A.

However, at least once, Jimmy ended up on the short end of the stick. I got to see it as I happened to be at the Everharts' one night when he came by to sell ZIF. ZIF was the brand name of a cleaning agent. It was sales scheme kind of like Amway, in which you bought products to sell to people in your community. Ellen Sullivan, during the time she was at Hampton Baptist, started selling ZIF.

On this night, I was talking and drinking coffee with Lucille and Phil Sr. when Jim Ailor either knocked at the door or just walked into the kitchen. After chatting for a few minutes, Jim told the Everharts that he was selling a super cleaning agent that Ellen Sullivan had turned him on to. Jim went on to say why a bottle of ZIF was just what they needed to make their house spick and span. It was a high concentrate liquid, and they could buy a half gallon or full gallon with a hand-held spray bottle, which would last them months. Jim was actually a pretty good salesman. Little did he know that he had met his match!

After finishing his spiel, Phil Everhart told Jim that he was interested but wanted a demonstration of how good it was. Jim agreed. Phil pointed to a wall in the kitchen and said, "How will it work on that? I see a little dirt and grime."

Jim spent about ten minutes scrubbing and when finished, I have to admit it looked pretty nice. Phil then pointed to the refrigerator and asked how ZIF would work on it. Jim spent another ten minutes on the refrigerator. During this demonstration, all of us kept talking, sometimes about the cleaning and sometimes about life in general.

Long story short, Phil pointed out a dozen spots in the kitchen that needed cleaning. Jim spent about ten to fifteen minutes on each, while we all carried on in conversation. An hour later, Jim asked, "Well, what do you think?"

Phil said, "It looks nice, Jimmy, but I am going to have to think about it for a few days." Jimmy looked a little disappointed but left with a smile. When he was gone, Phil said, "Well, that was fun!"

The Everharts never purchased any ZIF. Lucille remembers that Bruce Everhart also tried his hand at selling ZIF. I don't know if he had any better results.

Ellen, who was no more a "saleslady" than Jim a "salesman," didn't manage to sell much of the stockpile she had purchased when signing up. She soon realized that she was not going to sell any of the product with Jimmy being one of the few she was able to recruit.

I was working at the Peninsula Baptist Association at the time, and part of our ministry was helping people get food and other needed items. Ellen finally came to me and asked if I could use any or all of the cleaning supplies that were cluttering up her garage. I took it off her hands and stored it in the PBA garage. Some of it we used for cleaning the office, but most of it was put in food boxes and given to needy families. So in the end, Ellen's supplies were put to good use . . . but not for a profit!

My final interaction with ZIF came when Jim Ailor became my boss as the director of missions for the PBA in the early 2000s. One morning, Jim came into the office and said that he had something for me. It was an old spray bottle of ZIF that he had found in his house. For a while, I kept that bottle as a reminder of Jim's night at the Everharts'.

• Playing cards was a big evening activity for many years. Bill Sasser, John Lee Robbins, Cliff Morris, Don Miller, and I would often go by the Ericksons and play bridge with Alice and Wayne. Jane Dennard and I played bridge many weekend nights at the home of a newly married couple who were friends with Jane.

• Alice Matthews (later Erickson) attended the College of William and Mary. She was very popular and attended a lot of fraternity parties. I remember Alice telling me that the frat houses kept bottles of milk in the fridge for party nights. Alice didn't drink liquor, but they wanted her to come to the parties and thus the milk.

Trip May came as a summer youth minister in 1972. He had the youth group perform a play, *Murder in the Cathedral*, about the life and death of Thomas Becket. I played Becket, who was killed by three knights at Cantebury Catherdaral.

One of the scenes in the play shows the three knights defending their actions while the body of Thomas Becket is lying at their feet. I told Trip that there was no way I could get through the scene without moving and/or opening my eyes. Trip said that they would have one of the knights throw a cloak over my body.

That would have worked fine except that during the scene, the knight forgot a line, and so another knight kept repeating the cue.

It struck me as funny. I started to laugh silently. Unfortunately, my mirth grew so great that the cloak started trembling. Realizing that only made me laugh more. It became a vicious cycle. And that is how I turned a poorly acted serious play into a hit comedy!

- Most of the youth would sit in the balcony each Sunday morning along with a number of adults. One of the modes of training was that the older youth acted as ushers and took up the offering in the balcony.

Bryan Lilley started coming to Hampton Baptist in the 1960s when he was in the Langley Air Force band. He started dating Barbara Gunter. Barbara and I graduated from Hampton High the same year. In those days, the young adults would go out to eat after church on Sunday night.

I got talking with Barbara Gunter's younger sister Deborah at Brian's funeral. Deborah had been about twelve when Barbara and Brian were dating. She told me that she remembered tagging along with all of us when we went out to eat because Barbara was her ride home. She said that it made her feel "grown up" to go out with the young adults.

After marrying, Bryan and Barbara had three kids who were very active at church. Their son Ed is my good friend today, and Chandler, Ed's son, has worked for me as a summer missionary (Smishy) at the PBA. That's right—the grandson of the couple I hung out with in the 1960s is old enough to work for me. In fact, Chandler Lilley graduated from high school in May 2024.

It gets weirder. Ed Lilley is a pastor at a local church. He is one of a group of ministers (including Jay Russ and Brenden Lawson, Jay and Claudia's son) that meet with me for lunch each Tuesday. Ed was in North Carolina recently for a church function of some sort. A woman there was playing the piano for the event. When she found out that Ed was from the Peninsula, they started

Barbara Gunter (2)

Brian Lilley as a waiter at a youth banquet (3)

talking. Somehow, it came up that Ed had been in Harbor Lights, the musical group at Kecoughtan High School. The woman told Ed that she too had been in Harbor Lights. The subject of churches came up, and she said that she had gone to Hampton Baptist when she was in school. This, of course, led to a long conversation. The pianist's maiden name was Vick! It was Brenda Vick, and she was still involved in church music.

There were a lot of public school teachers who attended the church, including Mary Etta Brown, who was both a teacher and later the principal of an elementary school. Kathryn Thomas was my fifth-grade teacher at Willis-Syms-Eaton Elementary. She was an excellent teacher. Many of you were already aware of this.

I said "a lot of public school teachers." That is not quite true. There were (and are) so many public school teachers who were members of HBC that I would not even try to list all of them. (Plus, this book is already way too long!)

- I remember in later years, I was in Jim Allison's Sunday school class. Jim did a great job of teaching every Sunday, but the event I remember the most only happened once a year. Tommy and Tracy Ward would invite the class over for an oyster roast in their backyard. That was some good eating!

The above comment reminds me of a discussion I had with Melanie Beck after the end of the annual Work Camp. I was telling Melanie how much I missed the Thursday night suppers at Work Camp. It was a roast beef meal cooked by the Emmaus Baptist ladies. I had forgotten that I had talked about some of my other favorite meals and cooks before. So Melanie and I made a list of five of my favorite meals (later expanded) that I would love to have cooked for me one night a week after I retired. This was the list, and several are from Hampton Baptist:

- Jo White (Stevens Memorial) got my summer team to do a backyard VBS at a trailer park for about twenty years. Jo would always have the team over for lunch during the week. I would often hear from former Smishies (including from HBC) wanting to know if Jo did "takeout." Later, when Jay Russ became the pastor at Stevens Memorial, he got to enjoy her cooking too.
- JoAnne Barbour made sure that I got one great dinner each week for many years. This was, of course, the Wednesday night meal at HBC. In more recent years, Cheryl Elder and Sandy Tidwell has kept this going, and I greatly appreciate them both.
- Ellen Sullivan would cook special meals for me and the friends I brought with me to Tylertown.
- Alice Rich was my go-to cook whenever I did a senior adult program with lunch at Riverside Baptist and later Temple Baptist.
- Faye Morse who cooked the roast beef on Thursday nights at Work Camp.

SEARCH INTERNATIONAL

In the early 1960s, John Robbins, Bill Sasser, Don Miller, Cliff Morris, and I decided to form an organization dedicated to learning and trying new ideas. I think the main thing we wanted to do was have fun together, and we needed a "cool" reason to do this. We got together one night at my house to refine our plans.

The main idea we hatched was embodied in the word *new*. We wanted to find and explore new horizons. And thus, we would use the word *search* in the title of our new organization. It was mostly Hampton Baptist people, although it was not restricted to church members.

The founding members of Search International:

John Robbins	Bill Sasser
Kenny Caldwell	Don Miller
Mike Haywood	Allen Turnbull
Cliff Morris	Jack Miller
Bill Worster	Kenny Higgins
Jack Shepherd	Wayne Matthews
Sydney Garris	Ted Taylor

Yes, before you point it out, Search began as an all-male organization, but that soon changed, as you will see from an early document I still have.

It was founded in 1962. To be honest, we did not do much more than sit around and talk about possible projects to research. The neatest thing we did was to enlist older, qualified adults to give us advice on our projects. We called them our Technical Advisors, or TAs. While a lot of our ideas were rather far-fetched, our list of Technical Advisors was truly high caliber:

Wayne Erickson	Alice Erickson
Phil Everhart Sr.	Lucille Everhart
Sam Ailor	Martha Ailor
John Dennard	Chester Brown
Chester Robbins	John Dawson
Woody Patrick	

It is possible that a few of them never knew they were TAs. We tended to add people to the list without checking with them first. I have an early list of both members and TAs:

John Lee Robbins	Don Miller
Mike Haywood	Bill Sasser
Allen Turnbull	Kenny Caldwell
Sydney Garris	Billy Byrd
Wayne Matthews	Jack Shepherd
John Hicks	Diane Roth
Cliff Morris	Mike Williams
Allen Turnbull	Allen Stagg
Dave Wood	Margie Whitcomb
Jane Dennard	Brenda Vick
Ted Taylor	Vernon Rollins
Jim Ailor	Phil Everhart Jr.

Margie Whitcomb at VBS (2)

Our list of achievements was not all that great, but we did a few interesting things:

- Built a sandbox for Lucille Everhart's kindergarten class at church
- Investigated a UFO sighting in Toano (This was one that supposedly caused motor vehicle engines to inexplicably cut off.)
- Dug for old fossils at a location in Hampton where a new apartment complex was being constructed
- Worked with VIMS to install an underwater habitat in the York River (Our claim to fame on this project involved one of the original *Mercury* 7 astronauts, Scott Carpenter. Chet Robbins got him to look at some of our diagrams of the project. Carpenter made notations about the drawings and signed it.)

Jim Ailor, who could be counted on to add excitement and controversy to any adventure, formed a counter organization to Search. He called his Found. Found's charter stated that the main mission was to undermine Search, opposing anything Search stood for and being its general adversary! I do want to point out that both Jim Ailor and Phil Everhart Jr., co-founder of Found, later became members of Search.

- I had a lot of good friends at Hampton Baptist, including Bill Sasser. Everyone enjoyed having Bill around, and he added a lot to the group. The one thing he did not add was his automobile. Bill very seldom offered to drive us to any function or destination. His go-to comment was "I'm riding on empty!" This was said so often that if Bill's name came up for any reason, someone in the group would say, "I'm riding on empty!"

I remember going to a Redskins football game one year in the late 1950s. Jack Shepard's father drove us. Besides Jack, his dad, and me, the group included Don Miller, Bill Nelson, and Cliff Morris. I actually do not remember much about the game, although I think the Redskins won, and I did get Eddie LeBaron's autograph.

Eddie LeBaron was the quarterback of the Washington team then and later became the first starting quarterback for the Dallas Cowboys when they entered the league. Things were so laid back at the time that anyone could walk onto the field after a game and mingle with the players.

The other detail about this trip was brought back to me by Don Miller a few years ago, when we would meet on Fridays for lunch. He reminded me that we drove through Maryland on the way home and stopped at a restaurant to get a bite to eat.

Gambling was legal in Maryland at the time, and there was a row of slot machines along one wall. I had an extra quarter and played it. Much to everyone's astonishment, I hit a small jackpot, winning about twenty-five dollars in quarters. I was able to pay for everyone's dinner, which back then, probably didn't amount to the cost of gas for the trip.

THE ROYAL AMBASSADOR "SAND BOWL"

Ted Taylor started going to HBC when he was stationed at Langley Air Force Base. I do not remember how he got started at HBC, but he became a good friend to a bunch of us, including Cliff Morris, Don Miller, John Robbins, and Bill Nelson. Ted was a terrific basketball player and helped improve HBC in the city church league.

For a while, Ted lived in an apartment in the old Darlene Estate. One year, a group of us went to Ted's apartment to watch the college bowl games on January 1. Two of the games were being played at the same time, and Ted really wanted to see both of them. So the day before, he purchased a new portable TV set. We watched one game on the larger console set and the other on the new portable.

Ted went back home to Harriman, Tennessee; married his childhood sweetheart; and worked a for his church, as the supervisor of a large gym and family center. Ted and Don Miller have remained close and in contact over the years.

Ted Taylor and Ricky Wallace (left) looking over a note from a washed-up bottle we found on the Haunted Woods beach (1)

Ted Taylor helped me with RA meetings during the time he was at Hampton Baptist. Ted made several of the camping trips to the Haunted Woods. One of the other events he made was our annual "Sand Bowl" game at Nags Head. This occurred on a Saturday around New Year's Day at Jockey's Ridge.

We would take a football to the top of the sand dune and mark out a playing field (obviously not on level ground). Usually, it was Ted and me against the RAs in a game of tackle football. It was played at a slow pace, as we had to negotiate both the slope and the sand. It was always a fun time. We tried to keep the game at the very top of the ridge, but more times than not, we were rolling down the side of the dune, either from being tackled or from losing our balance when going out for a pass.

One year, Wayne Everhart took his surfboard with us, anchoring it to the top of my car. Others who participated besides Ted and Wayne were Ricky Wallace, Craig Michael, Bruce Everhart, Phil Everhart Jr., Jimmy Ailor, Bill Sinclair, and other RAs.

Ted Taylor, Wayne Everhart (getting sand out of his hair), and Ricky Wallace at Nags Head (notice Wayne's surfboard on top of my car) (1)

JIM AILOR FILMS THE BIBLE

Several years later, Jim Ailor out-did me at Jockey's Ridge. This was during his high-school years. Jim decided that he was to going to make a movie of the Book of Revelation, also titled *The Book of Revelation*.

Jimmy recently told me that he remembers building a mock-up of the scenes in the garage at the Ailors' house. He and his "crew" (probably Phil Jr., Roddy, the Whitcombs, and who knows who else) made a model, which was four feet in diameter. They built a throne made out of clay in the middle. People and creatures were also made out of clay. The model was built on rollers so that it operated like a lazy Susan. They rigged lights to shine on it as it spun. Jimmy had an eight-millimeter camera with a zoom lens. The big scene showed "heaven" in rotation while the camera zoomed in and out on the characters.

They watched the movie when it was finished. This was, of course, at a time when you could not immediately preview your film work. Jim said that the biggest problem with the heaven scenes filmed in the garage was that you could see a lawn mower in the background!

They filmed most of the scenes locally but decided to take the cast to Jockey's Ridge to film the crucifixion at the top of the sand dune. Phil Everhart Jr. played the part of Jesus. Jimmy said he made Phil carry the cross to the top of the sand dune. Many years ago, Jim showed me the film after it was finished, and I must say, it was not too bad. The scene at the top of Jockey's Ridge was impressive. Jim does not know if the only copy of the film is still in existence.

THE "GOING-AWAY" PARTY THAT MIGHT HAVE KEPT ME FROM GOING AWAY

The cake waiting for me at the Parsons' house (3)

A surprise going-away party, which wasn't really a surprise, might have kept me from getting drafted when I was at Christopher Newport College in 1967. Here is how it all came about.

In the mid-1960s, I was playing in the church basketball league with Hampton Baptist. Our team would have included Billy Byrd (who was usually the coach of the basketball and softball church teams during that time). Other players would have included Ted Taylor, Don Miller, Cliff Bowen, Bill Sasser, and John Robbins.

In one game that season, I had gone up for a rebound. Fortunately, I got the rebound. Unfortunately, someone on the other team undercut me at the back of the knees, and I took a tumble, landing on my right shoulder. The shoulder popped out of joint, but as I was getting up, it popped back in, and I continued to play.

From that time on, for the next several years, if I did any sort of sharp, throwing movement, the result was a partial shoulder dislocation. Smooth movement of the arm was OK, just not any kind of jerking motion. I could bowl with no problem, but I could not make a throw to first base in softball without the shoulder separating. I learned to live with the problem, and the shoulder popped out a lot.

It happened enough times that I became good at fixing it. I am not sure how I learned this, but the procedure I used involved a twelve-inch softball. I would keep one in the trunk of my car. That way, if my shoulder popped out, I could get the softball, tuck it under my arm, and rotate the shoulder around the ball until it fell back into place. It worked nicely and without any pain.

In 1967, my second year at Christopher Newport, I got a notice to go to Richmond for a pre-draft physical. My doctor gave me a note explaining my shoulder condition, but I still had to report for the physical, where a military doctor would consider the note and my shoulder.

On the evening before I was to go to Richmond, my friends were going to throw a surprise going-away party at the home of the Parsons. I was told that there was a pool party at the Parsons' and that everyone was coming. It turned out, I had a dinner date with Barbara Selman that night and said I could not make the party. Bill Sasser told me I still had to come because it was supposed to be a surprise but the party was for me. I said I would make my dinner date early and then we would come by.

When I got to the party, which was already in progress, Barbara and I walked behind the house to the pool. Neither of us had planned on swimming, and so we didn't have bathing suits with us. When I got close to the pool, someone yelled, "Who wants to throw Haywood in the pool?"

I knew the answer to that question, and so I turned around and started running back toward my car. I was looking back at the people chasing me and didn't see the tree until my shoulder hit it.

Next thing I knew, I was lying on my back. This time, my shoulder was not just partially dislocated; it was totally out of joint. John Robbins yelled to those crowded around me that all we needed was the softball in Haywood's trunk. I gave John Lee the keys, and he got the softball. It didn't work.

We finally decided that John Lee would give me a ride to the emergency room, and if necessary, someone would give Barbara Selman a ride home. (That became necessary because I was at the ER for a good while.)

Mary Sue Dietrick, Barbara Selmon, me, and John Robbins at an HBC youth banquet (3)

I remember a few things about the hospital visit. One was that the doctor told me he was going to give me a shot containing one of the major street drugs of choice at that time: Demerol. He also told me that putting the shoulder back in joint would not hurt but that night might be painful. He was right on both counts. The doctor did not even take off his shoe; he put his foot into my armpit, grabbed my hand, and pulled it up with a twist. He put my arm in a sling and sent me home—or back to the party rather.

When we got back to the Parsons', most everyone had left except for the family, John Lee, and John Dawson. I saw the cake they had ordered and ate a piece of it before departing. At that point, I was feeling good enough to drive home. I felt great until about 1:00 a.m.; after that, I was awake all night.

The next morning, I drove to the selective service office and talked with Mrs. Bovey (anyone remember her?). She sent paperwork to the officer in charge, and then she told me to go home. I would be contacted in the near future. End of the story: I later got a notice that I didn't have to go.

The other good thing that came out of having my arm in a sling for six weeks is that it didn't pop out as often as it did before. That is not to say that it never happened again, but that is another story. To this day, some people think I ran into the tree on purpose, but that is giving me too much credit for advanced planning. All I was doing that night was trying to avoid getting caught and thrown in the pool!

Chapter 30

John Robbins, me, and Allen Turnbull pose at Old Rag Mountain, where we camped out for the night. (This was a time when a group of us, including Don Miller and Cliff Morris, spent several weekends camping out in the mountains.) (1)

THIS IS OUR STORY, THIS IS OUR SONG

Jane Rollins and Jeannie Hankinson at Nags Head (1)

The old Sand Sharks Scuba Diving Club used to go on a yearly trip to a place in North Carolina called Hawker's Island. We would either stay at Ma Hawker's motel or camp out on a smaller island, usually for a long weekend. During these trips we would often go to eat at a great seafood restaurant in the vicinity called Captain Bill's.

One year, back in the 1960s, I was at Captain Bill's with our club members. Suddenly I heard my name being called out from across the restaurant. "Mike Haywood!" I looked up and saw Jane (née Rollins) and Dick Whittington waving to me from across the dining room. It turned out that they had first gone to Captain Bill's on their honeymoon and returned from time to time. That was one of life's unexpected but enjoyable encounters.

Alice Erickson takes the GAs to my PBA office to interview a real, live missionary! Peggy Godfrey, Jill Godfrey, Susan Lilly, and Amy Hurt are also pictured. (5)

Margie Whitcomb on the York River during a trip to Williamsburg (1)

Don and Vickie Ellis at a costume party (2)

Margie Whitcomb, me, and Ted Taylor at a Search
International meeting at my house (1)

Search International on a fossil dig: Sydney Garris, me, and John Robbins (Photo by Ted Taylor)

Alan Hurt bobbing for apples (2)

Another Milford Rollins–led trip to Nags Head: Dianna
Copple, Milford, Vernon Rollins, and that may be John
Ailor on the far right (1)

Vernon Rollins filming at Nags Head (1)

Chapter 31
Church Nights 1991–1996

1991
"A LOOK BACK ON THE
HISTORY OF CHURCH NIGHTS—
A HIGHLIGHT OF THE HIGHLIGHTS"

This Church Night was exactly what it was called. A skit, song, or commercial from each of the past Church Nights was recreated. We even got to see a couple of episodes that had been cut from their original program due to time restraints.

Bill and Nancy Lee Trimble performed a new skit called "Driving Miss Dottie!" Lynn Mayberry played the *Pink Panther* theme on the piano during the 1981 remembrance.

The folder of Church Night material that Bill gave me is missing three years. For two of those, I was able to glean the title and a couple of bits from this script. Unfortunately, the third missing year came after this one, in 1994.

1992
"CELEBRATING HAMPTON BAPTIST'S
200TH ANNIVERSARY"

- Sampson and Delilah were the hosts of the homecoming parade.
- Chester and Mary Etta Brown were the grand marshals of the parade.

- Edward Brown was the driver of his parent's float and kept trying to speed it up.
- Frank Schneider was selling HBC calendars (see pictures on following pages).
- Jimmy Michael performed a commercial.
- Thirty years ago, in December 1961, Dr. John Garber retired after thirty-seven years as pastor, and on January 1 of 1962, Chester Brown became the new pastor.
- Jay and the youth group depicted a mission trip to Stone Mountain, Georgia, where the youth helped renovate a church building and run a Vacation Bible School.
- The handbell choir performed.
- One of the floats was the "Turkey Hunt." (This was a repeated activity that Jay began for HBC youth; later, Jay and I adapted the Turkey Hunt as a PBA youth event.)
- Dr. Ann Rosser crowned Martha Ailor (chair of the Bicentennial Committee) homecoming queen.

Sandra Bundick helping with Vacation Bible School (2)

In 1991, Hampton Baptist published a calendar as part of the celebration of its 200th anniversary (1791–1991). Inside the calendar was the hymn that Gary and Chester wrote for the event. The caption reads:

> We would like this hymn to be our gift to Hampton Baptist on its 200th anniversary. We dedicate it to the Glory of God in the hope that He may use it to bless the congregation of this church so that our future may be as wonderful as our past.

1993
SANDRA BUNDICK'S
FIVE-YEAR ANNIVERSARY

Church Night Committee: Bonnie Montjar, Mike Haywood, Gary Powell, Jan Blair, Gene Jordan Jr., Renee McCormick, Frank Lawrence, Willie Curtis, David Glass, and Dottie Wallace

Sandra Bundick was called as the secretary of Hampton Baptist in September 1987.

"Tonight, we are going to show you the 'mess' that might have been in 1992 if Sandra had not been here to keep us straight." (The Victory Singers leave when Gary Lewis tries to make coffee. Bill Hurt throws darts at a map to decide where WMU circles will meet.)

Sandra would work on the pronunciations of the names of new members to make sure Chester knew how to pronounce them. Bill used the following names of members who joined in 1992 to show how they might have been mispronounced if not for Sandra.

(Continued on page 374.)

Hampton

1791

FOUNDED ON FAITH · 1791 HAMPTON

Bicente

ptist Church

1991

ial Year

Laborers together with God

Hampton Baptist Church Staff

Important dates for April: 14th - Virginia Choral Society; 20

Lower Right: Dr. Chester L. Brown, Pastor. Born in Gloucester County, Virginia. Holds the B.A. and D.D. degrees from the University of Richmond, the B.D. degree from Southeastern Seminary, and the D.Min. degree from Union Seminary in Richmond. He had further study at the University of Edinburgh.

Lower Left: Dr. Anne P. Rosser, Associate Minister. Born in Richmond, Virginia. Holds the B.A. degree from Westhampton College and the D.Min. from Union Theological Seminary.

Upper Left: Mr. William G. Hurt, Minister of Education/Administration. Born in Roanoke County, Virginia. Holds the B.S. degree from V.P.I. and the M.R.E. degree from Southern Seminary.

Upper Left Center: Mr. Gary E. Lewis, Minister of Music/Organist. Born in Two Rivers, Wisconsin. Holds the B.M.Ed. degree from the University of Wisconsin and the M.C.M. degree from Northwestern University.

Upper Right Center: Mrs. Sandra M. Bundick, Secretary. Born in Accomack County, Virginia. Studied at Goldey Beacom College, Wilmington, Delaware.

Upper Right: Mr. Julious L. Russ, Minister to Youth. Born in Ft. Huachucca, Arizona. Holds B.A. degree from Mars Hill College and the M.Div./ M.R.E. degree from Southeastern Seminary.

ation WMU Meeting; 28th - Children's Day in Sunday School

Ministering in His Name .

In 1950, Hampton Baptist Church revised its constitution to provide for "life deacons" and "term deacons."

There are seven life deacons. When a vacancy occurs, the election of life deacon must be from those who have served three or more full terms as a term deacon and shall be made on nomination of the deacons and elected by the church.

There are be thirty term deacons who serve a three year term and then must sit out one year before being eligible for re-election.

It is the duty of deacons to visit the members of the church and to encourage the members in worship and service. It is also their duty to distribute the elements of the Lord's Supper, and together with the staff, exercise general oversight of the work of the church.

Pictured are six of the current life deacons. Front row from left: William A. Pleasants, Jr., T.W.E. Hankinson. Back row from left: James Paul Allison, Lewis C. Parsons, Jr., Francis W. Jones, A. W. Patrick, Jr.. The seventh life deacon (not pictured) is Milford Rollins.

GOD OF EVERY GENERATION
GENERATION

Chester L. Brown

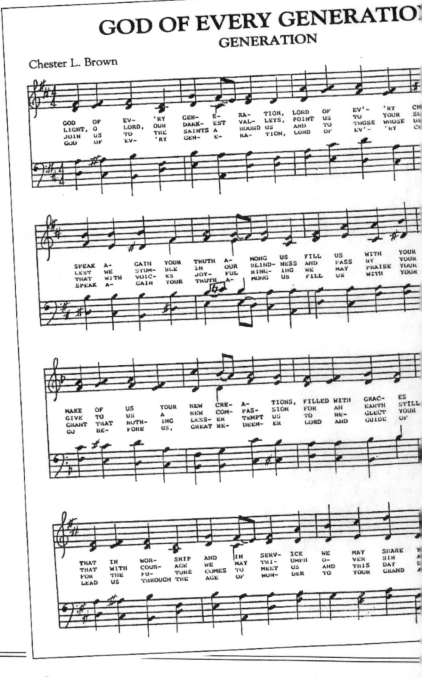

God of Every Generation . . .

We would like this hymn to be our gift to Hampton Baptist on its 200th Anniversary. We dedicate it to the Glory of God in the hope that He may use it to bless the congregation of this church so that our future may be as wonderful as our past. The copyright is being secured in the name of Hampton Baptist Church.

Chester Brown
Gary Lewis

(Continued from page 365.) Can you identify the correct last names? (See answers on page 377.)

Sarah Éclair
Claudette and Matthew Differ
Martha Bird
Richard and Wanda Lace
Amy McInwheel
Lindy McInwheel
Juli Macenroe
Will Macenroe
Elizabeth Mitchale
Bonnie and Shane Moundjoy
Debbie, Brooke, Jim, and Jimmy Pickett
Leith Sailor Smith
Betsy Thimble

1994

Church Night Committee: Richard Pulley, Jack and Ruby Sheppard, Carlisle and Mary Tiller, Becky Glass, Ann Bane, Bill Williams, Pam Hallissy, and Mike Bjorklund

There was no script for 1994 in the packet Bill gave me. Since this year came after the 1991 history of Church Nights, I had nothing to fall back on. The committee was listed on a single sheet of paper. Another loose slip of paper listed some people in skits and a few events. This might be for 1994, although I am guessing. Here are the names listed on that piece of paper:

Stan Ewing, Anna Moore, Bonnie Madre, Bill Pleasants, Lewis Parsons, Mike Haywood, Richard Pulley, Tom Forrest, Bev Doyer, Sidney and Gene Jordan, David Glass, Nancy and Bill Trimble, Bill Williams, Phil Everhart, Bert Kirby, JoAnn Rawls, Woody

Patrick, Roland McKendree, Cynthia Otte, Francis Jones, Eddie Hankinson, Roy Powell, Frank Bryant, John Bane, Eddie Forbes, Gary Powell, Susie Castle, Pam Hallissy, and Martha Owens

1995
"CHECKS HE WROTE—
EDDIE HANKINSON: 40 YEARS OF SERVICE
AS CHURCH TREASURER"

Church Night Committee: Bill Williams, Phil and Willie Curtis, Mike Haywood, Gary Powell, Martha Ailor, Frank Schneider, and Bill Hurt

In the introduction, Bill Hurt mentioned that in one of Chester's annual letters, he remarked that "he didn't know when Church Night got out of hand."

The youth sang several songs, including "We Need a Red Pencil for our Church Budget," "Come to Church and Give Your Money," and (for Chester Brown) "Tiptoe Through the Tithers."

Dr. Garber had asked Eddie to become the church treasurer forty years before. Eddie said that he had written about 45,000 checks for HBC.

Here is a script for one of the gags:

Eddie sits working at a desk when Edward Brown comes in carrying a deer head.

Eddie: Where do you think you're going, Edward.

Edward: To see my dad. I want to show him my latest trophy.

Eddie: Oh, no. Sorry, but you can't do that.

Edward: (confused) Why not?

Eddie: Because the buck stops here!

1996
"ANGELS IN THE SKY"

"Tonight, we are looking at the 'angels' among us who took care of the church in 1995."

- Church Night Committee: Frank Lawrence, Bev and Billy Forbes, Gene and Sidney Jordan, Suzanna McKendree, and Lynn Latham
- Programs handed out by David Cox and Will McKendree
- Narrators: Lynn Latham, Bill Forbes, and Bill Hurt
- Lights by Frank Schneider
- HBC had 18 standing committees with 139 people.
- Committees included Premises, Flowers, Auditing, Baptismal, Library, Lord's Supper, Nursery, Personnel, Recreation, Counting, Recording, and Finance Planning.
- In addition were the people in the choirs, as well as Sunday school teachers, the WMU, men's organizations, office volunteers, and Gift Wrap Booth workers.
- Skits were performed by Phil Everhart Sr., Roland McKendree, Baxter Lee, Monika Malone, Susie Castle, Phil Everhart Jr., Roddy and Suzanna McKendree, Woody Patrick, Tracy Ward, Mary Elizabeth Brown, Mike Haywood, Bill and Nancy Lee Trimble, Jimmy Michael, George Grotto, Jean Thiel, Edward Brown, Raynelle Ewing, Bev Forbes, Sidney Jordan, Bill and Jane Hurt, Debbie and Joe Spencer, Pearl Lineberry, Edward Brown, Betsy Trimble, and Bert Kirby.
- Mary Elizabeth: "The youth won first place in the PBA softball league this year. I think we should build a softball diamond!"

1993 QUIZ ANSWERS

Sarah Éclair (Blair)

Claudette and Matthew Differ (Duffer)

Martha Bird (Feathers)

Richard and Wanda Lace (Mace)

Andy and Lindy McInwheel (McIntire)

Juli Macenoe (McKendree)

Will Macenroe (McKendree)

Elizabeth Mitchale (Michael)

Bonnie and Shane Moundjoy (Montjar)

Debbie, Brooke, Jim, Jimmy Pickett (Puckett)

Leith Sailor Smith (Taylor Smith)

Betsy Thimble (Trimble)

Amy Hurt (3)

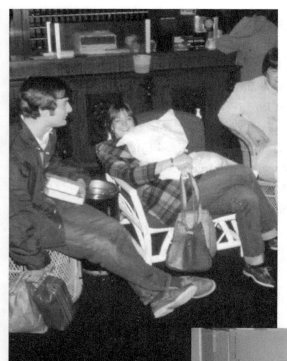

Left: Wes Lawson and Trudy McBride on a youth outing (Whatever else was going on, you could count on Trudy to make it zanier and more fun.) (3)

Right: Jill Godfrey, Sharon Goodwin, and Becky Parsons (3)

Jill Godfrey, Heather Ewing, and Cynthia Hammond share a joke. (3)

Beth Robbins at VBS (2)

Iris Rollins (not sure what is going on here) (2)

Peggy Price (2)

Ken Matthews, Mary Etta Brown, and Camelia Everett at Eastover (3)

Peggy Price and Betty Sasser at VBS (2)

Laura and Alystra Little at a Halloween party (2)

Susan Forbes (2)

Sharon Melson with the senior adults (2)

Doris Williams, Mary Oldershaw, and Virginia Trescott (2)

Thomas Goodwin, Greg Schneider, and Bret Godfrey (2)

Chapter 32
Royal Ambassadors

Royal Ambassadors (RAs), Girls Auxiliary (GAs), and Acteens were a big part of growing up in church. Obviously, most of what I remember is about the RAs, but I have been told some stories about GAs and Acteens.

Some of you might remember that for a long time, the boys' organization, Royal Ambassadors, was under the leadership of the WMU. That meant that in my early years, I had a female RA leader, Mrs. Sparrow. In the 1950s, the RAs were officially put under the men's organizations. I was not around for that change because I had joined the Boy Scouts and dropped out of RAs.

During the time I was not involved, HBC might not have even had an RA chapter. I do remember that during my junior-high years, hearing in Sunday school that there was going to be an organizational meeting to start a new RA chapter at Hampton Baptist. I decided to attend that meeting.

There were only two of us there: me and Dave Carter, who would be the RA leader. I remember being excited about what Dave had to say about what RAs would involve. Dave thought it would be a great experience; he asked me to tell others and promised that the church would also publicize. He was convinced that our numbers would grow quickly, and he was right.

I don't remember who was at the next meeting, but it was more than just Dave and me. Pretty soon, Bill Nelson, Don Miller, Jack Shepperd, Kenny Matthews, and several others were attending on a regular basis. Dave was a good leader and teacher, and he made us look forward to our RA meetings.

The first extracurricular activity that I remember Dave Carter involving us in was the Peninsula Baptist RA baseball league. At our first practice, we met a new guy—a big fellow, who would help Dave coach the team. His name was Wayne Erickson. He was teaching a boys' eighth-grade Sunday school class, but I had not met him yet. Wayne (and Alice) would play a big part in my life from that point forward.

I don't remember the baseball team I played on being highly successful, but I do know that it was a lot of fun, and we enjoyed being together. Dave and Wayne had a knack for making things enjoyable. Several incidents remain etched in my memory.

In our first game of the season, I was at second base, and Bill Nelson was at third base. As we were getting ready to play, I noticed several rocks in the dirt around the base. I reached down, picked up two rocks, and looked toward the trees growing behind third base. I figured I could kill "two rocks with one throw" and so let loose with both, aiming at the outfield side of third base.

I saw where one of the rocks landed in the bushes but did not track the other one. I was still looking that way when someone in the outfield yelled, "Nice throw, Haywood!"

My eyes focused on Bill Nelson, who was rubbing the back of his head. Because the outfielders saw it, I had to admit to Bill that I was the perpetrator and apologized.

At another game, our pitcher (I can't remember who) was having a tough time in the first inning getting the ball across the plate. Someone—perhaps Wayne Erickson, although I don't really remember—suggested I give pitching a try. "Why not?" I thought and took the mound.

I still remember all these years later. The batter did not swing at my first pitch, but it was a perfect strike, right down the middle. "Hey," I thought, "this isn't that hard. Maybe I'm a natural-born pitcher." Eight pitches and two walks later, I knew I was *not* a pitcher. In fact, I am not sure another pitch was within a foot of the plate. Needless to say, that ended my pitching career forever (at least until slow-pitch softball)!

I have never been a motorcycle fan, and in fact, I think I only ever rode on one once. Jack Sheppard had purchased a motorcycle that summer. He was going to ride it to Newmarket Baptist, where we were playing a Saturday game. Jack convinced me that I needed to ride with him, and I did. I will admit it: I was scared to death all the way to Newmarket.

Once Jack and I got there, I decided that I would ride back with either Dave or Wayne and didn't care to ride a motorbike ever again. (And I don't think I ever did.)

It turned out that I didn't have to worry about riding back with Jack. The motorcycle returned in the back of the truck, and Jack departed in an ambulance. It was a close play at home. I can't remember if Jack was catching or running home to score. The opposing player was a pretty big guy, and he and Jack collided at home plate. The other player was fine, but Jack was lying in agony in the dirt with a broken leg. Jack handled it well, and we all got to sign his cast. Most importantly, I didn't have to come up with   an excuse not to ride home on the motorcycle.

The other incident involving a Hampton Baptist guy with a motorcycle was a wreck. Sydney Garris was the one riding. I don't remember why, but he was thrown off. He was laid up for a long time because when he landed, the edge of a drink can cut into a muscle in his back. I remember visiting Sydney and how he could not get out of bed due to the injury.

The final story I remember is funny but a little embarrassing for me. It was a close game, and Bill Nelson was playing third. Wayne Erickson had to ump because the league could not get an official that day. There was a close play at third, and Nelson felt that he had tagged the runner out before he got to the base. Wayne the umpire called the runner safe. Bill and I and a few others argued a little; we thought Wayne had missed the call. Wayne remained calm and said it looked to him like the runner was safe. After a few seconds of arguing, the rest of us settled down, shut up, and got ready for the next batter. Not Bill Nelson. He wouldn't let it go and continued to argue.

Me carrying Jack Sheppard (I am not sure why!) (1)

Since Wayne was umping, Dave Carter was coaching the team. Dave let Bill gripe for a few more seconds and then told him that was enough and no more lip. But Billy continued to run his mouth. Dave gave him one more warning and told Bill that if he did not shut his mouth, he would be out of the game.

Now Bill swung his ire toward Dave, telling him that he couldn't throw him out because we only had nine players. Dave responded, "That's it, Bill. You're out of the game!"

That shut Bill up and surprised the rest of us. Bill started walking off the field.

At that point, I decided that Bill was my good friend and if Dave was going to throw him out of the game, he could darn well throw me out too. So I started to walk off. I was going to make a statement!

Dave saw me walking off the field and yelled, "Haywood, what do you think you are doing?"

I lost my nerve and stopped in my tracks. Fortunately, I thought of a face-saving answer. "We only have eight players left. That means we have to forfeit."

Dave replied, "Get back to second, Haywood! We'll play with eight players."

And with that, I turned around and walked back to second without a word. So much for my great show of support for a teammate.

During the first year of Dave Carter's leadership, I had been attending both RAs and Boy Scouts. Then my scout troop moved its meeting to the same night the RAs met. This time, I opted to stay with my church friends and didn't look for another troop to join. That ended my Boy Scout days.

Dave, Wayne, and probably a couple of other adults took us on several camping trips. Usually, these were in a wooded area of Gloucester. (This was not the Haunted Woods. Those trips would come later when I was the RA leader.) We would play a game around the fire that Dave called "Filter Through."

It was simple. One person—we'll call him "Bob"—would have one to two minutes to get as far away from the campfire as he wanted. Then everyone else would fan out and try to catch Bob. Meanwhile, Bob would try and get by the rest of the group and make it safely back to the campfire without being tagged. Everyone other than Bob had to be so many feet away from the fire.

Once, on the way to our camping spot, we got a bit lost but finally made it to a big pond. Dave pointed to the other side of the pond and said that was where we would make camp. We would have to follow the dirt road around the pond before we could get to the campsite.

Bill Nelson, Don Miller, and I, as well as a couple of others, decided we would swim across the pond, leaving our packs and equipment in the car. It was not that long of a swim, but it was fun and refreshing until we got to the other side. Upon arriving in the shallow water at the campsite side, we discovered the lake bed was full of clam shells.

We tried to be careful as we waded toward the shore, but Bill Nelson managed to deeply cut his foot on a broken shell. It bled profusely. Wayne and the rest of us stayed at the site and set up camp while Dave took Bill to find a local doctor. A couple of hours and many stitches later, they returned. It was still a fun trip, but Bill couldn't do a lot. In fact, he got a real bedroom to sleep in at the house of the family who owned the land we camped on.

Several years later, Howard Stone became the RA leader for the church and enlisted me, in college at the time, to be his helper. Working with Howard was super, and he taught me a lot. However, he soon changed churches. For about a year, there was no RA program before I was asked to set one up. I was not sure what I was doing but decided to accept the challenge.

My first organizational meeting was a replica of the one in which I first met Dave Carter. At our first meeting, only Ricky

Wallace showed up. I followed the same path that Dave Carter had paved and told Ricky we would work on getting a group together, which we did. Between the people Ricky knew, several of whom did not go to church, and the families I knew, we soon had a good-size group. This included, among others, Phil Everhart Jr., Jim and John Ailor, Bill Sinclair, Roddy McKendree, Lee Feathers, Craig Michael, Bruce and David Whitcomb, Billy Bosta, and Michael Vick.

Ted Taylor, who was stationed as an airman at Langley, started coming to church at this time. We became close friends, and I got him to help out with the RAs. It was during this period that Milford Rollins told us about the Haunted Woods, and it became our main camping destination for several years. We went to several other places, such as Peaks of Otter and Gloucester, but the Haunted Woods was our regular haunt (pardon the pun). Stories of the Haunted Woods can be found in my book *Tales My Father Told Me*, but I am going to repeat two of them here.

Ted Taylor, Don Miller, and I were taking the RAs on a specific camping trip to the Haunted Woods. Jim Ailor caught me at church the Wednesday night before the RA meeting and told me I needed to come up with an excuse so that he, Phil Jr., and I could go over early on Saturday morning. He said we needed to leave about an hour before the rest of the guys. I didn't even bother to ask why but arranged for Ted and Don to take the rest of the group after us. My excuse was that the three of us were going to do some snorkeling off the beach.

I arrived at the Ailors' on Saturday morning, ready for anything. Jim met me at the front door and said I needed to drive him up the block, over to Phil and Lucille Everharts'. Ailor said he and Phil wanted to show me something.

It was a bit bizarre, even for these two clowns. They had constructed a full-size coffin. It had been sitting in the Everharts' front room, and Lucille told me she would mighty glad to get rid of it. Both the Ailors and the Everharts didn't seem to mind what the boys did with the coffin, as long as they did it somewhere else!

The coffin was large enough that we had to put it in the trunk of my car. Of course, it was much longer than the trunk, so we had to leave it open, with one-third of the coffin sticking out. We tied it in and then loaded up the rest of our gear. I figured we would not run into a whole lot of traffic this early in the morning. It turned out to be one of the more interesting ninety-minute drives of my life.

The following scene played itself out a dozen times on the ride over. I drove a little under the speed limit, keeping an eye on the rearview mirror to make sure nothing fell out of the trunk. From time to time, a solitary vehicle would overtake us. About the time they got a car's length ahead and realized what they thought they had seen in our trunk, they would brake and fall back just behind us. After getting a better look at the coffin, they would shake their head and speed off. I wondered what would happen if we were passed by a state trooper, but we arrived at the Haunted Woods beach without further incident.

Jimmy and Phil had a plan. We took the coffin down to the beach, where we found a natural hiding spot. They told me to do all of the RA activities on the other side of the beach that day. Then we changed into our bathing suits and spent a half hour snorkeling. We were still in the water when the other two cars pulled in.

As the rest of the group were arriving, I pointed out to Jim and Phil that it had been hard for the three of us to carry the coffin to its hideaway. They agreed to let Bill Sinclair in on the secret, which would give us four people to carry the coffin later that night. We managed it, but just barely.

We'd followed our usual procedure: made camp and messed around for the rest of the day, taking time to cook lunch and dinner. During the evening, we'd played some night games and made a campfire, where we made s'mores and told stories. I tried to lay the ghost stories on a little "thicker" than normal.

Over the years, we had found the perfect spot to make camp, as long as there was no rain in the forecast. About a quarter mile down the beach from the parking area was a stand of trees near the water's edge. A clearing in the middle of the copse made a natural space to lay out sleeping bags.

By midnight, everyone except the four of us had gone to bed. We'd even kept Ted and Don in the dark on this one. When the last person had headed for the clearing, we doubled-timed it to the coffin. I do not know what type of wood those guys had used, but whatever it was, it was heavy! Somehow it seemed to have gained weight. I began to wish we had gotten Ted and Don to help too. To make matters worse, we had to carry it twice as far that evening.

When we got back to the fire, Jim, Phil, and Bill set up the scene. They placed the coffin at the water's edge, sticking it half-way out of the water. When all was in place, we let out a series of blood-curdling screams. As soon as the first of our group appeared at the edge of the clearing, we took off down the beach, stopping only when we were out of sight. It was marvelous fun.

The four of us crept back along the edge of the marsh and watched. One by one, the sleepy campers appeared at the treeline. When they got closer and saw what it was, they began calling for us to show ourselves. I don't think they were terribly frightened by the coffin, but it did take a few minutes before they approached the water.

Now, it is quite possible that the coffin added to the local legends of the area because the best part of the coffin story is only conjecture. This is what happened: We were all so tired that I told everyone to go to bed and that we would take care of the coffin in the morning. What I didn't reckon on was the tide. During the night, the tide came in and the coffin went out. When we got up in the morning, the coffin was nowhere to be seen. We looked up and down the beach. Most likely, it floated out a little ways and sank. If so, it might have given some future snorkeler or swimmer a scare.

And then there is another possibility. They had constructed the coffin well, and it might have floated for a good distance. It could have possibly beached itself on some other deserted beach or even in someone's shoreline backyard far from our campsite. Sometimes, I like to contemplate the stories that might have circulated about the mysterious coffin that washed ashore one morning!

There were a few other interesting trips we took to the Haunted Woods. On one of the earliest excursions, we hiked into the forest, looking for anything of interest. We found an old, deserted house in the middle of the woods, with no path or road leading to it. It was two stories and in bad condition. A bed frame in one of the bedrooms was somewhat ornate. We kept talking about taking it home, but we never did.

A group of us, youth and young adults, spent a startling night in the house. It was quite an evening, with a lot of card-playing and very little sleeping. There was a hole in the ceiling of one of the downstairs rooms, making a crude "chimney," and we built a fire under it.

Before the overnighter, we'd all agreed that no one would bring weapons. We knew that weapons would be a bad mix in a potentially emotional situation. Everyone promised, but everyone lied. When we arrived at the house, every single person took out a knife of some sort and kept it close throughout the night. At least no one had brought a pistol! Still, I am glad that no one from the surrounding area showed up, or they would have had a rude reception.

Our other rule was that no one would go out alone to take a leak. Even so, when two or three got up to relieve themselves, usually the rest of the group went too. The only exception was when one of us actually fell asleep during the night. In the wee hours of the morning, Jim Ailor awoke to find no one in the house. He thought that the skeletons in armor had taken us all, but then the whole group walked back in from a bathroom break!

Opposite page (photos by Lucille Everhart and Jim Ailor):
 Upper left: Tim Rollins, John Ailor, Cliff Morris, Mike
 Vick, Larry Brumfield, Roddy McKendree, and Bruce
 Whitcomb (No weapons? Right!)
 Upper right: Mike Vick, Bruce Whitcomb, Mike
 Haywood, Larry Brumfield, Roddy McKendree, Phil
 Everhart, Tim Rollins, and John Ailor
 Middle, right and left: Tim Rollins and John Ailor
 Bottom left: Phil Everhart, John Ailor, and Jim Ailor
 Bottom right: Jim Ailor, Phil Everhart, and John Ailor

Later on, I coached baseball as an RA leader. We were in the PBA RA league and did well, tying for first place one year in the mid-1960s. (We ultimately lost in the playoffs). At the end of that year, to thank me for coaching, the team threw me a party in the

Fisherman's Cove, and Jimmy made me an award using Charlie Brown. Members of the team included John and Jim Ailor, Roddy McKendree, Phil Everhart Jr., Bruce and David Whitcomb, Jimmy Allison, Mike Vick, Craig Michael, Timmy Rollins, Tommy O'Bryan, Zeb Goodwin, Lee Feathers, and Gary McCord.

Roddy McKendree (3)

John and Jimmy Ailor presenting me with an award (3)

Jim Paul Allison taught me a lesson at an RA baseball game that has stayed with me all these years. He was at a game in which Jimmy was playing. My friend Don Miller was umping. I felt that Don had missed a call at first base, and I let him know loud and clear what I thought. I told him I thought he was a lousy umpire. Jim Paul confronted me as I returned to the sidelines and told me I should not have acted that way.

"But it was a really bad call," I protested.

"That's not the point, Mike. Don is your friend, and we should never treat our friends that way."

I have tried to never forget that.

Billy Bosta (top) and Craig Michael (below) (3)

Left: Jimmy Allison pitching with David Whitcomb behind (3)

Below: Mike Vick (3)

Right: Gary McCord (3)

Below: Timmy
Rollins (3)

Lee Feathers (3)

Jimmy Allison and Bruce Whitcomb (3)

Above: Roddy
McKendree
practicing for an RA track
and field day (Is that Dave
Carter in the white hat?)
(3)

Right: David
Whitcomb (3)

Left: Phil Everhart Jr. (3)

Right: Jim Ailor
(3)

Chapter 33
How Haywood Came to the PBA

Jimmy Ailor, Phil Everhart Jr., Roddy McKendree, Bill Sinclair, Tommy O'Bryan, Billy Bosta, and a tale of treasure all had a big role in this incident, which led to my being called to the Peninsula Baptist Association. It also involved a headache, but mostly, it was the leading of the Holy Spirit. At the time, I was working for the local welfare department, dealing with cases of neglected or abused kids. This was emotionally draining, but it was a job that had to be done, which made it worthwhile.

Earlier in life, I had felt that the Lord wanted me in some sort of direct Christian ministry, but nothing had been forthcoming. And so I had kind of pushed it to the back of my mind. It was also during this time that I began working with the younger guys at church, in particular the Royal Ambassadors. This group included the above mentioned and several others. Because I had also been scuba diving for many years, one of my interests was underwater shipwrecks and treasures. I tried to tie this subject in with the other activities in which I engaged the RAs.

One of the shipwrecks I had researched took place near our neck of the woods. It was a Spanish fleet that had gotten caught in a hurricane during the mid-1700s. One by one, the galleons and frigates had been driven ashore along several Atlantic coast states. The first ships to take the brunt of the storm happened to be in more populated regions, and their wrecks had been fairly well salvaged soon after.

Ships ran ashore at Topsail and Drum Inlet in North Carolina. There was but one ship left, however, she too was soon cast upon the sand by wind-driven breakers. This ship, *La Galga*, came ashore in a remote stretch of coastline along the North Carolina-Virginia border. This is the only ship whose treasure the sea and sand has never given up.

At the time, there was an inlet called Currituck, which has since washed over. A few tantalizing leads came to light, but no major salvage had ever been attempted. Some of the articles I had read discussed these bits and pieces of evidence. Local residents on either side of the old Currituck Inlet would, from time to time, find gold doubloons along the shoreline and even inland.

This is a story you can check out in your own local library. Look for information about Spanish ships, including the La Galga, being blown ashore during a 1750 hurricane. The last ship broke up at the shoreline near the Virginia-North Carolina border, where Currituck Inlet was located. Thus, it would seem that the ship was wrecked just off the coast there.

We decided we wanted to have a go at some of those doubloons, if not the whole treasure. Our problem was that we did not have a boat, and no roads led all the way to the site. Therefore, I devised a different plan. We would drive my car as far as the roads could take us. Then we would park and hike down the beach. All we needed was a partially filled backpack for such things as food, water, and a sleeping bag. Why partially full? Well, that way we would have room for all the gold doubloons and silver pieces of eight we would most certainly find on our journey. (I had no doubt that God would reward His faithful servant—me—who was spending all this time with the church youth!)

So that is what we did. It was a beautiful day for a hike, and that part of the trip was a complete success. We had lots of fun, even though we didn't find a single coin of any sort that first day. We made camp on the beach at dusk. We were still confident of our success, though. Surely, the surf would wash up some coins for us to find tomorrow. The return trip was a replica of the day before: lots of sun and wind and surf, but no treasure. To be honest, I am not sure we got anywhere near the shipwreck site.

However, the two days of walking through soft sand in the heat finally took a toll on my head. By the time we were within a mile of my car, the only thing I had to show for the two-day adventure was a splitting headache. You know the type—the kind that makes you not want to talk to anybody about anything. That was me. All I wanted was to get to the car and take a couple of the aspirin I always carry in the glove compartment. Then I would drop the guys off, go home, and sink into oblivion.

The last half hour, I was moving on sheer willpower. With perfect timing, the little man inside my head waited for each of my footsteps to hit the sand. Then he would bring his mallet down on the chisel wedged into the back of my brain. I tried to walk with a light step, but it didn't fool the little man. He always knew when to strike the next blow. (This was almost like one of those Excedrin commercials, which show the little man in the head, except that I was looking forward to a couple of Bayer aspirins, not Excedrin.)

I drew strength from a mental image of the aspirin bottle in the car. Actually, it was not a bottle at all. This was when you could purchase Bayer in small tin boxes that held twelve or twenty-four of those wonderful white tablets. Aspirin has always been a wonder drug for me.

When I got to the car, I found my tin of aspirin in the glove compartment. It was empty.

Once an RA, always an RA. This was at a PBA mission
event many years later: me, Phil Everhart, Jimmy Ailor,
and Tommy O'Bryan. (1)

Mentally yelling—only softly because the little man needed
only the slightest excuse to do his worst—I accused the Lord of
not giving me proper attention. After all, I had been willing to put
up with the guys for *two* days. (That included Jim Ailor, mind you!)
The Lord should have prevented any headaches. At least I was not
thinking about any treasure we had not found!

On the way home, the throbbing finally reached the point
at which it seemed to hold at a constant level. I knew then that I
would live. I drove back to Hampton as fast as possible, dropped
the guys off at their homes, and then headed for the local pharma-
cy, where I could purchase the required drugs.

Now, all I wanted at that moment was to go inside, buy the
aspirin, and escape as soon as humanly possible. The last thing in
the world I needed was a conversation with an old college friend.
Naturally, the only other person in the store was an old college

friend. I had not seen her in a couple of years, but I was sure she would recognize me. I tried to slip down an aisle on the opposite side of the store. I came around the end of the aisle and saw the aspirin display. She was standing beside it.

I had no choice. Plastering on a fake smile, I approached. I said hello and then proceeded to carry on one of the most mindless and hypocritical conversation of my life.

"Hi, how have you been?" I asked. *Haywood, grab the aspirin and only be as nice as you have to be to get what you need. Maybe she's in a hurry. . .*

"Fine, Mike! How are you doing?"

"Oh, I'm fine." *Can't you tell I have a headache? I don't want to talk. I want to go home!*

"That's great. Where are you working these days?"

"I'm working with the welfare department. I really love it." *Who cares where I am working? Right now, I couldn't care less about where I work or who I work with.*

"That's neat. My mom was telling me that the Baptists are looking to start a social work ministry on the Peninsula, working with young people. Maybe you should check into it."

I have a headache, and you want to talk about the Baptists?

OK, Haywood, be nice and tell her you think it's a great idea, whatever it is she's talking about. Lord, just get me out of here!

"Gosh," I said as I paid for the aspirin, "I would love something like that. Well, good seeing you. I have to run now."

Before she could say anything else, I scooped up my change and headed for the door. I began to feel a little guilty on the way home, but the little man with the hammer started to tap out a new tune, and I forgot the whole episode. It was a short ride to my home and couch. I popped two aspirin and drifted off into a solid sleep. The little man had moved on by the time I awoke and with him, my memory of the encounter at the drugstore.

If it had been up to me, things would have ended then and there. However, the Lord had other ideas. My friend talked to her mom, who talked with Reverend Kissinger, the director of missions for the PBA. George Kissinger then called my pastor, Chester Brown, who evidently said nice things about me.

George then called me in the middle of the week, when I didn't have a headache. I was truly excited about what he had to say. I listened intently and the rest is history. It took about six months, but the following spring it was official, and in May 1971, I began my career with the Peninsula Baptist Association.

George Kissinger, director of the PBA when I joined, is at the groundbreaking of the property on Hall Road. This was a mission church started by Hampton Baptist. Lewis Parsons is to George's left. On the far left, is Chet Smith, the first pastor of Hall Road Mission. (2)

Chapter 34
Three Special Services

All of the worship experiences at Hampton Baptist made a big impact on me and many others. There were other special worship events that left their mark, but I want to mention three in particular.

CHRISTMAS EVE
CANDLELIGHT COMMUNION

This yearly service was always a profound experience. A lot of churches do these, although most start earlier in the evening. At Hampton, the Christmas Eve service began at 10:30 p.m. with harp music and usually ended a little before midnight. Most years, they were so well attended that chairs had to be set up at the end of the pews. It always concluded with the lighting of candles and the singing of "Silent Night." The congregation would raise and lower their candles at certain parts of the song.

Chester Brown recently told me the story about how our Christmas Eve service got started. Chester said that after the 1960 vote to install him as pastor at the beginning of the next year, Dr. Garber came to him to with an interesting idea.

For many years, Hampton Baptist had what was called a "Watch Night" service on New Year's Eve. But there was a church in Norfolk that had begun holding a nighttime Christmas Eve service. From what he'd heard about it, Dr. Garber thought it was a good idea that could be implemented at HBC. He suggested that he and Chester go to the church in Norfolk to check out their Christmas Eve service.

This being his last holiday season as the pastor of Hampton Baptist, Dr. Garber thought it might be nice for Chester to begin a new tradition at the end of *his* first year. So, on Christmas Eve 1960, the current and future pastors attended that service. They were both impressed and decided that they would retire the Watch Night on New Year's Eve and institute a Christmas Eve service the following year. HBC mostly followed the same format, but in later years, Chester added some new components, including harp music to begin the service.

In late December, the weather was cold, of course, but not usually inclement. One year, however, we had an ice storm that knocked out most of the electricity in Hampton. One of the few places that had power was a small part of downtown Hampton, which included Hampton Baptist. The church got the word out that the candlelight service would still be held that evening at 10:30 as usual.

There was no electricity at my apartment, the wind was freezing, and a layer of ice coated the trees. However, the church was well lit and warm. The service was beautiful, and I was glad we had not canceled. At the beginning of the service, Chester remarked that they probably should have canceled but that this was his favorite worship service of the year! I could easily believe that.

It was a time when you got to see most of the regular attendees but also members who had moved far away and returned for this special occasion.

For the first couple of decades, the 10:30 p.m. service was the only one on Christmas Eve. At some point, many of the young adults with small children asked Jay Russ if the church could manage another service earlier in the evening. Jay spoke with the staff, who thought this might be a good idea. It was decided that Jay would be ideal to lead this service. People at both have said how special these services have been to them and their families.

ADVENT MEDITATIONS BOOKLET

This is not a worship service, but I think here is the best place to mention this special "devotional ministry" that Hampton Baptist provided for its members beginning in the early 1990s. Chester had come across something similar at another church and felt it was something that HBC could do well.

It was decided that the church would write and publish a booklet of daily Advent meditations. The staff would select Bible verses and various church members would write a devotional using one of those scriptures. These little books were always uplifting and illuminating. It gave many in our congregation a chance to share their thoughts and insights about the Advent season.

The following people contributed a written meditation in some of the later years:

O COME EMMANUEL: MEDITATIONS FOR ADVENT

Chester Brown	Stan Ewing
Martha Ailor	Corinna Powell
Jack Miller	Eddie and Bev Forbes
Steve and Amy Witcover-Sandford	David and Becky Glass
Jay Russ	Charlotte Dillow
Dan and Margaret Menser	Ben Sandford
Keith Ethridge	Ben and Linda Riddle
Nancy Sandford	Tom Matthews
H. O. and Monika Malone	Alystra Barefoot
Phil and Lucille Everhart	Bill and Brenda Cole
Erin Hallissy	Suzanna McKendree
Bruce and Martha Owens	Bill Hurt
Bill and Nancy Trimble	Frank and Mary Jane Ranson

MAUNDY THURSDAY COMMUNION

For many years, beginning in the mid-1980s, Hampton Baptist held a Maundy Thursday communion service. In it, the deacons acted out a tableau scene of the Last Supper. When the speaking parts were finished, the one portraying Jesus broke bread and gave it to the deacons representing the disciples. They in turn distributed the bread to the congregation. The same was done with the wine (which was actually grape juice).

It was always a very moving experience; however, my two most vivid memories are humorous. The first year that HBC offered this service, I was in the last year of my deacon term. Whoever was directing the reenactment asked me if I would play the part of Judas. In truth, I had made another commitment and had to decline. I am not sure if some people thought I'd done so because I didn't want to be Judas.

The next year, I kept that night open and was able to help with the scene. Because I had rotated off the deacon board this year, it was decided that I should play the part of Jesus; that way the deacons could play the disciples and serve communion to the congregation. I caught a lot of kidding about skipping Judas and waiting it out to play Jesus. (Honestly, that was not the reason!) I played Jesus for the next five or six years.

The second thing that I remember well involves my good buddy Jay Russ. Although he was not a deacon, Jay was portraying of the twelve disciples one year. This was during the period that I played Jesus. I was sitting alone at the table with the communion elements as the "disciples" entered one at a time. I greeted each with some kind of gesture, which might include a hug, a handshake, a pat on the shoulder, and so on.

Previous pages: GA coronation service: Martha Ailor is in the center (green dress), and that might be Ann Ailor on the left with the green cape and crown (2)

When Jay's character came into the room, I tried to do something different. We clasped hands overhead then lowered them to chest level while pulling each other closer. Once everyone had arrived, we sat and proceeded with the supper.

After the service, several relieved people came to Jay and me, all saying the same thing. They'd each had a moment of panic, thinking that we were going to give each other a high five! That would have surely ruined the solemn experience, but some wouldn't put it past us.

The next year, Jay and I were again cast to be in the Maundy Thursday program. At the first rehearsal, we made so many jokes and bloopers that whoever was directing the tableau got really frustrated. When the scene was really getting out of hand, one of the deacons told the director, "Don't worry, none of these things can happen on Maundy Thursday because the day before, Jay is going into the hospital for a hernia operation."

It was true! Jay had his surgery, and Maundy Thursday was carried off without a hitch!

GA AND ACTEEN CORANATIONS

The pageantry of these services always left me inspired. I remember telling someone when I was young that if I ever got married, I wanted the service to look like one of these coronations. Of course, no one ever had to worry about how to pull that off!

Chapter 35
The Godfreys

Bill and Virginia Godfrey were at the church for several years. Bill was the executive officer on a submarine stationed in the area. They were regulars at church, and all of their kids were active in the ministries for children and teens.

It was also during this time in the late 1970s that I began a Peninsula Baptist Association coed softball league. Hampton Baptist was trying to join that league when Bret Godfrey came to me and said that his mom was offering to coach the HBC team. I talked with Virginia, and although she knew nothing about softball, she was happy to be the coach so that the church could have a team in the league. (No one else had volunteered.) She went on to say that Bret would do the actual coaching but that she would occupy the official position, which had to be filled by an adult. That situation worked great, and it was fun to have her, and Bret, as part of the league.

(In fact, it was because of this that I changed the rules of our softball league: an adult must be present but the coach can be one of the players.)

During this time, the Godfreys became close friends with Chester and Mary Etta Brown as well as with the Ewing family. Raynelle Ewing and Virginia were especially close, as were their daughters, Heather Ewing and Jill Godfrey, and sons, Jon Ewing and Bret Godfrey. About a decade later, Heather and Jill accompanied me and others on a scuba-diving vacation in Key Largo. Jon, Heather, Bret, and Jill also helped with some of our retreats and other events for the hearing and visually impaired.

Jill Godfrey, Heather Ewing, and Karen Watts at a retreat for the hearing and visually impaired (in the new dining hall at Camp Piankatank) (1)

One of the ministries I was performing through the PBA at the time involved finding temporary foster homes. When I left the Hampton social services department to go to the PBA, that need was expressed to me by several of my coworkers, and I worked to find homes that could take in children temporarily.

I found out that Virginia volunteered in a city program aimed to provide relief for single mothers with special needs children. Volunteer families would babysit the kids for a couple of hours, thus allowing the single mother some time to do whatever needed to be done or have an hour or two to herself. It was a great program, and Virginia loved doing it.

I talked with Virginia a couple of times about the social services need for safe homes in which to place teens for short periods of time. The Godfreys did this for me a couple of times. One of

418

the other needs I had each summer was housing for out-of-state college students who were working as summer missionaries for the PBA. This ministry was one in which four to six college students came for ten weeks to work with the PBA. Most of the students who did summer mission work were from local churches and wouldn't need a place to stay. (This included several Hampton Baptist students over the years.) However, we would also get students from the Home Mission Board and from Baptist Student Unions. Those would be from other parts of Virginia or another state altogether.

The Godfrey family was able to take in two delightful young ladies. First, they had Belinda Crowley and after that, Marianne Williams. I spent a lot of afternoons and Saturday mornings going by the Godfrey home and chatting with the family during those two years (1979 and 1980). I specifically remember going to pick up my Smishy and eating pancakes with Virginia and the student they were housing at the time.

Belinda Crowley (Texas Tech University) was our new out-of-state Smishy in 1979, and she got us off to an auspicious start by wrecking one of the Godfreys' cars. Well, it was not as bad as it sounds. The first day I brought Belinda to them, I explained that I would provide transportation for her during the summer. Virginia said that might be needed from time to time, but for the most part, Belinda could drive their old car. Both Belinda and I were a little hesitant, but Virginia was adamant. Their insurance would cover Belinda, and it would make things easier on me.

Of course, Belinda ran into a bit of a situation the first week here. She had purchased flowers (I think for the Godfreys) and was driving home with the vase in the passenger seat. As she made the sharp turn onto their street, the vase of flowers started to tip over. Belinda kept one hand on the wheel and reached for the vase with the other. Unfortunately, in leaning toward the passenger seat, the hand on the steering wheel kept turning it, and before she knew it, she had side-swiped a telephone pole. (Brooke Puckett would be the second Smishy to tangle with a pole. At least in Brooke's case, it was her family's car. We were returning in a caravan from Camp Piankatank, where we had held a day event for visually impaired students. I was behind Brooke's car when she made a lefthand turn onto a side road and knocked down a yield sign on a wooden post. Since no one else was around, I told Brooke and the rest of the drivers to "drive on" as though nothing had happened. And that is what we did!)

Belinda called me and sounded a little shook up as she told me her story. I drove over to the house, not knowing what to expect. When I got there, Virginia was all smiles.

"Mike," she said, "You didn't have to come! It's not that big a deal. I'll get Bret hammer out the dent. He's good at it. I won't even have to report it to the insurance company. These things happen. Don't worry about it."

Bret Godfrey, Tom Bundick, Jon Ewing, and Mildred Barnes at Eagle Eyrie (2)

In fact, Virginia was so understanding about the whole thing that it helped quell Belinda's objections to driving the car ever again.

"Of course you will keep driving the car," she said. "It was an accident, and it was trivial. And if you hit another pole, we'll just get Bret to fix it again!"

Belinda tried to argue, but Virginia was having nothing to do with it. Belinda kept driving and without incident the rest of the summer. I think she was worried the next time she got behind the wheel, but she did fine.

Belinda was the perfect summer missionary to put with Virginia and Bill. The three of them were laid-back, quiet people, who would do anything in the world to help you out.

That incident probably best describes the Godfrey family. They loved each other, their friends, and the people they got to know. My own life was richer because I got to know them. Bill was always optimistic and a lot of fun. He even got me a sweater once.

Bill and Virginia always sat in the balcony at church, and after becoming their friend, I usually sat with them during the 11:00 a.m. church service. And of course, they were at most church events. I saw Bill a couple of times wearing a neat blue sweater. I told him how much I liked it. He told me that he had gotten it at the PX and that a lot of his shipmates wore the same sweater, and indeed, it had a military look to it. Bill immediately offered to pick one up for me if I wanted. I did, and the next week, he gave me a sweater. Not only did it look good but it was also very warm. I loved it and wore it until it became ragged.

One other memory is the Sunday morning I was sitting with them after I had helped a church with a lock-in the night before. Because there had been a big storm brewing, Bill had been on the submarine all night and had just gotten off duty that morning. Virginia was sitting between Bill and me.

Shortly into the service, I felt an elbow dig into my ribs, and I woke up. I mouthed a thank-you to Virginia and watched as she had to do the same thing to Bill, who nodded off on the other side. Long story short, Virginia spent the whole service elbowing both of us every five minutes or so. We were both sleepy enough that Virginia got a good workout that morning.

The following winter, I began taking vision-impaired students on snow-skiing trips at Massanutten. It was a big success and a lot of fun. During the first year of the program, I got Bret Godfrey to be one of my volunteer helpers.

The Godfreys' had become one of my own second homes. If I needed transportation or another chaperone or someone to look after a lonesome child, they didn't hesitate to pitch in.

The next summer, I got a delightful young lady named Marianne as an out-of-state summer missionary from Texas. Once again, I asked Virginia and Bill if they would house her, and they were more than happy to do so.

Bill and Virginia were the perfect summer parents for Marianne. Like the prior year, this meant that I would get a lot of pancakes and coffee at their house each morning when I drove over to pick up Marianne. (Bret needed the extra car this year, and so I was back to taxiing.)

They had one foster daughter in the home when Marianne came to live with them. Kim Sok was a Cambodian refugee who had first been housed with Iris and Willard Garris, but by this time, she had been with the Godfreys for a couple of years. One of the big events of this summer was going to be Kim's wedding. Kim was a quiet and pleasant young lady who loved to help out around the house, which she did almost to distraction.

Her only issue was in high school. Actually, it was in only one class—English. Kim worked hard, and by her senior year was getting a real feel for the language. In the middle of her senior year, she told me the following story, which illustrates how well she had assimilated English.

As an assignment for one of her classes, Kim and two other students had to make a commercial for a product of their choice. The other two girls were fluent in two other languages, let's say Spanish and French. They decided that they would individually give the same presentation in three languages: Spanish, French, and Cambodian (Khmer). Then, in unison, they would repeat it in English. They were going to do this in rapid-fire order. Kim was to go last in the individual presentations.

On the day of the presentation, Kim felt she had everything down pat. The three girls walked to the front of the room, displayed a picture of their product, and then launched into the verbal presentation. The French and Spanish versions finished, it was time for Kim to give her presentation in the Cambodian language. But when Kim opened her mouth to speak—nothing! She couldn't say a word in Cambodian because the only words that came to her mind were English. Finally, slowly and deliberately, she was able to "translate" in her mind the presentation from English to Cambodian. Kim said that for the first time in her life, she was happy to be embarrassed.

It took Marianne all of thirty minutes to fit right into the family. I left after having coffee with her and Virginia, convinced I was in for a summer I would not soon forget. I was right, but not in the way I ever would have hoped. The next morning, I made it to the Godfreys' in time for pancakes out on the screened-in side porch, and then it was off to introduce Marianne to the rest of the summer team.

The next two weeks were busy and fun. The team spent their days doing Vacation Bible Schools at low-rent housing projects and in the backyards of church members. Then we came together each night to goof off. Marianne missed a couple of evenings with us because she was doing something with the Godfreys.

Then one Thursday afternoon, Virginia called to tell me that she and Bill were heading out for the weekend. They had the chance to take an unexpected trip for a couple of days in Puerto Rico. They had asked Marianne to take care of the kids and just wanted to let me know. We talked for a while, and I wished them a good trip.

That Saturday night, the team was at my apartment. Marianne was not able to come over because she was with the Godfrey kids, but the rest of us were enjoying movies and games. Then the phone rang. I answered and could immediately tell that something was terribly wrong. Marianne was sobbing on the other end.

She told me that they just received the message that Bill and Virginia had been killed that afternoon. Their helicopter had crashed in the ocean between two islands.

I had suddenly lost two good friends, but of course, the biggest loss was that of two parents to the Godfrey children. I don't need to go into how devastated every one of us was. I know that I was simply stunned.

Bill's brother agreed to come down to take care of the family until things could get sorted out. Still, it was going to be a couple of weeks before he could arrive, and he asked if Marianne would stay at the house for the remainder of the summer to help out, which she was more than willing to do. I, of course, told her that caring for the children was now her main ministry for the rest of the summer.

I mentioned earlier that the Ewings and Godfreys were great friends. I was speaking with Raynelle Ewing as well as Heather Ewing Klose and Jon Ewing at a recent Wednesday night supper. (Yes, I am still getting my weekly best meal at Hampton Baptist.)

Heather and Jon played a large part in helping the Godfrey children through that difficult time. As all of us at HBC were taught, friendship is often fun and adventurous, but it is also therapeutic!

Heather and Jon each shared with me a story I had not heard before concerning the Godfreys. Heather said that Virginia would make her and other teens visiting the home do chores. Heather did her share of chores but Jon said he managed to avoid most of them.

Jon also let me know that I did him and Bret a service by placing girls at the Godfreys' during the summers. God always sent attractive Smishies my way; Belinda and Marianne were no exceptions. The two guys didn't mind that a bit! Jon, Bret, and Belinda served on one of our retreats for the hearing and visually impaired. Jon told me that he remembered pushing Belinda in the pool during that weekend. I do not remember that, but it was a fairly typical occurence at the retreats I ran so it would blend in with many such memories!

The Holy Spirit was on that household and began a merciful ministry of consoling and healing. As far as our team was concerned, Marianne had the most difficult assignment that summer. This tragedy did, however, help make our team grow even closer together.

Then the summer ended on an emotional, yet bittersweet high. Kim was married at Hampton Baptist Church the first week of August, with Pastor Chester Brown officiating. Kim asked Jill Godfrey and Marianne Williams to be her bridesmaids. I do not know if I have ever seen three more beautiful young ladies walk down the same aisle.

The scene that day was perfect, displaying the all-encompassing love of Jesus Christ. It reflected the fact that love can radiate through us, into any situation. Bill Godfrey would have been the one to give the bride away. No doubt in my mind that he and Virginia were there that day in spirit. In Bill's stead, Willard Garris walked Kim down the aisle and gave her away.

Although they never met, the Godfreys and the Sullivans reminded me a lot of each other. They were both military families, who were only at the church for a limited number of years. The real similarity was that they were low-key, personable, and willing to do anything to help out in any situation. They both greatly impacted my life. The Godfreys, like the Sullivans years before, had become close friends with the Browns, Ewings, Everharts, Ericksons, Suzanna McKendree, and many others.

Bill Godfrey left another legacy. The captain and crew of the submarine Bill was stationed on gave a gift in memory of Bill and Virginia. They presented Hampton Baptist with a pulpit Bible, which was used by the church for many years.

Virginia Godfrey and Raynelle Ewing getting ready for VBS (2)

Chapter 36

Above: Craig Waddell, Aaron Whittington, me, and Jay Russ at Work Camp (1)

Below: Annie Forrest with a kid on a mission trip (4)

Sidney Swiggart leading singing on a youth outing (3)

Martha Feathers (2)

Eleanor Oakley and Sandra Bundick at a youth Sunday school picnic (3)

The joys of mission trips: Sarah Trimble, Brenna Moore, and Beth Everett (4)

A Work Camp site with Jim Puckett and Aaron Whittington (4)

Natalie Forbes and Bobby Vann at the church (4)

Stan Ewing, Sam Ailor, Dick Everett, Joe Spencer, Frank Riggins, Williard Garris, and Bill Corlett on a deacons' retreat (2)

Senior adults at play and work: above—Mary Cibinic and Anna Ulsh with Dottie Lee Jones on the far right; right—Mary Cibinic (2)

Right: Lindsey
Matthews
(4)

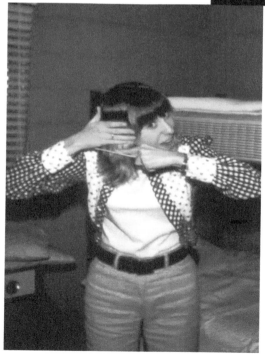

Left: Marianne Gaesser (3)

Chapter 37
Youth Week and Youth Sunday

This must be a VBS class preparing to send greetings to church staff, probably the year Jay Lawson was summer youth director by himself. (2)

The church includes a Youth Week and Youth Sunday each year. On Youth Sunday, the young people of the church teach all the adult Sunday school classes, and the youth pastor preaches at the worship service. In later years, there have sometimes been a series of senior-high preachers. The youth enjoy several socials during the week and may even lead the Wednesday evening service.

I can tell you about Youth Week for 1960 because the *Daily Press* published an article in the Sunday morning paper about the coming week. It listed who would be involved and what would be happening.

A rising senior, I was the "youth pastor" in 1960, and David Levy was the "assistant youth pastor." I can still remember that Sunday morning because I kind of put Chester Brown, then the associate pastor, on the spot, but he bailed me out nicely. The theme of Youth Week that year was "Christ—Youth's Example." I wrote my sermon and prepared to deliver it. The only mistake I made in preparation was not paying attention to the length of the sermon.

Dr. Garber, the pastor, presented me with a Bible to commemorate the official beginning of Youth Week. Then Chester took over as moderator. I delivered my sermon, which lasted all of five minutes. When I finished with prayer, Chester returned to the pulpit and spent about twenty minutes riffing on the theme and what would be happening during the week. He did this off the cuff during the 8:30 a.m. service. I wasn't able to add much content to the sermon between services, but at least Chester was prepared for the eleven o'clock.

The Sunday evening service had four speakers: Mike Haywood, Linda Miller, Sandy Aust, and Eddie Higgins. Music consisted of a solo by Jackie Norman and a quartet number by Carol Turnbull, Linda Miller, Kenny Matthews, and Tommy Northern. A churchwide fellowship followed.

David Levy spoke at the Wednesday evening service, and Barbara Gunter sang a solo. There was a luau-themed evening on Friday at the home of Mr. and Mrs. Milo Begor. Mr. and Mrs. A. W. Patrick entertained the youth with a beach outing at their summer home on Saturday afternoon.

> The other notable Youth Week that I remember was in the early 1960s. A group of young adults lobbied to get Margie Whitcomb as the youth pastor. She did a great job in that capacity.

I have the list of participants for a Youth Week in the early 2000s:

Senior Speakers: Mary Williams, Ellen Barnes, Molly O'Bryan, Erin Hallissy, Sara Martinez, and Richard Pulley

Ushers: Tommy Fields, Courtney Russ, Libby Cox, Megan Tucker, Megan Forbes, Patrick O'Bryan, Ben Hallissy, Kylee Jordan

O T Scripture: Will McKendree

Children's Sermon: Leigh Taylor Smith

Offertory: Reid Matthews

N T Scripture: Eric Stevenson

Sunday School Teachers: Justin Martinez and Chris Flowers; Kaitlyn Rejzer and Kylee Jordan; Megan Forbes, Katie O'Bryan and Kelly Sayers; Ellen Barnes and Jenny Fields; Richard Pulley and Ian McPhee; Courtney Russ, Ben Hallissy, and Lauren H(**); Casey McPhee and Rich H(**); Sara Martinez and Erika Fields; Will McKendree, Will Bane, and Philip Everhart; Tommy Fields, Leigh Taylor Smith, and Lloyd Everhart; Courtney Rejzer and Brando B.(**); Erin Hallissy and Libby Cox; Patrick O'Bryan and Ashley W(**); Mary Williams and Megan Tucker; Molly O'Bryan and Annie Forrest

Chapter 38
The Bible Bet and the Beard Barbered

In the fall of 1996, I made a bet with the youth to encourage them to bring their own Bibles to Sunday school. To win the bet, they had to achieve a collective 90 percent of Bibles brought for eight Sunday mornings. If they fulfilled the requirement, they could cut off my beard and moustache.

You probably remember the six-question report we had to fill out each Sunday: 1. Present? 2. On time? 3. Brought Bible? 4. Brought offering? 5. Studied lesson? 6. Attending worship?

I had maintained my beard since I'd grown it in 1976. If I lost the bet, I would get to keep my hair but had to remain beardless for one month. The contest would last for two months.

After the first Sunday, they had a 50 percent grade, and I was feeling pretty confident that I would be able to preserve my beard and moustache.

However, after their slow start, the youth really got into it, and they were soon consistently arriving with their own Bibles. Twice during the period, parents told me they had to head back home after leaving for Sunday school because one of their children—a teenager—remembered they had left their Bible at home. The parents told their teens to pick one up at church; there were always plenty lying around. The teens explained that the terms of the agreement required them to have their own Bible from home and that they wanted to see me clean-shaven.

Annie Forrest and Billy Everette were my only youth allies. Both Annie and Billy told me at the time that they wanted me to keep my facial hair and so would not bring their Bibles on purpose. They kept their vows, but incredibly, evenwith the slow start and my two supporters, the class reached the 90 percent threshold by the end of the eighth Sunday. The contest ended during the month of December.

Jay Russ and Bill Hurt thought it would be appropriate to do the barbering during Church Night. Bill wrote a script that centered around this event, and it was the centerpiece of the 1997 Church Night event.

CHURCH NIGHT 1997
"CUTTING HAYWOOD'S BEARD"

The Church Night skit began with me walking around the front of the sanctuary as though lost. I run into Bill Hurt and explain that I'm new to town and looking for a church to attend. Here are the ensuing highlights:

- Bill gives me a seat in a barber chair (belonging to Jimmy Taylor) and says he wants to tell me some of the special features of Hampton Baptist.
- Stan Ewing, Sunday school director, talks about Sunday school, drapes a smok over me, and fastens it at the neck.
- Bev Doyer tells me that there are a lot of single women in the WMU, but they all prefer men who are clean-shaven. She also says she has alerted the Prayer Chain about my upcoming ordeal. "Mike, you never know when you might need prayer."
- Jay Russ talks about Children's Church and Monika Malone about the Soup Kitchen.

- Bill Hurt talks about the upcoming winter Bible study about Samson and Delilah.
- Jay Russ talks about the Gift Wrap Booth and gifts me a box of Band-Aids.
- Sidney Jordan, Bev Forbes, and Pam Hallissy talk about the summer VBS.
- Baxter Lee pantomimes a portion of *The Barber of Seville*.
- Bill mentions that the youth recently performed a musical titled *Living on the Edge*.
- The youth come on stage carrying Edge shaving cream and garden tools.
- Corinna Powell stands in front of me with a pair of hedge trimmers. I ask her who she is. Corinna replies, "I'm Delilah!"
- At this point, the youth surround me so that no one can see as they do their work. The first time they break, I'm wearing a skull cap. Someone says, "I thought we were supposed to shave the beard, not the head!"
- They get back to work, and when they separate a second time, I'm wearing a wig and a gorilla mask. "I knew we shouldn't have used the Rogaine aftershave!"
- The third time they break, I have Band-Aids all over my face (and beard). "The lighting is not good in here. Grab the electric razor, and let's do it right."
- During the earlier gags, Jay Russ had shaved a line on my sideburns to show the youth how far up they could go. (Miraculously, they respected this boundary.)
- Each youth shaves a part of my beard and moustache with "The Barber of Seville" playing in the background. (They actually do a good job of not harming me.)
- Bill's final comment is "Well, Mike, as you can see, HBC is a church on the cutting edge!"

Kristi Ferris and "Delilah" (Corinna Powell) at a church youth event (4)

As agreed, I shaved the next morning before work and did the same for the next thirty days. I will admit that I was so used to the beard and moustache that I hated my new look. On the morning of the thirty-first day, I did not shave and waited eagerly for the facial hair to grow back.

The beard remained with me until the COVID crisis of 2020, when all the barber shops closed. I let things go as long as possible but eventually tried to trim the beard myself. I never could get the two sides even and would cut a little too much on the bushier side. Finally, I said, "Oh, why not?" I shaved it clean and started growing it back after that.

When I went for a walk past the home of Robert and Tracy Hudson, Tracy was sitting out in the yard. She took my picture to send "a beardless Mike Haywood" to some people in the church.

January 1997 at the PBA office on my first day without my beard (1)

Chapter 39
Church League Sports

When I first got involved in Hampton Baptist city league sports, Billy LaNeave was the coach of the softball team. I actually got to play one year of fast-pitch softball before the city switched to slow-pitch. I was happy with the switch.

That last year of fast-pitch, the games were played at Darling Stadium. Home plate was on the visitor side of the stadium, nearest the corner of Victoria Boulevard and Kecoughtan Road. That meant you had a short right-field line, but left field could be the length of the football field. Right field was bordered by the bleachers, but left field had no barriers.

Frank Earwood later told me about attending the yearly softball meeting for the city's recreation. Frank was the coach of the Fordham Independent Baptist Church in East Hampton at the time. Suey Eason, who worked for the city then, told the assembled coaches that he had been introduced to a new type of softball. It was called "slow-pitch softball," in which the ball is pitched underhand with an arc. The city recreation league implemented the style that year and never looked back.

Frank Earwood was a role model for a lot of Hampton Baptist youth and adults. Most of us remember him from our days of playing church league softball and basketball. Frank eventually became the pastor of Buckroe Baptist and later, Faith Baptist.

Frank was generally the official for church softball and one of the two officials for basketball. I think the thing that most of us remember about Frank is that he was fair, encouraging, and relational. He was also an excellent official and kept the games in control.

When I began the Peninsula Baptist coed softball league in 1977, Frank was one of three people I consulted. The other two were Jimmy Osborne, who ran the Newport News city softball leagues, and Jerry Compton, a member of Liberty Baptist and a recreation specialist for Fort Monroe and other East Coast army bases. Not only did they give great input, but all three became umpires for PBA softball. They were three of the reasons that the softball league was a success.

Lucky Elliott was coaching the Hampton Baptist basketball team the first year I played, along with Jack Shepherd, Don Miller, and others. During those days, the *Daily Press* would print the box scores of the church league games each week, which means I got my name in the paper. Bill Nelson, who was in his first year of college, saw a copy of the box score and wrote me the following: "Wow, Mike! Two points! How awesome!"

Shortly after I started playing with Hampton Baptist, Billy Byrd became our coach for both basketball and softball. He was a great coach. I remember playing a lot of coed softball games at Darling Stadium, Pembroke High, and Eaton Junior High.

Bill Nelson caused me a bit of a problem a couple of years later while he was still in college. He was home for the summer and working at the *Daily Press*. I have to admit that I was never a great hitter while playing softball for the church. (I also got flak for having a "shot-put" arm when throwing from second to first base.) But this year, I got the first and only homerun of my life. Being nice, Bill, who was at the game and who also worked on the sports pages of the newspaper, mentioned my homerun, along with a couple of others in that ballgame.

At first, I was excited to see my name in print. I was working for the Shipyard at that time, and my department had been working overtime two nights a week, Monday and Wednesday. Church league softball was played on Monday and Thursday nights. Only once did I give my boss an excuse about not being able to work one Monday, and you can guess which game that was. My boss happened to read the sports page! Fortunately, he was understanding and not upset, but I did get a lot of kidding about it.

You might remember from one of the Church Night quizzes in Chapter 4 that HBC had a bad-luck basketball team (1-11) in 1966. But that year's softball team fared much better, coming in second place in the league. There were seven teams in the league that season. Ironically, we did not lose a game to the first-, third-, or fourth-place teams but lost once each to the fifth-, sixth-, and seventh-place teams. Our record was 8-3-1. The first-place team, which we beat once and tied once, had a record of 9-2-1!

The members of that 1966 softball team are mentioned in the poem that Bill Sasser and I wrote:

AN ODE TO PAST DEFEATS

The year that passed was sixty-six.
It was a year we got our kick.

The year was hardly one week old,
when the basketball team began to fold.

Nine straight we lost, things looked bleak,
And then a forfeit marred our streak.

We ended the season at one and eleven.
I sure hope they aren't keeping records in heaven.

Then came the summer and on the scene
Was the pride of the church, the softball team.

Hampton Baptist Church

Old veterans and rookies, they came a'hopping,
And Dawson too with his flashbulbs popping.

We had many problems, both big and small:
Sheppard played in the mud, and Sasser couldn't hit
  the ball.

Everhart could hit the ball but never hit it fair,
And every time that Miller swung, he only hit thin air.

Lawson and Ailor played the field as if they were so tired.
Haywood's and Elliott's pitching left much to be desired.

Byrd was always on the ball, just like a Mickey Mantle,
But every time he reached for it, he couldn't find
  the handle.

Robbins could not buy a hit, Brumfield was too slow,
Erickson couldn't field the ball, and Riddle
  couldn't throw.

At least we were consistent in the year that passed.
We lost the first game that we played, and we lost
  the last!

What we've said has been in jest
Because we know we were the best.

Next year we're bound to go all the way,
So come on out and watch us play.

For a couple of years, the girls played in the volleyball church league, with games being played at the Thorpe Junior High gym (the old Hampton High School). I remember that Suzanna and Martha Dunn played one year.

Billy Byrd was a terrific basketball player, but in later years, he didn't get a lot of help from his friends, including me. The newer player who added a lot to our team was Ted Taylor. Ted was our friend in the Air Force who was a fantastic basketball player. We won a lot more games after Billy added Ted to the team.

I did a better job of organizing sport leagues (softball, basketball, and flag football) for the Peninsula Baptist Association. Hampton Baptist teams did well in those leagues, winning several titles, from the late 1980s on. By that time, Jay Russ had taken over coaching the teams. The league was initially for youth but beginning in the mid-1970s, was expanded to adults. All of the PBA leagues were coed.

Susie Castle, Sue Martinez, and Justin Martinez at adult coed softball (1)

Left: Alice Matthews Erickson showing her softball form in a game at Eastover (Alice played for HBC in the city recreation leagues.) (2)

Below: Don Miller was an ump in my youth and adult coed softball leagues. This batter is part of a Special Olympics team, one of several that played in the PBA league each year. I didn't require my umps to wear uniforms, and Donald took full advantage! He became very active in city sports officiating for both Hampton and Newport News. (1)

Above: Brooke Puckett, Molly O'Bryan, and Mary Williams (1)

Below: Brooke Puckett; Mike, Sue, and Justin Martinez; Debbie Puckett; Will McKendree; and Susie Castle (1)

Chapter 40

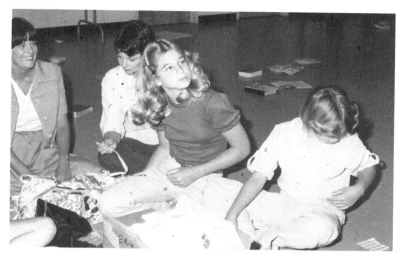

Virginia Godfrey and Teresa Diggs helping at VBS (2)

Jean Jones, Cindy Rollins, Mary Etta Mann, Nancy
Mitchum, and Dianna Copple at Nags Head—the latter three
got the helmets from an army surplus store. (1)

Above: Frank
Riggins and Jon
Ewing (2)

Left: Steve
Sandford serving at
a youth banquet (3)

Nancy Forbes during an outdoors VBS refreshment time (2)

Gene Kirby helping at VBS (2)

Sharon Diggs, Sue Coughenour, and the VBS visit the organ. (2)

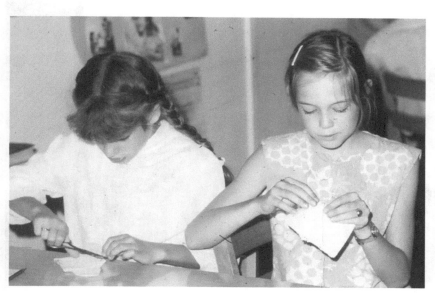

Trudy McBride works on a craft. (2)

Angie Russ and Jane Kirby (2)

Gene Kirby, John Erickson, and LaVonda Simpson at Eastover (3)

Wayne Erickson, Jimmy Michael, and LaVonda Simpson
(a Jim Ailor painting in background) (3)

Jill Godfrey,
Heather
Ewing,
Susan
Forbes,
Krista
Everett,
and Sandy
Everett (3)

Right: Linda Hurt
giving a ride (2)

Below: Nancy Lee
Jones (2)

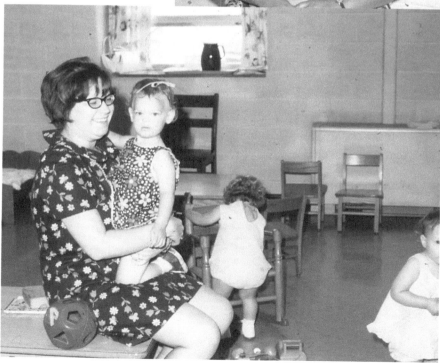

Susan Wallace, Beth Robbins, and Brenda Vick at the Fisherman's Cove (3)

Chapter 41
Chester Brown's Unique Ministry

When the steeple came down in 1999, we had to worship in the fellowship hall for a couple of months. During that period, one of the Sunday morning bulletins featured pictures of people who had grown up in Hampton Baptist and later pursued church ministry as well as current members in the ministry. As you might expect, it was substantial but not an exhaustive list.

Hampton Baptist had more members in ministry than any other church in the Peninsula Baptist Association. I suspect that it is more than most other churches anywhere. This trend began under Dr. Garber, but it really hit its peak during Chester's pastorate. Both Dr. Garber and Dr. Brown encouraged HBC members to seek where God might be leading them. It was not always into a church ministry, but it was often a service of some sort. (Although the shared youth ministry of Jim Ailor and Jay Lawson is a poster example, few of those who entered the ministry were cut from the same cloth.)

Bill Hurt came shortly after Chester, and he provided a steady and calm influence on the education of church members. This dovetailed nicely with Chester's modeling. In addition, Gary Lewis led a music ministry that lifted the soul and inspired us to want to do good for the Lord. When Jay Russ came to be the youth minister, his style of leadership and mentorship contributed to the same goal. All four of these staff members encouraged congregants to ponder where God might be leading them and then be willing to follow that leading.

Jay Russ put all of this in perspective during a recent funeral. Bill Hurt passed away in 2023 while I was writing this manuscript. Chester Brown, Jay Russ, and Paul Garber spoke at the funeral.

Bill and Jane Hurt's children—Linda, Amy, Alan, and David—were there. So were a lot of Hampton Baptist people.

After sharing a lot of remembrances, Jay told those gathered that we need to remember what the church has done for us. HBC developed more than forty people in a thirty-year span who went into the ministry of the church or other people-related careers (teachers, lawyers, physicians, nurses, social workers, etc.). He reminded us to celebrate our past but not forget that there is much more to be accomplished.

Hampton Baptist's other unique quality is that it became a place of refuge and healing for other pastors of the Peninsula who had to leave their churches for various reasons (generally, retirment, health issues, or church dysfunction). Chester and Hampton Baptist were always available to provide them rest and space. Chester would actually reach out and invite such pastors—whether they agreed theologically or not—to worship with us while they worked through their situations.

Another method Chester used to encourage pastors—those new to the Peninsula and those going through a rough patch—was to take them out fishing. Chester grew up on Sarah's Creek, and the water was his old friend. In later years, Jay Russ got to go on many of these fishing trips. Chester would grab Jay and the pastor in question and take them out in his boat. It was a time to get away for a while and relax—a time when questions could be asked and answered without judgment.

Some of the pastors knew a bit about boats and some of them knew nothing. Jay told me about one incident in which Chester was struggling to get a fish into the boat and asked the visiting pastor to take the wheel. This pastor knew nothing about boating and kept bumping the boat into a concrete piling. Chester began to grow frustrated but kept his voice calm as he tried to help the pastor navigate around the obstruction, without much success!

One great example of how Hampton Baptist encouraged us to follow the leading of the Holy Spirit is the friendship of Chester Brown and his pastor, George Kissinger. George was the pastor of Union Baptist when Chester went into the ministry. Although no one would accuse George and Chester of sharing the same theological grounding, there was a respect and affection between the two that was obvious to all. And that never changed to the day George died.

I was a product of this mentorship in which all members of the church were encouraged to discover how their gifts and services might be used. Often this realization did not result in an official, paid ministry position. Church members could find roles within the organizations of the church, perhaps being called to become deacons, Sunday school teachers, leaders of girls' and boys' programs, and even (one of my personal favorites) cooks for the Wednesday night suppers. The leadership we were given did not stop there but included guidance in how to be effective husbands, wives, and parents.

When I first started working with the PBA, George was my boss. For fifteen years, he was as responsible as anyone for my continued employment there. George led the service when Chester was ordained, and they were as close as two friends could be. They worked well together and always encouraged each other.

George retired in 1985 and moved back to Achilles, in Gloucester. Chester and I would visit him from time to time.

When Mary Etta was offered the position of principal at an international school in Cairo, Egypt (after Chester retired from HBC and Mary Etta retired from being an elementary school principal), they would go on to live there for seven years. Chester and I went to visit George one more time before he and Mary Etta moved.

The visit went well, and just before we left, Chester said, "George, I know that even though I didn't turn out theologically exactly as you would have liked, I want you to know that you had a profound influence on my life and in church ministry." George thanked him for the kind words.

At that point, I said truthfully, "And I want to say that the two of you have had a profound influence on my life and ministry."

George was in his nineties at that point but still sharp with a keen sense of humor. His immediately reply was "If that's true, then we are all in trouble!"

Below is a list of members who grew up at HBC and went into full-time Christian ministries. Most became pastors, but you will find singers, educators, music and youth ministers, Christian counselors, chaplains, and other positions of Christian ministry. (I know this is not a complete list, and I apologize to anyone I've left out.)

MEMBERS WHO LATER ENTERED THE MINISTRY (PARTIAL LIST)

1. Ailor, Jim
2. Blackwell, Johnny
3. Collier, Quimby
4. Dunn, James
5. Ellis, Chris
6. Farris, Eugene
7. Owens (Feathers), Martha
8. Garber, Paul
9. Goodwin, Thomas
10. Harris, Earnest
11. Haywood, Mike

12. Wilkerson (Jones), Jean
13. Kirby, Bert
14. Lambert, Margaret
15. Lawson, Jay
16. Lilley, Ed
17. Matthews, Tom
18. Mitton (Riddle), Becky
19. McCraney, Arnold
20. Morris, Owen
21. Mull, Dick
22. Nidiffer (Tillery), Jo
23. Northen, Betty
24. Ozment, David
25. Parron, Matt
26. Pulley, Ann
27. Pulley, Richard
28. Rawls, Thomas
29. Sandford, Ben
30. Sinclair, Bill
31. Taylor, Ted
32. Vann, Bobby
33. Whittington, Aaron
34. Yates, Robert
35. Wilson, Rick
36. Hartmann, Eleanor

PARTIAL LIST OF MEMBERS IN MINISTRY WHEN THEY JOINED THE CHURCH

1. Ethridge, Keith
2. Glass, Becky

3. Kinnard, Will
4. Latham, Lynn
5. Phelphs, Ron

MEMBERS WHO WORKED AS SUMMER YOUTH MINISTERS

1. Krista Everett
2. Brooke Puckett
3. Erin Hallassy
4. Bobby Vann

MEMBERS WHO WORKED AS "SMISHIES" (PBA SUMMER MISSIONARIES)

1. Jim Ailor
2. Susan Williams
3. Karen Watts
4. Sandy Everett
5. Aaron Whittington
6. Krista Everett
7. Brooke Puckett
8. Beth Everett
9. Lindsey Matthews
10. Chris Ellis
11. Corinna Powell
12. Ann Pulley
13. Billy Everett
14. Bridgett Wilson
15. Will Rawls
16. Bobby Vann

17. Megan Tucker
18. Kylee Jordan
19. Courtney Russ
20. Caitlyn Russ
21. Megan Forbes
22. Erin Hallissy
23. Leigh Taylor Smith
24. Billy Jones
25. Collin Chance
26. Lauren Farow

Read lines left to right   L

LINE 1
Jay Lawson, Pastor, Hilton Baptist
Thomas Goodwin, Student, Fruitland Bible College (NC)
Martha Feathers Owens, * Staff, Peninsula Pastoral Counseling Center
Thomas Rawls,* Student, Univ. of Richmond
LINE 2
Chris Ellis,* Student, Averett College
Eleanor Hartman, Assoc. Pastor, Hilton Baptist (NN)
Jim Ailor, Pastor, Hebron Baptist (Afton, Va.)
Johnny Blackwell, Retired Pastor (Waverly Baptist)
Keith Ethridge, *Assoc. Dir. HQ/VA
LINE 3
Jean Jones Wilkinson, Former Dir. Richmond Baptist Center
Paul Garber,* Retired Pastor (Gloucester Point Baptist)
Tom Matthews, Retired Music/Organist Rock Springs Presby. (Atlanta)
Betty Northen, Pastor, Oakdale United Methodist (Baton Rouge)
Mike Haywood,*Ministerial Staff, Pen. Bapt. Assoc.
LINE 4
Ronald Phelps,* Retired, Dept. Chief Chaplians, VA
Quinby Collier, Dir. Men's Programs, Teen Challenge, Mid-South
Robert Yates, Pastor, Vaughan Baptist, Vaughan, NC
Lynn Latham, Innercity Ministry, Orlando
Ed Lilley, Student and Youth Minister, Poquoson Baptist
LINE 5
Will Kinnard,* Assoc. Dir. HQ/VA
Becky Glass,* Staff, Peninsula Pastoral Counseling Center
Ben Sandford, Pastor, Big Bethel Church (Hampton)

* Present Members
Others not pictured: James Dunn, Ernest Harris, Bert Kirby, Margaret Lamberth, Becky Riddle Mitton
Orrin Morris, Dick Mull, Jo Tillery Nidiffer, David Ozment, Rick Wilson

Chapter 42

Above: Sydney Swiggart leading the youth choir: Linda Hurt, Laura Wood, Cindy Parsons, Cindy Garris, Kim Schneider, LaVonda Simpson, and Trudy McBride (3)

Right: Chester giving a service award (2)

Above: Sunday school
picnic (3)

Left: Susan Forbes
and Krista Everett

Above: Tonya and Sidney Pearce; below: Susan Lilly,
Sharon Goodwin, and Jill Godfrey at a costume party (2)

Dawn Lilley serving Leigh North, David Martin, and Ed Lilley (2)

Wayne Everhart (2)

Above: Anna Ulsh; below: Linda Hurt (2)

Top: Kitchen duty (2); above: Ben Sandford, Nancy Lee
Jones, and Nancy Sandford: Halloween 1976 (2)

Chapter 43
March on Buckroe

Jim Ailor keeps popping up in all these stories, but that has been true for all the years I have known Jim. During his college years, Ailor put his enthusiasm into what was known at the time as the "Jesus People." That term referred to any young person who was completely sold out to Jesus. And Ailor was! From Jesus cheers at the top of a building to a Jesus march on our local amusement park, Jim was the ringleader.

The march occurred the year that Jim was the youth director at Fox Hill Road Baptist. Jimmy later told me that he had figured the distance that Jesus had to carry the cross to Calvary. The trip from Fox Hill Road Baptist to Buckroe Beach was the same distance. And so the march began at the church, and we would return there afterward. It was a Saturday.

During the march to the beach, we stuck "reds" anywhere we could. Reds were Christian stickers about the size of a quarter. Jimmy had designed these red stickers with phrases such as "Turn to Jesus," "Freak Out on Jesus," "God Is Love—Jesus Shows It," and "One Way—Jesus." If I remember correctly, there were four stickers on a page. We would peel them off and paste them to telephone poles, mailboxes, street signs, and so on.

Opposite page: As reported in the PBA newsletter "The Plan"

"JESUS PEOPLE" MARCH TO BEACH

by JIM AILOR

on't know why we have to have Jesus March. I wish we didn't. don't know why the news media en't reporting the great demonrations of the Holy Spirit in urches across the nation. I n't know why you have to strike, have a sit-in, or demonstrate, march to reach the news med- but "we'll march all the way Washington if we have to, to ow the world we mean business," omised a band of 200 Jesus ople who disrupted traffic turday night during a Jesus rch from Willow Oaks Mall to ckroe Beach. The 4½-mile march lled the air with songs and sus cheers. One lady said, hen I saw the march I was fur- us, but the love that covered e march quickly changed my

mind." Some 400 attended the rally following, at the beach where song, praise and testimonies "turned many on" to Jesus. Three folk-singing groups; The Whispers of Love, The Campbels, and a group from Rock Church; led the rally.

The Jesus People declared all-out war on the devil. "The devil has turned the Peninsula upside down, and Jesus is going to turn it right side up." Some 8,000 tracts, Jesus papers, and "reds" were passed out.

Herb Griffith, youth director at Phoebus Baptist, said in awe, "Where did all these Jesus People come from?"

September: Busy Month

CHURCH TRAINING

REGIONAL CHURCH TRAINING CONVENTION is to be held at Parkview church September 14 at 7:30 p.m.

BAPTIST MEN

Associational Baptist Men's Meeting has been changed to September 25, 1972, at 6:00 p.m. at First Baptist Church, Newport News. Tickets for dinner are $1.00.

BAPTIST MEN'S WORKSHOP
September 15-16, 1972
Eagle Eyrie   Cost $9.25

SUNDAY SCHOOL

Immeasurable help to new Sunday School officers and teachers will be available at the "Associational Sunday School Launch" to be held September 18 and 19 at 7:00 p.m. at Temple church. Staff members are listed below.

General Officers - Rev. Jack
                         Price
Young Adults - Rev. Joe Vaughan
Adults - Rev. Robert Carlton
Youth - Rev. Nim Lawrence
Younger Children - Mrs. Elsa
                        Begley
Older Children - Mrs. Betty
                       Willett
Younger Preschool - Mrs. Annie
                     Lee Carlton
Older Preschool - Mrs. Britt
                       Burroughs

Now It's Ours - And the Bank's!

Pictured at left are: Mr. W. L. Carleton, Attorney for Peninsula Baptist Association; Rev. V. Allen Gaines, Associational Moderator, Mr. M. Hunter Riggins, Chairman of the Eastover Committee, and Mr. Tom Newton, Attorney for Gray Lumber company; as title to Eastover Plantation is formally transferred to Peninsula Baptist Association. Mr. Newton is associated with McGuire, Woods, and Battle of Richmond.

Peninsula Baptists are reminded that in order to utilize Eastover, certain guidelines must be followed. These were printed in the last issue of PLAN.

A FALL WORK DAY IS PLANNED. DATE TO BE ANNOUNCED SOON.

The Lord taught me a great lesson on that march: He is in charge, and He has a special role for Jimmy Ailor.

To be honest, I was not too excited about the march. It wasn't really my thing, and I didn't particularly want to go. I didn't think it would do a lot of good, and I felt that any non-Christians would ignore us or think we were loony. I only participated because Jimmy was my friend, and he needed a few adults (in age only) to be present. I figured it was going to be a waste of time, but what the heck?

Things began pretty much as I expected. We marched down the road toward the amusement park and beach, shouting Jesus cheers and singing hymns. The only people who paid us any mind were those who had to wait at an intersection for a couple hundred teenagers to cross. We committed a little "vandalism" on the way by sticking the reds all over the amusement park, but even that didn't get any dramatic response. We walked across the street and stood as a group at the seawall that ran along the road as we looked past thirty yards of beach to the water's edge.

Jimmy wanted a crowd to preach to, but we were not attracting one. I sat down, hoping he would soon give this up so we could all go home. Jimmy came beside me and said he was going to pray for the Lord to send some youth our way.

I thought, "Jimmy, the Lord is not going to send you anyone today. This is not the Lord's way." I had already made up the Lord's mind for Him. (Was that a chuckle I heard from up on high, over the sound of the surf?)

Jimmy started to pray. I wasn't praying. In fact, I was looking to our left, where a group of teens walked down the beach where the waves break. They were headed toward us. Watching the tall girl—with the long, flowing blonde hair, wearing cut-offs and sporting a dark tan—accompanied by a group of four or five guys, was as good a way as any to pass the time as Jim continued to pray.

Keep in mind, *I* am the one with no faith this afternoon. I had told the Lord what I thought about this whole thing. It didn't seem to me like the group of teens walking through the surf had been paying us any attention. They were too busy talking among themselves.

But then, just as they came parallel to us, the tall girl broke away from the group and headed straight for us—for *me* actually.

Her friends stopped for an instant and then followed behind her. She was definitely the leader. She was looking right at me, probably because I was the only one of us with his eyes open. Everyone else was busy praying. She walked up and stopped about three paces from me. I stood up. In a loud and belligerent voice, she asked just what "the hell" did we think we were doing.

Now, I have to be honest about this. I did no witnessing that day. What I did do was argue with her. I told her we were on a Jesus March. She told me how silly that was. Ailor had stopped praying and was standing just off to the side. I should have turned it over to him right then, but I was hooked into the argument and went toe to toe with this young lady. What I didn't notice until later was that our arguing had attracted a crowd of teenagers, probably larger than our original group.

Ailor waited until his audience had grown considerably, and then he politely asked me if he could say something. ("Well, sure. Isn't this whole thing your idea?") Then Ailor preached to this assembly of youth. I sat down again and reflected on the fact that Ailor's faith in the Lord had been validated. He had been sent a crowd as requested. And the Lord had used unbelieving me to help attract this crowd.

I do not know what results, if any, came from Jimmy's sermon that afternoon. I do know that he preached the Word that day. And I also know that the whole incident had a profound affect on me. (In fairness, I should also say that the young lady and I had an enjoyable and rational discussion after Jimmy finished. She was very intelligent and made some good points. I do not know if Jimmy's beachside sermon had any effect on her life, but I hope it raised some curiosity.)

Many years later, Jim was called as the director of missions for the PBA. One day, he walked into my office and said, "Mike, I have a gift for you."

He then threw a strip of reds on my desk, telling me he had found them at his house in an old filing cabinet!

Chapter 44
Senior Adults

Hampton Baptist has always treated its senior adult members well. They represent a wellspring of knowledge and experience. A lot of the "Hall People" I have mentioned were senior adults.

Two things stand out in my mind when I think of our senior adults: One is the amount of time that Bill Hurt and Alice Erickson put into garden tours, historic home visits, and special events at the church. Later, when Alice had moved on, Jay Russ and Bill Hurt regularly organized the senior adult events.

And two, I got to be a waiter at the annual senior adult banquet for about a decade. That was always a joyful event.

Baxter Lee is the emcee at a fashion show during a senior adult banquet. (2)

Right: Nannie
McKendree and
Madge Haywood (2)

Below: Ammie
Garber (2)

Church Picnic

Below right: Betty Corbett (5)

Below left: Betty and Frank
Tillery with Margaret (5)

Lucille Rollins on a house and garden tour (2)

Nannie McKendree (2)

Dexter Bird and Francis Jones (2)

Food, glorious food! (2)

Alice Erickson, Velma Jean Allison, Madge Haywood, and
Francis Jones (2)

Nannie McKendree and Madge Haywood (2)

Lucille Rollins, Freda Nelson, and Alice Erickson (2)

Chapter 45
Church Nights 1998–2000

1998
"LET THE PEOPLE RUN"

Church Night Committee: Keith Ethridge, Wayne Cox, Bonnie Madre, Frank Schneider, Kay and Gary Powell, Gordon Rawls, Peggy McBride, Nancy Sandford, Bob Sigler, and Traci Ward

Instead of a nominating committee to name officers and leaders of church programs, people could run for office at this Church Night, and the congregation would cast votes on Sunday morning.

- Stan Ewing and Anna Moore made campaign speeches for Sunday school director.
- Mike Haywood came in with a ballot box: "Any more ballots to be stuffed—I mean, ballots to be marked?"
- Bill Hurt: "You have a lot of ballots there. Perhaps you should bring in another box."
- Mike: "I have a better idea!" *(pulls out a shredding machine)*
- Phil Everhart Sr. and Tom Forrest campaigned for Premises Committee.
- Bonnie Madre: "We need names for the emerging two parties. How about 'Samsonite' for the liberals and 'Jericho Boys' for the conservatives?"
- Sidney Jordan and David Glass campaigned for the WMU and Men's Association.
- Bill Trimble and John Bane campaigned for church treasurer. "We need to build a golf course with no green fees for Jay Russ and a duck blind in the steeple for Dr. Brown."

- Gene Jordan, Bill Williams, Bert Kirby, Joanna Rawls, and Woody Patrick also made appearances.
- Mike Haywood (PBA) was the teacher for the Foreign Missions Week of Prayer.

[1999—No Script]

2000
"INDIANA JONES AND THE FALLEN STEEPLE"

Church Night Committee: Susanna McKendree, Bruce Owens, Jack and Ruby Sheppard, Nancy and Bill Forbes

- The opening scene showed the steeple falling because of Chester pounding the pulpit. Then Chester said, "Bill, our steeple just fell off, and it's irritating me. Please go out, and put it back in place!"
- Bill Hurt called Phil Everhart Sr., and they inspected the fallen steeple, finding a number of artifacts inside, and sent for Indiana Jones to help.
- The on-going gag was that someone from St. John's Episcopal kept trying to steal items from the steeple that might prove that HBC is older than St. John's.
- Some of the items found included a frying pan (Robert Hudson performed in a skit about the pancake breakfasts) and the old Sunday school attendance records of Bill Sparrow.
- Joanne Barbour was in a skit about Family Night suppers.
- In another skit, Jay Russ used a pickaxe on the ice in the baptismal in order to baptize Courtney Russ, who was wearing a lot of warm clothing. (Note: Baptismal water was freezing cold on the morning Courtney was to be baptized because the heat had not been turned on.)

- Sidney Jordan told about the church picnic. Nancy Forbes talked about VBS.
- Beth Forrest Jennings came to be the HBC interim music minister.
- Phil found a pictorial directory "artifact"; a St. John's member fought with Indiana Jones as the performance came to a close.

BILL HURT'S RETIREMENT CELEBRATION

In 2005, after all the annual Church Nights written and directed by Bill Hurt, the time came for Bill to retire. We were in a bit of a quandary because it was Bill who had always created the programs to honor any HBC retiree. Now the church needed a program to celebrate Bill—the man who had designed all the programs.

The committee appointed to plan Bill's retirement program came up with two good ideas, but it was obvious that neither would be appropriate: 1. Get Bill to write and direct his own retirement program. This idea had merit but was quickly voted down. 2. Chester Brown, who gave Bill the annual Church Night program to direct, was often its target—I mean, *subject*, so someone suggested that Chester produce and direct Bill's ceremony. This idea was also voted down.

Finally, Eddie Forbes and others came up with a suitable program to honor Bill Hurt's career. Fittingly, they based it on a TV show that was popular at the time, *Keeping Up Appearances* with Hyacinth and Richard Bucket.

It was at this retirement ceremony that Bill called me up front and gave me copies of all his annual Church Night program notes.

In 2006, we had the same problem of "no Bill" to direct Church Night, but that is a story for another time.

Chapter 46
And Then Came Jay

As you know by now, Jay Russ came to be the youth minister of Hampton Baptist in 1985. Jay had the youth participate in many PBA events over the years. He and I also initiated Tuesday luncheons for PBA ministers—mostly youth ministers—which continues today. Some of the current participants include Jay, Ed Lilley, Jay Lawson, Brenden Lawson, Matt Parron, and me.

Jay did me a big favor, for which I am deeply appreciative. There was a time in the mid-1980s that I, while trying to make sure I didn't show favoritism to HBC youth in PBA events, actually neglected playing a role in our church family. In 1987, Jay pointed that out to me and told me how to correct it by being his helper at the Wednesday- and Sunday-night youth meetings. After I agreed, he said it would further help if I became the youth Sunday school director. What could I say? He had me "dead to rights."

It is neat how things so often work together for good. The three guys in the middle of the photo on the previous page are Jon Ewing, Jeff Flowers, and Jimmy George at Eagle Eyrie. I am in the back row, between Laura Wood and Trudy McBride. Martha Feathers is on the far right. Lib Hutchby and Kim Sok are in the front row.

Jeff Flowers, Jay Russ, and Jimmy George were at Mars Hill College together. (This picture was taken before I met Jay.) Jimmy had asked me to find a summer youth position for Jeff through the PBA. I was able to direct him to Stevens Memorial. They all went from Mars Hill to Southeastern Seminary together. Jay, Jimmy, and Jeff are great friends today, and so is John Ewing. (3)

So I said "yes," and much of what follows is a result of that conversation. Jay had done me a great favor because over the next fifteen years, those roles led to some of the most enjoyable times of my life.

GAMES FROM THE JAY RUSS
YOUTH MINISTRY YEARS

I have already described some of the novel activities that Jay did with the youth group, but I'd like to mention a few more.

I will begin with a game that Jay invented in the mid-eighties. It's a ping-pong game that I had never seen before. All you need is the table, one ball, two paddles, and a lot of space to move around the table.

We begin with two players at each end of the table. Those two players can do a regular volley for the serve or simply choose who serves first. All the rest of the youth form a circle around the table. One of the two end players serves the ball, quickly lays the paddle on the table, and moves to his or her right or left. As soon as the first player touches the ball, the person to their left/right immediately runs to the spot, picks up the paddle, and prepares to return the ball from the player on the opposite side. After the second player returns the ball, he/she drops the paddle, and the next player moves to the end of the table. If a ball is misplayed, the game pauses, both ends rotate in the same direction, and the game continues with another serve. If the server makes a mistake, the player on their side takes over. When you make a mistake, either serving or returning, you are out of the game. This can become a very hard game as the number of players dwindles. When it's finally down to three players, one will have to run to the other side before the ball is returned.

I am sure that some other youth minister has played this same game with their youth group. However, in all of the recreation conferences I've attended and books I've read for decades, I have never come across a game even remotely close to this one.

Another event Jay pioneered that became a big hit with youth at Hampton Baptist Church and later the Peninsula Baptist Association was the Turkey Hunt. Begun in the mid-1980s, it comprised three to four HBC teams, each with their own vehicle. Sometime in the 1990s, Jay suggested that we make it a PBA event. We did, and it continued until around 2008. In a nutshell, this event involved a scavenger/treasure hunt on the Peninsula and surrounding area. It was not uncommon for a church van to put on a hundred or more miles during the Turkey Hunt.

We would start at a church or the PBA office. The basic ground rules were laid out there, and the first clue given to the teams. At a PBA Turkey Hunt, we would usually have between ten and fifteen churches participating, with well over 200 youth.

Generally, the Turkey Hunt comprised one of four scenarios:

1. Each clue would take you to a church or public area where you would search for a cut-out "turkey." After finding all the turkeys, you would rush (under the speed limit, of course!) back to where you started. Once you returned, you would have one or more puzzles to figure out, which normally had you to performing a skit or song.

2. Each clue would take you to a church where certain adults would give you a feat to perform (throw a hula hoop over a person standing ten yards away; drive four large nails into a plank without bending any of the nails, etc.). One year, the teams had to catch a live turkey, a task much harder than you would expect.

3. Another year, a few weeks before the Turkey Hunt, I drove all over the Peninsula while Jay sat in the passenger seat and filmed our travels. At each location, we hid items that the teams would have to find. This Turkey Hunt was based on the horror movie *The Blair Witch Project*. For another hunt, Jay and I drove all over the Peninsula and painted "turkey tracks" on trees, signs, and telephone poles.

4. Two different years, the clues led the teams to the PBA Eastover Retreat Center. Once there, additional clues told them where to dig for the buried turkeys. The second year of this, we buried the turkeys near the James River waterline, not realizing that we buried them at low tide. It was high tide when the teams dug for them at Eastover. That was interesting.

These were high-energy Saturday afternoons. Here are some of the other memorable events during Turkey Hunts:

Richard Castleberry (First Baptist Church, Newport News) took his youth to Fort Eustis trying to decipher a clue that was actually sending them to Todd Stadium.

Darlene took her youth group to Victoria's Secret in the mall.

One year, unbeknown to Jay and me, Hampton University was having a parade, which blocked off all the roads around Hampton Baptist, where one of the clues led. A couple of groups made the right decision and parked as close as possible and then walked the remaining blocks to the church. The rest of the groups rode around the perimeter for an hour trying to find an open route while calling Jay and me at the base church and using a lot of colorful language. (You might know the quote attributed to Einstein: "The definition of insanity is trying to do the same thing over and over again and expecting different results.")

During one Turkey Hunt, I was officiating PBA flag football at the Orcutt Baptist field. The teams had to come by, wait for a break in the action, and then run to me to get the clue.

Ed Lilley took his youth group to a store in the mall where the workers would give a clue to each team. Because they were a bit slow for Ed's taste, he jumped the counter, found the clues, and took one.

There have been numerous cases in which teams have found a hidden cache of clues, taken theirs, and then hidden the cache in the wrong spot!

UNIVERSITY LIFE

Here is a cautionary tale about who you can trust in life. Jay developed a simulation game for a PBA youth rally to help students prepare for college, hence the name of the game: University Life. The youth played it as a role-playing game. I got to play the part of a football coach who got his players favors from some of the professors. This was in the early 1990s, and it was a big hit at the rally.

Unfortunately, even in Baptist circles, not everyone can be trusted. Jay sent the game to an agency of the Home Mission Board. The staffer took the game, tweaked it, gave it a new name, and marketed it as his own. Jay never heard from the guy again.

Not *every* activity that he involved the youth in was an original Jay Russ creation. He took them to many area attractions as well as Baptist conferences and events.

For many years, laser tag was very popular with youth groups on the Peninsula. There was a big facility in Norfolk for this, and Jay took the HBC youth there often, and I accompanied them several times. The first time Jay and I took the youth there, we ran into a little problem. Most participants give a nickname for their electronic profile, which keeps a record of the number of times you have been hit as well as the number of hits you inflict. All the youth gave their nicknames with no problems. But when Jay and I entered our nicknames, we were told that "Lucifer" and "Devil" were not allowed!

On another occasion, Jay set up two teams. One consisted of four people: me, Jay, and two other adults, Mark Taylor and Talmadge Barbour. The other team, of course, was all the youth. That might not sound fair, and it wasn't—but not in the way you would think.

Jay worked it out with the folks running the facility that night to fix it so that our vests had only one sensor turned on. In addition, every time one of the adults fired their laser, the computers registered a "hit," whether we hit a target or not. It was fun to watch the youth lose their minds because they seemed to be missing shots, even at point-blank range. It was also fun to beat them up, but even more fun to see their faces after the game when Jay told them why!

CENTRIFUGE AND YOUTH MISSION TRIPS

Jay took the youth group on many trips during the year, including an SBC camp called Centrifuge and a mission trip, which usually involved construction and Vacation Bible Schools. These were usually in other states. Due to my Peninsula Baptist summer responsibilities, I was only able to make one Centrifuge, and I did go on a planning trip to Kentucky to help Jay set up the mission that would come later in the summer.

The photos that follow are from of those two summer events.

Lynn Mayberry, Kacie Martin, and Kristi Everett at Ridgecrest (4)

Sarah Trimble, Cary Matthews, Brooke Puckett, Katy Kruschwitz, Beth Everett, Trent Allison, and Debbie Puckett at Centrifuge (4)

Katy Kruschwitz, Nancy Kruschwitz, Lindsey Matthews, Ann Pulley, me, and Corinna Powell at Ridgecrest (4)

Mary Williams, Reid Matthews, Courtney Russ, Libby Cox, Megan Tucker, Leigh Taylor Smith, Katie O'Bryan, Erica Field, Billy Goins, and Will McKendree on a hike at Ridgecrest (4)

Matt Parron and Leigh North playing Uno (4)

The youth group on a mission, flanked by Don Barbour and
Jay Russ (4)

Sandy Everett and Chris Flowers (4)

Supper, the essential part of any trip, with Jim Puckett,
Scott Allison, Nancy Trimble, Kristi Everett, Debbie Puckett,
and Dick Everett (4)

Sara MacDonald and Leigh North (4)

Now, this is truly scary! Matt Parron, Susan Lilley, Bryan
Lilley, and Ed Lilley (4)

A momentary break on a mission trip: Nancy Trimble, Kristi Everett, and Debbie Puckett (4)

Nancy and Susan Forbes back at the church (4)

Music man with muscles: Gary Lewis (4)

Donny and Beth Barbour on a mission trip (4)

Brenna
Moore on
a youth
mission
Vacation
Bible
School (4)

I know that's Greg Bane and Sandy Everett, but who is the
guy in the middle? (4)

Sarah Trimble and Jim Puckett on a mission trip (4)

Marcus King (4)

Brooke Puckett,
Annie Forrest, and
Thomas Rawls (4)

Lindsey Matthews
and Scott Allison
painting (4)

Chris Flowers (4)

Mike Ellis and Jim Puckett (4)

Margaret and Dennis Allison (4)

Greg Bane
and Trent
Allison (4)

Beth Everett
with her
ever-present
smile (4)

Right: Matt
Parron (4)

Below: Trent
Allison, Talmadge
Barbour, and Greg
Bane; Matt Parron,
Ed Lilley, Mark
Taylor, and Steven
Cox in the back (4)

While Jay Russ was keeping the youth involved in so many of the PBA activities (and helping to organize and run many of them), he was also organizing and directing many youth events that were unique to Hampton Baptist Church. Jay was very creative in this respect. Keep in mind that he was inventing games and creative Bible studies every Sunday and Wednesday night during the year.

After arriving at HBC, Jay was put in charge of the Gift Wrap Booth, which helped raise money for upcoming youth events. It was well run and involved a lot of youth and adults. Anyone who helped with the Gift Wrap Booth at Coliseum Mall could probably write a book of their own about it. It was on-going for one month each year, the last day being on Christmas Eve.

A couple of other annual events that Jay led:

- Progressive suppers, when the youth ate an appetizer at one HBC member's house, a salad at another, a main course at yet another, and so on until dessert, with a continuous Bible study or mystery that was worked on at each home
- A Thanksgiving mystery when the youth tried to find out what happened to a turkey that was stolen by someone at the church, which included a video that gave clues
- Planning and overseeing Youth Sunday, when the youth would take on many of the ministries of the church

We should remember this about all the staff members at Hampton Baptist: In addition to all that they do for special events, they prepare for a Sunday worship service (actually two, one early and one late) each week of the year.

Chapter 47
Youth Sunday School

I had been well taught by my youth Sunday school teachers back in the 1950s and 1960s. Of course, some of you will remember that in those days, it was all-boy and all-girl classes. It was Mary Etta Brown and John Dawson, who were the senior-high Sunday school teachers in the 1980s, who decided that the guys and girls could meet together. And so they did, and it's been that way ever since. The HBC youth Sunday school was run by some stellar role models. Some of the teachers in later years included Mary Etta Brown, John Dawson, Francis Jones, Lib Hutchby, and Eleanor Oakley.

They were all excellent teachers, but Mary Etta, Francis Jones, John Dawson, and John Bane seemed to retain their special relationship with the youth even into their older years. Francis and both Johns eventually passed away, but Mary Etta continued teaching in the youth department.

When I stepped in as the superintendent in the late 1980s, Mary Etta and John Bane were teaching the eleventh and twelfth graders and still doing a marvelous job. I would sit in on their classes after opening assembly. I had worked with John Bane, a lawyer, in my years with the juvenile probation office. He was one of the best lawyers for juveniles that I ever came across. My first Sunday as superintendent, I sat in on his class, and all the guys kidded John that Jay Russ had sent me to check up on him and make sure he was doing a good job!

Sue Coughenour in
Sunday school (3)

John had two special gifts in teaching Sunday school. He had served in the army during the Vietnam War, and he had great stories about his service there that he related to the Sunday school lesson. Sometimes his stories were funny, sometimes serious, and often inspirational.

John had another gift that I admired. The youth were always trying to lead him off track from the lesson and talking about Vietnam or any other subject. John would answer their irrelevant question with some commentary, and suddenly, without the class realizing it, he had gotten them back on track!

I have to tell you one more story, which impressed me once I realized what was actually going on. Molly O'Bryan was a delightful young lady, who went with me, Jay, and other youth to Austria on a mission trip to work with Craig Waddell. What I noticed in Sunday school was this: Molly would often ask a question about the lesson that seemed to having nothing to do with the current point. She would often be kidded and, of course, someone would mutter the word *ditzy*.

A few minutes later, John's teaching would lead to the point Molly had been asking about earlier. When she asked her question, she was three steps ahead of everyone else in the class. After I noticed this, I would always try to think ahead and see that Molly was ahead of the game.

In Sunday school, Mary Etta was the solid rock she has always been. Of course, it helped that she was an elementary school principal. She had a great grasp of the Bible and understood young people. She loved the youth and always tried to leave them with a greater grasp of the lesson.

My favorite story about Mary Etta is a humorous one but shows what incredible self-control she possessed. One Sunday, John Bane, Mary Etta, and I were with all the youth for the Sunday school hour. We had a good discussion going on. One of our members had brought a young man, about seventeen years old, as a guest that day. The young man was from a very conservative church, and at one point, he spoke out on the subject of women in the ministry. "Women should remain silent and not teach men," he said.

John and I remained silent and let Mary Etta reply. I will not 'o her words justice but what she said essentially was that he had a ht to his opinion but that not everyone would agree. And that is e the matter rested.

One more Sunday school story from that era: As probably everyone knows, I cannot carry a tune in a bucket. However, I still like to sing. This past spring, I was at Stevens Memorial one Sunday morning, and at the start of his sermon, Jay Russ called me up front and gave me a shirt that said, "I might not have any music ability but that won't keep me from singing!" He said that he and Angie had come across the shirt during a trip.

During the Sunday school opening assembly at HBC, the youth would sing a lot of contemporary worship songs. I sang with them. One Sunday, a dozen of them came to me and said, "Mike, we have a great idea. You let *us* sing, and you listen!"

Well, I really could not argue with that.

Chapter 48

Karen Watts, Mary Elizabeth Brown, and Kathy Moore in the wheelbarrow race (2)

Ye Ole Sack Race (Beth Spencer on the far left) (2)

Sword Drill! (2)

A young Beth Everett, Aaron Whittington, Cary Matthews,
and Daniel Williams on a Jay Russ-led HBC mission trip (4)

Above: Chester Brown presents Bibles to Beth and Teresa Diggs. (2)

Right: Mrs. Wiggs and Jim Michael during a presentation

Chapter 49
Helping with Early PBA Ministries

In May of 1971, I became a home missionary working for the Peninsula Baptist Association. I had been working for the Hampton social services department for the two years before. For the next forty years, I would serve on the Peninsula, directing a large number of ministries for the PBA. A majority of our churches became a working part of these ministries.

Beginning in the late 1980s, none were more active in PBA events than Hampton Baptist Church and its congregation. One of our goals was to involve teens, young adults, and adults in these ministries.

Jim Ailor, Bill Sinclair, Lynne Everhart, Jay Lawson, Allen Feathers, Jimmy Allison, Laurie Schneider, Howard Stone, Wally Hicks, Gene Kirby, Cindy Garris, and Elizabeth Patrick were a big help to me in my early years with the PBA.

When I left the social services department, I was given three specific requests by leaders of city organizations. First, I had been asked by the director of the Big Brothers agency in the city to start a "Big Sisters"-type organization when I went to work for the PBA. (Lynne Everhart was the second person I recruited for that.)

The second request was for emergency foster homes. During my time with social services, there were many occasions when we didn't have an available foster home for a child in custody. Usually, it was only needed for a short period of time: one day to one week. We often ended up using a home that had been certified but was not really one we wanted to use. I worked with the courts and social services in providing temporary homes in which to place a child until social services could find an open foster home. Dick and Camelia Everett were the first family from any church to foster. Later, Hampton Baptist couples included Quimby and Sandra Collier, Lib and Jim Hutchby, Vernon and Cindy Rollins, and Bill and Virginia Godfrey.

The third request came from Wallace Hicks, who was just getting ready to retire. Wally was the chief juvenile probation officer for the city of Hampton. Wally was, of course, a member of Hampton Baptist. He and Jim Thomas (his replacement and a member of Ivy Memorial Baptist) asked if I could do a retreat for boys on probation. I set one up the first summer I was at the PBA in 1971. We used Camp Piankatank, and Jim Ailor was my camp pastor and one of the counselors for the retreat. The next year, we offered a camp for girls on probation, with Lynne Everhart serving as a counselor. The following year, we did a coed retreat for youth on probation in the Hampton, Newport News, and Yorktown areas. Laurie Schneider, Lynne Everhart, Bill Sinclair, and Jim Ailor helped with that one.

The next ministry I got into was working with vision-impaired students. I was asked to set up retreats for the Virginia School for the Deaf and Blind in Hampton. (Later, we got students from the Rehabilitation Center for the Blind in Richmond.) This involved Hampton Baptist folks in two big ways. I set up the camp for the Hampton school. (Another HBC member, Frank Bryan, became the principal at the Virginia School for the Deaf and Blind several years later.) We started small, with a one-day outing to Eastover. I ended up leaving the PBA for one year and had to turn the Eastover day trip over to someone else.

Laurie Schneider
at Camp
Piankatank (1)

Laurie Schneider is pictured above at Camp Piankatank on a retreat in 1974 that the PBA held for boys and girls on probation. Laurie was typical of the many Hampton Baptist youth who helped me in the early years of my ministry with the Peninsula Baptist Association. Each of them had a great love for their church, serving in ministry and being available for one another whenever needed. Always with a smile and a helping hand, they would do whatever was asked of them, be it at a church event or a Peninsula Baptist ministry activity. I am not sure if they fully realized how great an impact they made in these ministries. They simply represented the hands and heart of Jesus Christ to the world around them. I think all of the good I was able to do through the PBA came about because these teens (as well as those from other churches) who helped set me on the right path to doing ministry.

Eagle Eyrie: Laurie (above) and Kathy Moore (right), who helped me with PBA ministries later on (3)

Jean Rozema, Jane Kirby, and Becky Parsons enjoy snack at VBS. Jean took my place when I was on a year's sabbatical from the PBA in 1973. (2)

My replacement was another member of HBC. Jean and Don Rozema attended church for several years in the early 1970s. Don was an army dentist at Fort Monroe. Jean was tapped as my substitute when I took a leave of absence from the PBA in 1973. So Jean ran the event, although I was able to go as a volunteer. Allen Feathers was also on the trip.

I returned to the PBA in 1974 and ran the ministry from that point on. Jay Lawson came on the outing for the blind in 1974. In 1975, we held a two-day retreat for the visually impaired at Camp Piankatank and then expanded to three days from 1976 until the early 2000s.

The list of Hampton Baptist members who helped over the years with the retreats for the hearing and visually impaired included the following (I know I must be leaving someone out): Jim

Ailor; Bill Sinclair; Lynne Everhart; Tracy and Trudy McBride; Jill and Bret Godfrey; Jon and Heather Ewing; Kathy Moore; Martha and Allen Feathers; Ed, Susan, and Dawn Lilley; Laurie and Greg Schneider; Lynn Oakley; Sandy and Krisi Everett; Susan Forbes, Randy Ware, Brooke Puckett, Laura and Mary Williams; Daniel Williams; Corinna Powell; Mary Elizabeth Brown; Karen Watts; Susan Williams; Cindy Garris; Ann Pulley; Cindy Hammonds; Chris Ellis; and Billy Everett.

In 2001, Mary Williams led a retreat for the visually impaired with a group of Austrians and my summer team at Eastover Retreat Center. She did a fantastic job running that retreat.

Also, for about ten years, I worked with the Virginia School and the Wythe Exchange Club to take vision- and hearing-impaired students on snow-skiing trips. Many Hampton Baptist youth helped with these trips including Bret Godfrey, Mary Elizabeth Brown, Karen Watts, Tracy McBride, Susan Williams, Kathy Moore, and Jim Ailor.

Mary Elizabeth Brown on a snow-skiing day at Massanutten (1)

Left: Kathy Moore at dinner
on the way home (1)

Below: Susan Williams
working with a
vision-impaired girl (1)

Tracy McBride works with Velma. (1)

Chapter 50
Eight Special Ministries

While doing a lot of church-related ministry and activities for the HBC youth, Jay Russ also involved his youth group with many ministries of the Peninsula Baptist, making these events successful. From the time that Jay came to Hampton Baptist, he was a welcome partner in helping to plan and run these worthwhile and needed ministries.

WORK CAMP

Darlene Scheepers, Emmaus Baptist's youth director at the time and now Hampton Baptist's administrative assistant, began a ministry of repairing houses on the Peninsula during the early 1990s. Jay Russ got the HBC youth in on Work Camp from its inception. Jay designed one of the first camp T-shirts and served as a worksite leader.

I remember two special stories about Work Camp. I already told you about the time Corinna Powell wore a two-piece bathing suit to Water Country (see Chapter 6), so let me tell you a story about when Jay Russ got me big time!

This was 1999, and I was the site leader at a house where a lot of work needed to be done. The crew worked really hard during the first part of the week. We had run into a few problems with a city inspector but had been able to sort them out and keep working. But on Thursday morning, I drove our crew to the house. Official city tape was draped across the front porch. On the door was a notice that said the house was condemned and off limits.

I was confused and frustrated because no one from the city had informed us. I just stood there at the front of the house, looking at the yellow tape and the sign, growing more frustrated by the minute.

Finally, Chris Ellis said, "Mike, look at the back of the notice."

"How is that going to help?" I said in exasperation but doing as he suggested. On the back was written the following:

> Psych! Got ya, Mike!
> ——Jay Russ

Earlier that year, the steeple on the church had come down in a storm. The sanctuary had been damaged and could not be used for a long while. There was a similar sign on the sanctuary door, but I had not paid attention to it except to be aware that we could not go into the sanctuary.

Jay knew one of the city inspectors, who gave him a blank notice of "condemnation," which Jay filled in and pasted on our Work Camp door. He told Chris Ellis to tell me to read the back of the sign in case I did not. I have to admit that Jay got me this time, good and proper!

Jay would serve as a site supervisor each summer. He also led many of the programs during the camp. We had help from lots of churches as well as HBC. Some of the adults who served as both chaperones and site leaders from Hampton Baptist included Phil Everhart Jr., Jim Puckett, Jon Ewing, Tommy O'Bryan, Martha Owens, Bruce Owens, Steve Sandford, Amy Sandford, Margie Ware, Aaron Whittington, and Erin Hallissy.

John and Margie Ware at Emmaus during Work Camp (1)

Lots of youth, like Beth Everett, came on Work Camps but also worked hard repairing homes on other mission trips with Jay Russ (4)

Right: Caitlyn Russ ripping up a front porch (1)

Below: And then replacing it with help from Mallory Scheepers and Travis Wash (1)

Charlene and Charlie Patterson watch as teens improve their Bruton home

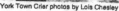

York Town Crier photos by Lois Chesley

Sandy Everett wipes grease from the kitchen walls prior to painting

Workcamp '95 helps rescue Bruton home

By Lois Chesley
Town Crier staff

Charlie Patterson and his daughter, Charlene, of the Bruton section of York County, played host and hostess to a group of 18 teenagers recently. Even though a party atmosphere could have been fostered, the intent of this gathering was far more serious.

The Patterson's home on Queens Creek Road had fallen into serious disrepair, and Charlie Patterson's pleas for assistance through various county agencies fell on deaf ears. Enter two teams from "Workcamp 1995," a project co-sponsored by the Peninsula Baptist Association, Youth Ministry and York-Poquoson Social Services.

The project, now in its third year, offers youth from regional Southern Baptist churches an opportunity to perform community service in their own community or neighboring communities. For one week recently, from Monday to Friday, these youth, along with volunteer adult project leaders, undertook three housing rehabilitation projects in York County and one in Poquoson.

The Patterson home required extensive repairs, but the group rose to the challenge under the leadership of overall project manager Ed Aadahl and his son.

Please see HOUSE, page 2

Work campers repair home

By Lois Chesley
Town Crier staff

During the hottest week of the year, which included 100-degree temperatures, most folks sought the comfort of an air-conditioned environment or headed for the local swimming pool. Not so for a group of young people who participated in "WorkCamp 1997."

This annual, week-long housing rehabilitation project is co-sponsored by York-Poquoson Social Services and the Peninsula Baptist Association Youth Ministry. Now in its fourth year, the project brings youth from several Southern Baptist churches to this area to repair the homes of low-income residents.

Last week, these youth, along with adult project leaders, undertook five housing rehabilitation projects in York County, one in Poquoson and two in Newport News. The annual event is a collaborative, community-based effort involving youth, adult volunteers, church and community groups, businesses, schools and local government agencies.

A York County home in the Bruton area was the largest project undertaken by the group this year, explained Mike Haywood, Youth Director for the Peninsula Baptist Association.

"We have 32 youth here on this site alone," he said. "This year, we have a total of 106 workers on the different sites and 10 cooks to prepare meals."

The home being repaired belongs to Myrtle and Eugene Wallace, an elderly couple who recently experienced health problems. Their situation made it necessary for them to move in with their daughter.

According to Haywood, the total project at the site involved building a wheelchair entrance ramp, removing and replacing the roof, replacing the flooring, repairing the ceilings and painting the interior. In addition, the group planned to provide a new back door entrance and replace the commode and floor in the bathroom.

At the completion of the renova-

Chris Ellis, Brenden Lawson and Corinna Powell replace commode in the bathroom

tions and upgrades, the couple will be able to return to live in their own home.

It is only through the volunteer efforts of many individuals and the support of our community that such a project can be planned and implemented. As in the past, WorkCamp 97 has relied heavily on the generosity of local churches and community groups to provide funding for the housing materials and supplies.

Cheryl Ferreira, Volunteer/Resource Coordinator at

York-Poquoson Social Services, has worked closely with the Peninsula Baptist Association Youth Ministers in the planning and coordinating of the WorkCamp since 1994. She explained that through social workers, "referrals of low-income families in need of significant housing repair are made to the Peninsula Baptist Association Project Leader, Harald Aadahl." He is the Youth Minister at Orcutt Baptist Church.

Please see **CAMP**, Page 2

FISHING TRIPS FOR THE
VISUALLY IMPAIRED

Daniel Williams, Laura Williams, and Betsy Trimble (4)

In the late 1980s, I began a new ministry through the PBA. We had been doing a lot of activities with vision- and hearing-impaired students in our area (from the Virginia School in Hampton) as well as residents of the state Rehabilitation Center for the Blind in Richmond. For the rehab center, we would charter a fishing boat and go out into the bay for a day of fishing.

A good number of students from other churches participated, but because Hampton Baptist was so close to the docks, HBC youth were a big source of help.

We gathered at the church about two hours before the trip, where we would have a time of fellowship. Jay and other adults would make ice cream sundaes for everyone. Then we would pair up with our newfound friends and head for the docks, where we would board the boat. After the fishing day was finished, our guests would head back to Richmond with coolers full of fish, and the rehab center cooks would prepare them a fish dinner. (About thirty fish were spared one year, when a young lady from Richmond named each fish she caught and made us throw them back into the bay.)

Among the HBC youth were Daniel Williams, Laura Williams, Mary Williams, Betsy Trimble, Chris Ellis, Billy Everett, Kathryn Brown, and Karen Watts.

Billy Everett and Chris Ellis taking a fish off the hook (4)

Jay and I making sure the fish are fresh and edible! (1)

Kathryn Brown went on several of the early trips. The
Chamberlain Hotel is in the background. (1)

INTERNATIONAL STUDENTS

In September of 1993, I visited Craig Waddell who, at the time, was the pastor of a church in Linz, Austria. Russ and Pam DeYoung, at North Riverside (where Joe Strother was the pastor and I had my PBA office), told me that if I was going to Austria, I had to also go to Latvia. I agreed and visited both countries. That was the beginning of a thirty-year international relationship that has been rewarding and fun.

Mary Williams (4)

Jay Russ has fooled me on many occasions, but one of the best happened in August 1993, just before my trip to Austria and Latvia. Jay had invited me over to his house for supper. Never one to pass up a free meal, I accepted.

When I arrived, Jay told me we had to go by the church and pick up a few extra chairs because more people were going to eat with us. We drove to the church, and I immediately noticed a lot of cars in the parking lot. Jay said that he didn't know about any meeting, but the lights were on in the sanctuary. Before collecting the chairs, Jay said that he wanted to see what program was going on in the sanctuary.

I peeked in the side door, with Jay just behind me. Suddenly, I felt myself being pushed into the sanctuary. That was when I noticed Jim Ailor and Jay Lawson among other friends inside. Even I could figure this one out. It was a surprise party—for me.

I had not realized that this was my twentieth anniversary at the PBA, but Jay had arranged a celebration. I was completely taken by surprise. I sat down and listened to a lot of nice things about me, done in a funny way. Lawson and Ailor performed a Blues Brothers routine. Jay and Tommy Lawson sang "Friends in Low Places" ("where the pastor don't go and deacons chase the youth away, but that's OK. . . ."), a song we learned at Rec Lab.

One of the kind things that Jay did, which helped with my upcoming trip to Austria and Latvia, was to arrange a money tree, on which people could clip monetary donations. That was really helpful, and I got just over $700 (which was worth a lot in 1993!).

Jay Lawson and Jimmy Ailor doing a Blues Brothers routine at the anniversary (4)

The first year I brought internationals this way was in 1995, when two Latvians and more than a dozen Austrians (and Romanians) came to work with my PBA summer mission team. The Austrians were here for three weeks, and the two Latvian girls, Liga and Ieva, came for ten weeks as Smishies.

We had several of our own youth also working as Smishies that summer. Brooke Puckett, Sandy Everett, and Aaron Whittington helped make the summer a success for Ieva and Liga. Brooke and Sandy came with me to pick them up at the Norfolk International Airport. One of the first things that Aaron did that summer was go with me and the girls to the Mariners' Museum. Aaron will confirm that the two Latvians, sixteen years old, were not all that interested in the museum until we got to the gift shop! Actually, the summer was great. Brooke and Sandy have stayed in contact, via Facebook, with the two Latvians since then.

Ieva and Liga stayed with two families in Newport News, but with the arrival of the Austrians that summer, Hampton Baptist got fully immersed. HBC families kept most of the Austrians that first year in 1995, and they continued to do so for many years after.

The following are those who took in visiting internationals in 1995: Peggy McBride, Sue and Wayne Cox, Jane and Dick Whittington, Sidney and Gene Jordan, Nancy Lee and Bill Trimble, Susie Castle, and Mike Haywood.

In 2000, Jay and I took Ann Pulley, Sara Martinez, Molly O'Bryan, Laura Williams, Mary Williams, Betsy Trimble, and David Cox, along with several others including my book editor, Dara Ailor, to Austria to do a camp with Austrian teens. The camp went well, but more importantly, this trip solidified a plan that Jay, Craig Waddell, and I made for bringing internationals to the Peninsula for many years after.

Starting in 2001, internationals began coming over to work with Hampton Baptist and the Peninsula Baptist Association for several weeks each summer. Although there were a few summers that they did not come, internationals were with us most years.

Austria 2000: standing—Craig Waddell, Mike Haywood, Molly O'Bryan, Laura Williams, Mary Williams, David Cox, Ann Pulley, and Jay Russ; crouching—Sara Martinez and Betsy Trimble

HOSTS FOR VISITING INTERNATIONALS

2001—Austrians, Iraqis, Romanians, Croatians: Sue and Wayne Cox, Virginia and Richard Pulley, Jane and Dick Whittington, Terri and Bob Fields, Angie and Jay Russ, Nancy Lee and Bill Trimble, Lucille Everhart, Sue and Mike Martinez, Bev and Tommy O'Brian, Susie Castle, Sidney and Gene Jordan, Pam and Jim Hallissy, Marion and Frank Supplee, Becky and David Glass, Lynne and Ken Goetzke, Suki and Jim Peirce, Julie and Ron Rejzer, Bev and Eddie Forbes, Debbie and Jim Puckett, and Mike Haywood

In 2001, students from Croatia, Austria, Iraq, and Romania came over with Craig Waddell. In the following photo, the internationals participate in a Wednesday-night youth meeting at HBC. The basic idea of this initiative is to throw a ball of string to another person while calling out their name. The catcher then does the same, and so on. At the end of the exercise, Jay talked about how we are all connected; as long as everyone holds on to their part of the string, the connection will remain strong and intact. Jay then had someone drop their part of the string, which caused the whole configuration to become loose and disjointed.

Nikki and Justin Martinez in the center, and Molly O'Bryan in the lower right (4)

We also did a lot of fun activities, as shown below, when the group was getting ready to play disc golf at a course in Norfolk. The girl next to Jay Russ is Trenice Durio, who was on my summer mission team and the daughter of Troy Durio; Troy ran the PBA Friendship House.

Sara Martinez, Bashar, Kristina, Benji, Trenice, and Jay Russ (l)

This has been a fabulous ministry, and the folks at HBC helped to make it work. Not only did a number of families provide homes, but everyone welcomed the groups into the church family. This ministry continued into the 2000s.

VIRGINIA SCHOOL FOR THE DEAF & BLIND

Hampton Baptist youth and adults got involved with the Virginia School for the Deaf, Blind, and Multi-Disabled (VSDB) the same year I did. We had done retreats for the school (as well as the Richmond Rehabilitation Center for the Blind and others in public schools) starting in 1973. For years, the retreats were the extent of this ministry. But about the time that Jay Russ arrived, we were asked by Dennis Ruffin, the coach at the Hampton school, to bring church teenagers to play the boys and girls basketball teams.

The hearing-impaired team would normally play other schools for the hearing impaired in Virginia and neighboring states. At one time, VSDB also played private schools in our area, but eventually, those games dried up. I had worked with Dennis on some activities at the school, and he asked if some of our churches could play their teams in what would be considered an officiated "league" ball game.

By the way, one of the area officials who would often work the games between the school and the churches was HBC's own Don Miller. Don always did a great job.

So I would get eight to ten churches to play basketball at VSDB. The church teams would be a little cocky going into their first game, but they were consistently the ones coming home with bruises and defeats! I think the churches won about one in five games throughout the years.

Jay brought the Hampton youth out to play every year of the league. They won a couple of games during the 1990s. I have to say that Hampton Baptist played one of the most exciting games at VSDB. It was during a tournament, and I do not remember the score. But I do remember that the game ended in triple overtime, with Hampton losing after a would-be game-winning shot spun out of the basket at the buzzer.

Jay also took the youth to play the visually impaired in a sport called "goal ball." The basics of this game involves rolling a ball about the size of a basketball but with a bell inside. If you are sighted or have partial sight, you must wear a blindfold. The game is played on a basketball court with three players on each side. You try to roll the ball past the other team, keeping the ball in bounds. The church team didn't win many of these games either, but they were a lot of fun.

Lloyd Everhart, Phil Everhart, and Will Bane playing goal ball at the school (1)

The other event in which Hampton Baptist and other churches interacted with kids from VSDB was a twice-a-month supper. This was a big deal because most VSDB students came from all over the state and lived in dorms and ate all their meals at the school. These dinners were usually on a Tuesday or Thursday night, and about

forty-five students (visually impaired, hearing impaired, or mul-
tihandicapped) would come to the host church. The WMU would
prepare dinner, and afterward, the students and church youth
gathered to play games and interact.

CHURCH HOSTED DEAF AND BLIND CHILDREN

On the evening of March 16th, our
church hosted a pancake supper for children
from the Virginia School for the Deaf and
Blind. About 115 people were in attendance,
and a fine experience was had by all. Following supper, the deaf group went to the
Adult I Department while the blind group
stayed in the Fellowship Hall. Specialized
entertainment was provided for (and by!)
each group.

Mike Haywood, Cynthia Hammond, Tracy
McBride, and Kathy Moore are presently working with the group, along with volunteers
from other churches. Mike hopes to involve
more of our youth in this ministry in the
future. Also active with this group is
Phil Everhart. Phil is Chairman of The
Hampton Mayor's Committee on the Handicapped.

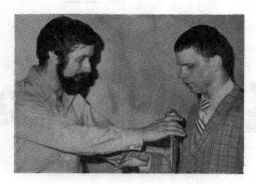

Bill Sinclair, in much later years, with two Happy Class members at the pool at Eastover (1)

HAPPY CLASS

Another ministry that the HBC youth were very involved in was the Happy Class. This is a Sunday school class for mentally challenged youth and adults that was taught at Liberty Baptist Church. (Today, there are two classes: the Happy Class for the lower functioning and the Wise Disciples for the higher functioning.) In 1981, Sarah Wise, who started the class, asked me to run a retreat for them in May.

We used Eastover, and I gathered a large group of youth from various churches, including HBC, to help out. Those retreats ran into the early 2000s with some volunteers each year coming from HBC. Bill Sinclair was the first young person from HBC to come on the retreats. In later years, Courtney and Caitlyn Russ, Meghan Forbes, Kylee Jordan, Ann and Richard Pulley, Caitlyn and Courtney Rejzer, Bobby Vann, Meghan Tucker, and Molly O'Bryan among others helped at the retreats.

Sarah also asked me to also help out once a month by teaching the Happy Class at Sunday school. I did this into the late 1980s, using youth from several churches. During those years, we used puppets a lot in our teaching.

Then, when I became the youth Sunday school director for Hampton Baptist in the late 1980s, I thought it was a golden opportunity. It came at the perfect time because the multi-church group of teens I had been using for Happy Class had all graduated and gone to college.

I spoke with Jay Russ, and he liked my idea. The Sunday school teachers also felt it was a worthwhile ministry and wanted their classes to participate. It would mean missing one Sunday a month, but since we could rotate through all the classes, it would only happen two or three times a year.

When I started as the youth Sunday school director, the fifth- and sixth-grade class would come to the youth department's opening assembly. This included singing (which, thankfully for all concerned, I had nothing to do with) and a devotional, which I delivered each Sunday. After the devotional, the fifth- and sixth-grade class would go to another part of the church where their classroom was located. I don't remember how this got started, but I think Jay said it had to do with getting the class acclimated to the youth department. Brenda Cole and Raynelle Ewing were teaching this class for most of this time.

With this arrangement, I divided the department into three groups. (The Happy Class was fairly large, and this gave me a good amount of help.) The three groups were fifth and sixth grades, middle school, and high school. We didn't teach during the summer because of my schedule. This meant that from September through May, each group would teach Happy Class three times a year on the second Sunday of the month.

The lessons were well planned and biblically based, although I always thought that the one-on-one interaction and prayer made the biggest impact. All of the groups planned a good class, although I must say that the lessons prepared by the fifth and sixth graders were usually the most meticulous.

It didn't take long for our youth to capture the hearts of the Happy Class members. I copied something that Jay Russ used to do with the youth at HBC. At the end of each Sunday and Wednesday night meeting, Jay would say, "Everyone has to get ten hugs before you can leave." When we arrived and left Happy Class, I told our volunteers to introduce themselves and shake hands with ten members of the class. (Hugs were optional, as some in the class had an aversion to hugging.)

Every now and then, due to the Hampton Baptist Church schedule, a class would not be able to make it one of their months. On those occasions, I would go by myself and teach. Every time that happened, the class would shout out when I walked in: "Where is your group?"

There was even a Hampton Baptist spin-off on teaching Happy Class. Matt Parron from HBC went to Parkview Baptist to be the youth minister in the early 2000s. Matt got with me and worked it out so that his youth group could teach the class some months.

One thing I enjoyed was the amount of creativity that was put into the planning and teaching. A few special classes remain in my mind:

- Lindsey Matthews once prepared the lesson all on her own.
- Aaron Whittington planned a lesson around a video he had filmed. He would play part of the video and then engage the class in discussions.
- Brenda Cole, Raynell Ewing, and their younger class always came up with neat crafts to use with the lesson, and the Happy Class members could take them home.

- John Bane once brought a carton of plastic eggs filled with items related to Easter to the youth Sunday school. His class decided to use the eggs at its next Happy Class visit. It was a big hit.
- One of the classes came with a digital camera and took pictures of everyone there. Then they made a collage and framed it. That collage is still hanging on one of the Happy Class walls.
- We would often hear individual prayer concerns from the class to take home and pray about during the week.

Molly O'Bryan at the Happy Class retreat (1)

Courtney Russ and Jimmy Palmer at the Happy Class
retreat (1)

Kylee Jordan and Meghan Tucker (1)

Meghan Tucker and Bobby Vann (1)

The most important part of the Happy Class retreats was the one-on-one interaction between the class members and our Sunday school youth. You can see that in these photos. I do want to mention the game being played by Courtney Russ and Jimmy Palmer, both blindfolded, in the top photo on the opposite page. Two players wear blindfolds, and the rest of the group make a fixed circle around them. One blindfolded person is designated the "chaser" and the other tries to keep away from them. You can see that both are holding a soda can, which is full of rocks or pennies. The only rule is that whenever the chaser rattles his/her can, the other must do the same. The game is over when the chaser tags their opponent.

SPECIAL CAMPS

Jay did one thing that absolutely kept me from losing my mind. (Actually, he often did this!) For several years, my PBA summer team did a camp for kids from low-rent housing areas. Part of my problem was that the camps were set up for a specific number of Christian club kids between the ages of seven and fifteen. On the Monday morning of camp week, buses would pick the kids up and transport them to Eastover. When they arrived, inevitably, there would be more campers than planned for, they would be as old as seventeen, and a third of them had never been to the club meetings during the year. To say the least, it was a rough week.

My summer team, often with help from Jim Ailor and his church in the D.C. area, would be the counselors. It was draining, emotionally and physically. After the first year and for the rest of the years the camp ran, Jay would bring the HBC youth over on Thursday after lunch. They would take care of everything for the next three hours. Three hours might not sound like much, but that break was what got us through the rest of the week. One of the main activities was a confidence course, with two climbing walls, that Jay and his group led the campers through.

Hampton Baptist youth who worked for me and served as week-long counselors included Sandy Everett, Brooke Puckett, Lindsey Matthews, and Aaron Whittington. Those coming with Jay as the Thursday afternoon lifeline included Jim Puckett, Sarah Trimble, Laura Williams, Betsy Trimble, and Bridget Wilson.

Next page (top): Laura Williams, Bridget Wilson, Betsy Trimble, Juli McKendree, Brooke Puckett, Sarah Trimble, and Jim Puckett helping at a PBA camp at Eastover

(4)

Below: This is a group who led the low-rent housing camp in the mid-1990s. A large number of this particular group was from my summer team and from Jim Ailor's church, Guilford Fellowship. Dara Ailor is the third from the left. Sandy Everett is in the middle, and Brooke Puckett is in the red on the right. The girl next to Brooke and the girl with the globe shirt are Ieva and Liga from Latvia. (1)

SMISHIES

Smishies, or summer missionaries, was a ministry that the PBA started in the late 1960s. I was put in charge in 1974. In the early years, there were four to six college students who came from several of our area churches. (In later years, this number would increase.) We also had out-of-state Smishies who came through the Baptist Student Unions (now called Baptist Collegiate Ministries) or the Home Mission Board (now called the North American Mission Board).

At the request of churches, this team would put on outdoor Vacation Bible Schools, ministries with special populations, camps and retreats, and work with internationals. In later years, sports camps, held at various churches, were a major focus. Smishies would also serve as leaders at such events as Work Camp and the GA camp at Eastover.

I continued to work with these summer mission teams until I retired from the PBA in 2012.

The list from Hampton Baptist who served as Smishies for one or more years include Jim Ailor, Susan Williams, Karen Watts, Sandy Everett, Aaron Whittington, Kristi Everett, Brooke Puckett, Lindsey Matthews, Chris Ellis, Beth Everett, Billy Everett, Corinna Powell, Ann Pulley, Bridget Wilson, Will Rawls, Bobby Vann, Kylie Jordan, Courtney Russ, Erin Hallissey, Caitlyn Russ, Meghan Tucker, Megan Forbes, Leigh Taylor Smith, Collin Chance, Lauren Farrow, and Alexander Brown.

For about twenty years, I would get one or two college students from out of the area to work with my summer mission team. Hampton Baptist folks were among those who provided homes for these Smishies. Dick and Camelia Everett, Virginia and Bill Godfrey, Sidney and Gene Jordan, Cindy and Vernon Rollins, and

Martha and Sam Ailor were among those who took in one or more of these summer missionaries.

Above: Ann Pulley and Corinna Powell with VBS kids (1)
Below: Bridget Wilson (4)

SPORTS CAMPS

One other PBA ministry at which Jay Russ and the Hampton Baptist youth were invaluable was our summer sports camps. These began as a single week event and grew to the point where I was leading ten to fourteen at various churches each summer.

In the early years, when there was only one camp per summer, I could get a lot of youth ministers to help out, and having enough teenage volunteers was no problem. Several youth ministers, such as Matt Parron, Ed Lilley, Ben Sandford, and Jay Russ, would always help on those weeks. As the number of weeks grew each summer, it became necessary to involve more and more teenagers to help run the camps. Hampton Baptist would always send a good number of helpers. Once we went to multiple camps each summer, the numbers of campers (at each camp) dropped. But during the 1990s, we reached a high-water mark of 275 campers one year at Immanuel Baptist Church.

No surprise here. Jay Russ is teaching golf. Patrick O'Bryan is on the far right. (1)

For several years, we used Orcutt Baptist as the venue. (1)

The leaders of the Orcutt Baptist camp (1)

2001 with the Austrians: This was not the largest camp, but it was getting close. Chris Ellis, Jay Russ, and Craig Waddell can be seen in the front. (1)

Chapter 51
Vacation Bible Schools

This was an event to which I was not often able to contribute, although from time to time, I got to speak to one of the classes about being a missionary for the PBA. Bill Hurt was in charge of the VBS, which always began with a parade through downtown Hampton. Most of the help came from the ladies and youth of the church. Some of the regulars were Jane Rollins, Jane Dennard, Lucille Everhart, Jane Kirby, and Jane Hurt. This was always a well-attended event, which helped model Christian living to kids. The following photos will give you an idea of what went on and who was involved.

Jane Rollins entertains the kids at the summer Vacation Bible School. Jane, a schoolteacher, was always very creative with both costumes and activities. (2)

Susan Forbes above and Patricia Wallace below helping with crafts at VBS (2)

Betty Lou Helbig above and Dot Turnbull (1966) below (2)

Nancy Eure (1966) above and Doris Smith McKlenney
below (2)

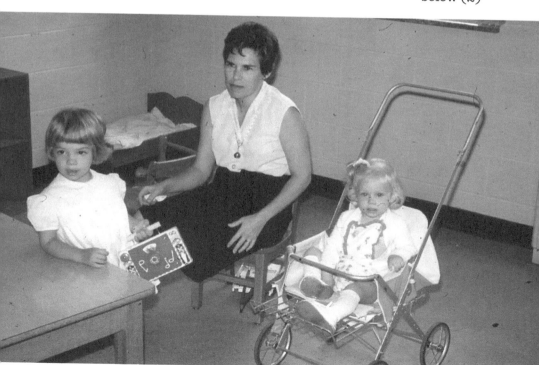

Pat Corlett above and Margie Ware below (2)

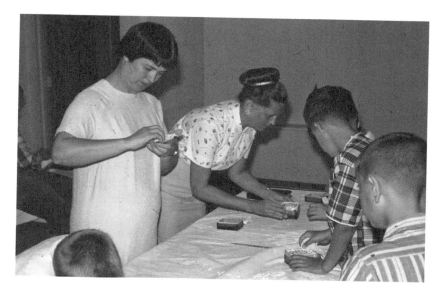

Aileen Riley and Mrs. Gaesser (2)

Michael Curtis (2)

Chester and Mary Etta enjoying snacks with the
Bible-schoolers (2)

Gary Lewis with VBS; Teresa Diggs in the background (2)

Cindy Garris doing crafts with the VBS (2)

Tommy O'Bryan goes to Bible school (2)

Baxter Lee dressed for success (2)

Above: Christine Vick helping with artwork (2)
Below: Jane Rollins (2)

Patty Price (2)

Becky Riddle and Karen Watts (2)

Hampton Baptist Church

Marge Michael (2)

Claudia Nock and Vickie Ellis (2)

Wanda Sayers (2)

Jeannie Wornom (2)

Mike Haywood—look! No beard. (2)

Cindy Rollins (2)

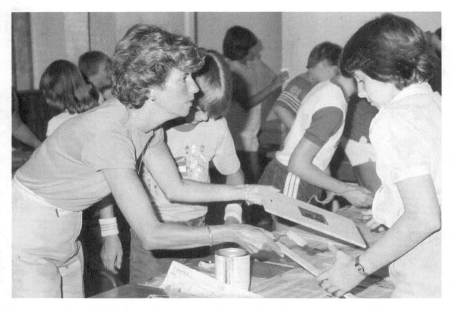

Toni Wilkins above and Mary Etta Brown below (2)

Above: Raynelle Ewing (2)

Left: Corinna Powell cleaning up after class (4)

Above: Chester Brown sharing Snoopy with Bible-schoolers (2)

Marge Michael (2)

Chapter 52
Other HBC Ministries

For this chapter, I want to focus on a few ministries for helping those outside the church walls.

A NIGHT'S WELCOME

HELP, a city agency that works with the homeless, started a program in the 1990s to provide food and shelter during the colder months. They recruited churches in the city to open their facilities to the homeless for a week at a time. It was called "A Night's Welcome." Hampton Baptist was one of the churches that responded and has continued to do so ever since. Carson Yates first involved HBC in this ministry, and he headed the endeavor for many years. (Phil Everhart Jr. is currently one of the leaders of this ministry.)

People who need a place to stay the night may arrive in the early evening in time for a hot dinner. Cots or pallets are set up in the fellowship hall where they can spend the night. They are given toiletries, such as deodorant and toothpaste, and other needed items, such as washcloths and blankets, for the evening. In the morning, the guests are given breakfast before they head out into the city for the day. The churches reopen at 6:00 p.m.

A dozen people help prepare and serve the two meals. Two to three people remain overnight as attendants. There are at least fifty people from the church involved each year. For many years, Lisa Smith, Gene Jordan, Eddie Forbes, Tommy O'Bryan, and I (three of the five of us) worked together for a four-hour shift, usually after midnight.

OFFICE SPACE

Hampton Baptist provided office space for several outside ministries, including mine. I'd had an office at the Peninsula Baptist Association headquarters for fifteen years. In 1985, I moved my office to North Riverside Baptist. It was during this time that Lynn Latham, the PBA's community services director, had her office at Hampton Baptist. In 1995, due to some construction and reconfiguration at North Riverside, I also moved my office to HBC, where I stayed for ten years.

The director of Southeast Prison Ministries had an office at HBC at the same time. One of the perks of working at HBC was the fantastic buffets the prison ministry provided once a year to show their appreciation for the office space. Sandra Bundick, the office secretary, told me my first year there that I did not want to miss this buffet, especially the shrimp. I love shrimp and never missed one of these luncheons in the ten years my office was at Hampton Baptist Church.

Even though Jay Russ's office and mine were back to back in the old fellowship hall, there were no disruptions or failure to accomplish our work. (This came as a surprise to many people!) The big catastrophe during that time came the morning that Sandra Bundick came into the old fellowship hall and told Jay and me that we had to leave the church immediately.

I jumped to the wrong conclusion and thought a bomb had been found at the courthouse, which is across the street. Fortunately, I didn't comment on that assumed scenario before Sandra told us that the storm that was raging had blown the steeple off. It was leaning by the church's front door, right next to the office!

The fallen steeple: I would like to point out that looking at front of the church, you will see that the steeple fell to the LEFT! (1)

Lynn Latham at VBS (2)

FISHERMAN'S COVE

In 1966, HBC began a coffeehouse ministry called the Fisherman's Cove. Coffeehouse ministries were popular in churches during this time, and the one at Hampton was a big success. It was located in the last room to the left when you're headed to the side parking lot. It would serve soft drinks, coffee, ice cream, and other snacks. It was open on Friday, Saturday, and Sunday nights (after church services). It could also be reserved for special occasions. Artwork and murals covered the walls, which caused at least one big powwow of the deacons, as you read in Chapter 6. Although anyone could visit the Fisherman's Cove when it was open, it catered mainly to teens and young adults.

Opposite page: top—Suzanna Dunn, Marianne Gaesser, and Susan Wallace (3); right—Betty Northern on the left and John Lee Robbins on the right (3)

VIETNAMESE CHURCH

Hampton Baptist provided space for a Vietnamese church plant in the 1970s. The Vietnamese church had a good turnout and continued to thrive well into the 1990s. At the same time, the church family took in refugees from Vietnam and Cambodia. The pastor was Rev. Vang Le. For many years, David Watts was the HBC liaison.

SAME (SO ALL MAY EAT)

SAME, So All May Eat, is a ministry that feeds anyone who shows up at noon on Mondays. It has been run for many years by Amy Whitcover Sandford. One thing Hampton Baptist has always done well is cooking and serving food, for any occasion!

HALL ROAD MISSION

Hampton Baptist branched out in a new direction when they established Hall Road Mission in Fox Hill in the early 1970s. Chester Smith was the first pastor of Hall Road. In 1980, Fred King was called to be the pastor. Fred later became the pastor of Tabernacle Baptist in Newport News. During its years of existence, Hall Road was a beacon of light in the Fox Hill area.

Chapter 53

"An Anniversary Carol," or "Giving Jay the Dickens"

Jay Russ's tenth anniversary was celebrated in 1995 with recognition and, of course, a skit. In this case, the skit was an adaption of Charles Dickens's *A Christmas Carol*. I got to play Jay Russ. The Angel of Youth Activities Past was played by Ed Lilley; Darlene Scheepers was the Angel of Youth Activities Present; Marcus King played the part of the Angel of Youth Activities Future.

The skit began with Jay considering leaving the youth ministry. He falls asleep, and the Angel of Youth Activities Past appears. He brings back past youth members, who come forward, one at a time, to relate a short "Jay" story. Then the angel says, "Think about what Ed Lilley was like in the fifth grade, and now he is a youth minister!"

The Angel of Youth Activities Present comes and announces, "Jay, you and I are going on a Turkey Hunt." They get in a "van" and go looking for a clue. They find a Youth Minister's Physical Fitness Kit, which contains a golf club, a softball bat, another golf club, a frisbee for disc golf, yet another golf club, and a golf ball.

The next clue leads to a Youth Minister's Survival Kit. They pull crutches out of the kit, and someone reads the tag: "'Ridgecrest—Suicide Hill: Wendy Maybury, Krista Everett, Brooke Puckett.' There's space here for more names. Anyone want to try?"

A wrist brace includes a note that says, "To be used in case someone gets hurt when we're NOT wrestling at Eastover."

A box of gauze bandages includes instructions that say, "In case of accidental hit by a sledgehammer, apply directly to the wound."

A vomit basin's note says, "We sure could have used this on our mission trips to Georgia and Kentucky!"

Jay falls back asleep, and the Angel of Youth Activities Future appears. Jay wakes up, and the angel says, "I've got your future right here!"

At the end, Jay goes back to being a youth minister and receives a certificate that reads: "This certificate is good for one group hug from the HBC youth!"

Chapter 54
A Baker's Dozen of the Best One-Liners

I know that for every great one-liner I remember, there are a dozen I have forgotten, and they may have been even better! But for what it's worth, here is a baker's dozen of my favorites.

1

Bill Hurt once told me about dropping off a costume for a Christmas play that the teens were performing at church. Bill took the costume to the home of the young lady who would be playing Mary, the mother of Jesus.

Bill had to explain himself to the girl's father, who was a rather rough character and didn't go to church.

"Oh," the father said, "are you going to make her an angel?"

Bill told me that luckily he kept his mouth shut, but the first answer that came to mind was "No, we are going to make her a virgin!"

2

One year, we were having a meeting at the Ailors' about an upcoming youth retreat. We had divided into two groups, one of which would choose the location and the other, the theme. I was in the theme group, and we decided to make *sex* the main topic. Meanwhile, the second group was discussing holding the retreat at a campground in the Richmond area.

As my group was debating specific discussions on the subject of sex, someone in the other group, very loudly, blurted out, "What I want to know is, just how far can we go?"

3

Sam Ailor's opening comment to my class on the first day of the new Sunday school year (I am sure this was an annual comment): "My last name is Ailor. That's 'Jailor' without the 'j'."

4

I helped Jay Russ run a mystery progressive dinner one year. At the first home where we had appetizers, each team was given a logbook detailing the mystery to be solved. Jay explained that at each home, additional information would be given. Teams could ask two questions, the answers to which might or might not help in solving the mystery.

After this introduction, Jay invited each team to ask their two questions. Billy Everett's team came up, and Billy asked, "We can ask two questions, correct?"

Jay replied, "Yes, you are allowed two questions. What is your second question?"

Billy tried to argue that his first question did not count. I think you probably know how that turned out! He almost asked a second question in his argument but caught himself before he finished.

5

About my third year at the Peninsula Baptist Association, my supervisor, George Kissinger, was asked to preach at Hampton Baptist one Sunday morning. In public settings, he often referred to me as "the boy."

He made this comment at the eleven o'clock service:

You know, I have really enjoyed working with your own Mike Haywood at the PBA. I tried to get him married off for the first couple of years he was with us. However, I have now decided that the boy is worth more to me single than he would be married.

6

Chester mentioned me once from the pulpit on a Sunday morning. Though not a compliment, it was funny. (Hey, any recognition is better than no recognition!)

On this occasion, Chester was speaking for a member's ordination service. He used the analogy of a little green man landing in a flying saucer on Queen Street. The little green man might look at all the churches in the vicinity, and Chester mused what he might learn just from observation.

Once he finished that analogy, he then said, "Let's move on from our little green man because he is not real. Everyone knows there's no such thing as flying saucers. That is, everyone except for Mike Haywood!"

7

In a sermon many years earlier, Chester was preaching after our area had been hit by a hurricane. This must have been sometime in the 1960s. He did not mention any names, but he did tell us about a woman who had called him after her roof had been blown off. Chester said that the woman had stopped coming to church for a year prior.

On the phone, she told Chester how she had prayed for God to protect her house during the storm. She wanted Chester to tell her why God had not done as she'd asked. He went on to tell the congregation that he did not verbalize it, but his thought was "Well, perhaps He was busy with His regular customers!"

8

Chester told on himself from the pulpit not too long ago. He said that many years ago, he had been having a theological discussion with Dottie Lee Jones. Chester said that he did not think that Dottie Lee understood what he was trying to say, which made him frustrated. At one point, Chester said, "Dottie Lee, you just cannot understand what I am saying!"

Dottie Lee replied, "Young man, I am perfectly capable of understanding anything that you are capable of adequately explaining!"

9

This is more of a "say no more" than a one-liner. Back in the day, when the saying "What Would Jesus Do?" (WWJD?) was popular, someone put the following sign on Sandra Bundick's desk in the church office:

WWSD—What Would Sandra Do?

10

On a youth retreat many years ago, Jay Russ designed a skit to teach the proper way to think and act as a Christian. The "contestants" in the skit were asked questions about what they would do in certain scenarios, and there were three possible answers. One answer would be funny, one would be the typical worldly reaction, and the third was the Christian response.

For the worldly answer, Jay or I could reply, "Well, you can go to hell!"

Mark Taylor gave the best funny answer of the night. When asked "What would you do if you had a tough moral decision to make?" Mark said (he made this up on the fly, which was easy for him), "Well, I always call the psychic hotline!"

11

Because I can't think of a better place to put this anecdote, there was the time that Gary played a real "downer" for the invitational hymn at the 8:30 a.m. service. Sandra went to Chester afterward and told him that the hymn was too depressing to end the service. "Pick a livelier hymn to sing for the invitation at the eleven o'clock service," she said. So that is what Chester did!

12

(Per Jay Russ) Chester was asked by a new pastor in the PBA, "What is the secret to remaining a pastor at the same church for so long?"

Chester answered, "You have to love *all* the people *all* the time. And when you don't, you have to convince them that you still do!"

13

As recounted in the previous chapter, to celebrate Jay's tenth anniversary, we performed a skit, based on the Charles Dickens story, that revolved around Jay giving up youth ministry.

In the skit, the Angel of Youth Activities Past brings back past youth members, who tell a story about Jay. The angel said, "Think about what Ed Lilley was like in the fifth grade, and now *he* is a youth minister!"

Chapter 55

Deacons

A deacons' and spouses' retreat held at Eastover in the mid-1980s: Jules Miller, Sam Ailor, Dottie Lee Jones, Dick Everett, Camelia Everett, Nancy Sandford, Maynard Sanford, Gary Lewis, Velma Jean Allison, Lucille Rollins, Marion Hankinson, Freda Nelson, Celia Dawson, Nancy Lee Trimble, Billy Trimble, Jane Kirby, Eddie Hankinson, Milford Rollins, Francis Jones, Jim Paul Allison, Bill Nelson, Alice Erickson, Wayne Erickson, Mae Hammond, and Gene Hammond (photo by John Dawson, who was obviously also in attendance)

The deacons at HBC were a group of men and, later, women who served the church in many ways. Several of them served in other areas of ministry as well, including Sunday school, youth, and so on. Others made up the group that I call Hall People. Wherever you met them, they would go out of their way to encourage you and make you feel important. This was a trait that never went out of style!

Dick Everett, Raye Mathis, and Freda Nelson (3)

Jules Miller, Milford Rollins, and Jim Allison (3)

Chapter 56
Conclusion

Above: Chester at a PBA function; Claudia and Jay Lawson in the background (5)

Right: Iris Rollins (2)

Above: Vacation Bible School (2)

Left: Trudy McBride (3)

Bill Hurt above; Jane Rollins and Martha Feathers below
(2)

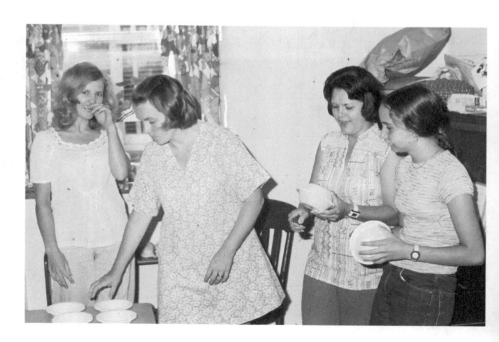

John Dawson (5)

(2)

Jane Hurt (2)

Angie Russ (4)

Left: Randy Ware (3)

Right: Linda Hurt (3)

Susan Lilley above and Faye Everett at Bible school below
(2)

Becky Riddle (3)

Beth Everett on a youth mission trip (4)

Celebrating

Thirty – nine years

of the Pastorate of

Dr. Chester Brown

1962 – 2001

Chester Brown retired at the end of 2001. I think this is as good a way as any to end this unofficial narrative.

CHESTER BROWN

On this occasion we give our love and thanks to Dr. Chester Brown for serving as Pastor of Hampton Baptist Church for thirty-nine years.

Dr. Brown graduated from the University of Richmond with an A.B. degree in 1952. He entered Southeastern Theological Seminary that fall. He was employed by Hampton Baptist Church as a Summer Assistant to Dr. Garber during the summers of 1953, 1954 and 1955. After receiving his B.D. in May 1955, Dr. Brown was ordained to the gospel ministry at his home church, Union Baptist Church, Gloucester County, on June 12, 1955.

Having the desire to pursue further study, Dr. Brown entered New College, University of Edinburgh, Scotland, for two years of post-graduate study in church history. Hampton Baptist Church called Chester Brown as Associate Pastor with his services to begin on January 1, 1958. He served in this position until Dr. Garber retired on December 31, 1961. Dr. Brown was called to be Pastor of Hampton Baptist Church as of January 1, 1962.

Recognizing his success as pastor and his pursuit of higher education, the University of Richmond awarded him the honorary degree of Doctor of Divinity in 1975. He was enrolled in graduate studies at Union Theological Seminary, Richmond, Virginia, on a part-time basis while carrying on his duties as Pastor of Hampton Baptist Church. He was awarded the Doctor of Ministry Degree in 1977.

We are pleased to have his family share in this celebration tonight: his wife, Dr. Mary Etta Brown who recently retired as Principal of Paul Burbank Elementary School and who will be a Curriculum Coordinator at the American International School in Egypt beginning in August; his daughter, Mary Elizabeth who is the owner of Friendship Imports; his son, Edward who is a Regional Manager of Major Minor Systems, Inc.

We are grateful to Dr. Brown for his ministry at Hampton Baptist Church since 1953 and for his many contributions to the life of this community and to our denomination on both the state and the local levels.

Radisson Hotel

June 20, 2001   *6:00 PM*

Master of Ceremonies   *Mr. Joseph H. Spencer*

Welcome   *Mr. A. Woodfin Patrick, Jr.*
Chairman of the Deacons

Blessing   *Rev. Anderson W. Clary*
Pastor, Queen Street Baptist Church

Dinner

Seminary Remembrances   *Dr. Paul R. Garber*

Staff Reminiscences   *Mr. William G. Hurt*
Rev. Jay Russ

Religious Herald Reflections   *Dr. Michael J. Clingenpeel*
Editor of The Religious Herald

Travel Recollections   *Mr. Andrew D. Greenwell*

Music   *Mrs. Elizabeth F. Jennings*
accompanied by her father, Dr. Thomas Forrest

Representing the Community   *The Honorable Mamie E. Locke*
Mayor, City of Hampton

Deacon Remembrances   *Mrs. Margaret H. Hatchett*

Presentation of Gift   *Mr. A. Woodfin Patrick, Jr.*

Recipient of Gift   *Dr. Thomas H. Graves*
President, Baptist Theological Seminary at Richmond

Acceptance of Gift   *Dr. Chester Brown*

Benediction   *Dr. William D. Booth*
Pastor, First Baptist Church

WORKERS TOGETHER WITH GOD

TRUSTEES

Francis W. Jones	Eugene M. Jordan II	A. Woodfin Patrick Jr.

LIFE DEACONS

T.W.E. Hankinson	Francis W. Jones	Roland L. McKendree Jr.
Cynthia P. Otte	Lewis C. Parsons Jr.	A. Woodfin Patrick Jr.
	William A. Pleasants Jr.	

TERM DEACONS

Term ends Dec. 31, 2001	Term ends Dec. 31, 2002	Term ends Dec. 31, 2003
Martha M. Ailor	Billy R. Cole	Margaret L. Allison
Beverly N. Doyer	Beverly D. Forbes	Stephen W. Barnes
William W. Everett	Kenneth H. Goetzke	Susan C. Castle
Stanley E. Ewing	Pamela G. Hallissy	William A. Corlett
Russell E. Fox	Susanna D. McKendree	Faye G. Everett
David E. Glass	James R. Pierce	Elizabeth V. Heard
Eugene M. Jordan II	James E. Puckett	Erin E. Kinnaird
Martha F. Owens	Robert L. Sigler	John M. Miller
Stephen P. Sandford	W. Mark Taylor	Thomas P. O'Bryan
Deborah K. Spencer	Jesse B. Wilkins Jr.	Nancy P. Sandford

CHURCH OFFICERS

Nancy B. Forbes	Clerk
William F. Trimble	Treasurer
Philip A. Curtis	Financial Secretary
A. W. Patrick, III	Moderator

ORGANIZATIONS

Stanley E. Ewing	Director, Sunday School
Martha F. Owens	Assistant Director, Sunday School
Nancy Lee Trimble	Director, WMU
William M. Kinnaird	President, Men's Association
Francis W. Jones	Chief Usher
E. Wallace Hicks	Assistant Chief Usher

Hampton Baptist Church

Chester Brown, *D. Min., D.D., Pastor*
Jay Russ, *Associate Pastor*
William G. Hurt, *Minister of Education/Administration*
Thomas Matthews, *Minister of Music Organist*
Sandra M. Bundick, *Administrative Assistant*

Chester Brown Retirement Committee

Cynthia P. Otte, *Chairman*
Velma Jean Allison, Lewis R. Parsons
Deborah K. Spencer, *Chairman this event*

This book has been fun to write, and it brings back great memories about the special people who made up the congregation and staff of Hampton Baptist Church. I realize that I have left out a lot of people, memories, and events, and I can only say that I am sorry about that.

I really believe this congregation taught me and others so much about what life should be about. We were taught to find our way in life; to follow the example of Jesus Christ; to help others, both friends and strangers; to develop our character (Luke 2:52); to love the life we have been given; to always look for new friends; and to view life as an adventure. We were taught to believe that the Holy Spirit is always walking with us and will bring us the guidance, strength, and "peace that passeth understanding" that God has promised us.

There really is adventure waiting out there, just beyond your line of sight. Be sure to look just up the trail a bit, past that stand of trees, over the far ridge; in that book you have in your hand; with that new kid you've just met; at that person who needs a little help; and in the memories of the senior citizen who lives down the street, in a retirement home, or perhaps in your own home.

And if some neat things happened in your life because of HBC, but they are not recorded in this book, that's OK. Because as my pastor and friend Chester Brown once said, "It's OK if we forget the good things because God will always remember." Hopefully the unintentionally left-out people and events are embedded in your own memory.

Thanks for being my friends. Thanks for your ministry to one another and to those outside the church.

For the rest of your life, go in peace, go in love, go with God.

Mike Haywood
November 2024